FROM TRADITION
TO GOSPEL

BY

MARTIN DIBELIUS

D1319126

CHARLES   SCRIBNER'S   SONS

New York

Translated from the Revised Second Edition of
Die Formgeschichte des Evangeliums in collaboration
with the author by Bertram Lee Woolf.

B-8.67[MCol]

Printed in the United States of America

AUTHOR'S PREFACE

When this book first appeared in German in 1919 its purpose was to introduce and establish the method of literary criticism which has since been called " Formgeschichte ". As it stands in the present edition its purpose is to describe and develop this method. In Germany the principles and consequences of this book have been the subject of scientific discussion during the last fifteen years. I have also lectured upon them in England, in Oxford in 1926 and in Manchester in 1933. The positive and negative criticisms which I have received have forwarded my work and made a further development of the method advisable. It is therefore a great pleasure to me to be now able to address the English-speaking reader in his own language, and I should not like this translation of my book to be published without expressing my hearty thanks to Dr. Bertram Lee Woolf for all the care and attention which he has given to my work.

The method of Formgeschichte has a twofold objective. In the first place, by reconstruction and analysis, it seeks to explain the origin of the tradition about Jesus, and thus to penetrate into a period previous to that in which our Gospels and their written sources were recorded. But it has a further purpose. It seeks to make clear the intention and real interest of the earliest tradition. We must show with what objective the first churches recounted stories about Jesus, passed them from mouth to mouth as independent narratives, or copied them from papyrus to papyrus. In the same manner we must examine the sayings of Jesus and ask with what intention these churches collected them, learnt them by heart, and wrote them down. The present-day reader should learn to read the individual passages of the early tradition in the way they were meant, before the time when, more or less edited, they were included in the Gospels.

The method of Formgeschichte seeks to help in answering the historical questions as to the nature and trustworthiness of our knowledge of Jesus, and also in solving a theological problem properly so-called. It shows in what way the earliest testimony about Jesus was interwoven with the earliest testimony about the salvation which had appeared in Jesus Christ. Thereby it attempts to emphasize and illuminate the chief elements of the message upon which Christianity was founded. Interest in these problems unites English and German research. I should like the English edition of this volume to be regarded as an expression of this fellowship.

MARTIN DIBELIUS.

TABLE OF CONTENTS

GLOSSARY OF THE PRINCIPAL TECHNICAL TERMS

ARETALOGY
: Miraculous action or divine manifestation. (cf. ἀρετή, a manifestation of divine power, 2 Pet. i, 3.)

CHRIA
: An epigram or saying ascribed to a particular person and originating from a particular situation.

FORMGESCHICHTE
: The literary criticism of the forms in which ideas, thoughts, reports, descriptions, etc., are passed on orally or in writing.

GNOME
: A word of various meanings, best perhaps understood as epigram, wise-saying.

KERYGMA
: The subject-matter of the gospel, the message of the sermon, the preaching itself.

LEGEND
: A narrative about some sainted person. The term "legend" does not in itself raise the question of historicity.

MYTH
: A story which deals with a *particular* relation and action of a god. A full and careful definition is given on page 266.

PARADIGM
: A short illustrative notice or story of an event, not more descriptive than is necessary to make the point for the sake of which it is introduced.

PARENETIC
: Hortatory, dealing with exhortation.

TALE
: A story told *primarily* for its own sake.

N.B.—The word *Fromm* and derivatives have been translated as a rule by *religious, religiousness*, etc., as better than the frequent rendering *pious* and *piety*, etc. It should be understood, however, in the sense of inward or personal religion, unless the context makes this impossible.

Chapter I

FORMGESCHICHTE, OR THE CRITICISM OF LITERARY FORM

There is a theory that the history of literature is the history of its various forms. This may be true of literature properly so-called, but it cannot be applied indiscriminately to every kind of writing. It has, however, special significance when applied to materials where the author's personality is of little importance. Many anonymous persons take part in handing down popular tradition. They act, however, not merely as vehicles, but also as creative forces by introducing changes or additions without any single person having a " literary " intent. In such cases the personal peculiarities of the composer or narrator have little significance ; much greater importance attaches to the form in which the tradition is cast by practical necessities, by usage, or by origin. The development goes on steadily and independently, subject all the time to certain definite rules, for no creative mind has worked upon the material and impressed it with his own personality.

What we have said is true also in marked degree of the humbler forms of literature. By this phraseology I mean that lower stratum which accords no place to the artistic devices and tendencies of literary and polished writing. Unpretentious literary products find their readers in circles not touched by literature proper. Yet the former like the latter are meant for a definite publicity and are not written merely for the circle of the author's acquaintance. Here we have a difference between even unpretentious literature and writings which are entirely private. To-day this difference is easily grasped, for the

fact of publication through press and trade distinguishes petty
tracts, popular calendars, and brochures issued by societies,
from mere personal notes on the one hand, and from writings
manifolded by the printing press or printed as " manuscript "
on the other. But in the case of ancient writings this criterion
cannot be applied, for we have no certainty as to the method
of their publication. In regard to Paul's letters, which were
copied and recopied many times for use by the restricted
public of the Christian Church, we may raise the question
as to the moment when they ceased to be private writings
and became a lowly form of literature. Again, in the case of
many writings of the New Testament, we cannot say to what
extent they were originally intended for publication, a term
which, in this connexion would mean general use in the
restricted circle mentioned above. If we knew in what way
the so-called Epistle to the Ephesians was first made public,
we should soon reach agreement as to its character. Primitive
Christian literature passed through all the stages between
private notes and the borders of literature proper. Only two
or three of its documents approximate to the literary standards
of Philo and Josephus. All the rest is either quite non-literary
or of minor literary significance. The evolution took place
without direct influence from literature proper. We may
therefore speak in a special sense of a " primitive Christian
literature ", whereas the " early Christian writings " of a later
date can be classified—at least as regards their form—amongst
Hellenistic literature.

In prosecuting a research in the history of the Form of
the Gospels, we must concern ourselves first of all and most
of all with only one section of primitive Christian literature,
namely the synoptic Gospels. Without a doubt these are
unliterary writings. They should not and cannot be compared
with " literary " works. Nevertheless they are certainly
not private notes but are designed for a definite publicity
even if it be only humble. But the literary character of these
books shows certain marks which differentiate them from

other primitive Christian writings. The literary understanding of the synoptics begins with the recognition that they are collections of material. The composers are only to the smallest extent authors. They are principally collectors, vehicles of tradition, editors. Before all else their labour consists in handing down, grouping, and working over the material which has come to them. Therein also their religious presentation of the material comes to essential expression. Thus they make their influence felt with much less independence than, say, the composer of the Fourth Gospel and much less also than the author of the Book of Acts. The latter is indeed himself an evangelist, but he is much more bound by his material in the Gospel of St. Luke than in the Acts of the Apostles. Here he acts as an author, but in the Gospel rather as a collector and editor. For this reason St. Luke more than the other synoptics shows the strongest literary character. Thereby it can be estimated in how lowly a degree after all St. Mark and St. Matthew may pass as authors. These matters are no longer in doubt and thus we may draw the following conclusions, although these are by no means generally recognized.

The position taken by the evangelists in forming the literary character of synoptic tradition is limited. It is concerned with the choice, the limitation, and the final shaping of material, but not with the original moulding. The form in which we hear of the words and deeds of Jesus is due only in a certain degree to the personal work of the evangelist. Owing to a philological and theological tradition we ourselves have become accustomed to ascribe to the authors and their prejudices a large responsibility for the tradition as a whole, just as if we were dealing with Belles Lettres. This error is ancient. Even Papias in the second century is entirely of the view that the evangelists were authors who shaped their narrative with literary freedom according to their knowledge of the events. In reality the personal factors had but little significance in shaping the tradition, at any rate as far as the Gospels of Mark and Matthew are concerned, and it is very doubtful whether much depended upon the personal factor in the earlier history of the tradition. Here we touch upon a further question with which our present enquiry will deal at much greater length. It is that a critical reading of the Gospels shows that the evangelists took over material which already possessed a form of its own. They joined some paragraphs together which beforehand had possessed a certain independent completeness.

The criticism of the Form of the Gospel, i.e. of this material, does not begin, therefore, with the work of the evangelists, for it has rather already reached a certain *completion of development* by the time we have reached the form of the evangelical books. What now takes place is the further development of this category of writing up to the collecting of a tradition that had grown " wild " and that had been consciously corrected. The apocryphal Gospels have apparently preserved such collections. What took place previously was the formation and the growth of small separate pieces out of which the Gospels were put together. Even these little pieces obey the laws of Form-construction. They do it all the more as in the development of *their* form the individuality of an original writer played no real part. To trace out those laws, to make comprehensible the rise of these little categories, is to write the history of the Form of the Gospel.

The first edition of this book in 1919 was intended as a working basis for reading the Gospels from the point of view of the development of their form. A few years earlier the title of the work had been used in a significant manner when Eduard Norden in 1913 gave to his book " Agnostos Theos " the subsidiary title " Researches in the Formengeschichte of Religious Language ". This book was intended to deal with a type of speech of a soteriological character. Hence his researches were to a large extent on that level of literature where the individual taste of the author determined the final form of the material which had been handed down.

Research into popular non-literary writing with which the Formgeschichte of the Gospel deals had, in many regions, already gathered experience and developed methods. Johann Gottfried Herder was the pioneer of such movements in the sphere of biblical literature. As an interpreter of biblical writings he intuitively put forward many axioms which only at a later date were to reach significance for criticism. His understanding of the popular mind revealed to him the special character of religious popular literature, and his understanding of human nature showed him what was the typical character of such writing. His understanding of folk poetry enabled him to recognize the naïve and creative element in the biblical writings. Of course, he was not able always to distinguish between æsthetic appreciation and literary evaluation, hence the researches of the nineteenth century into the sources of the Gospels were not able to carry his work further, because they were immediately concerned with historical results. But ever and again in the middle of this period of historical work, the consciousness came forward that in the case of some of the biblical writings, and especially in those of the first century of our era, the subject was not literature created by the mind of the author, but formulations which necessarily come from the presence and activity of a circle strange to literature. In this sense Franz Overbeck differentiated primitive Christian literature from patristic literature. In the same way Georg Heinrici defined the contents of the synoptic Gospels as collected material, and he differentiated them, and the other New Testament writings, from literature proper. They were to him the sources and the witnesses of a missionary activity. The possibility of analysing this collected material was first systematically proved in the sphere of the Old Testament where it was traced back to the minutest perceptible forms of tradition. By their researches Herrmann Gunkel and his school made the analysis of the "smallest details" an axiom of research.

A method of handling popular categories in accordance

with the history of their form (in the proper sense of the term), i.e. in accordance with the way in which these categories could be distinguished in the writings of the Old Testament, was only reached when, from the form in which the detail was cast, a conclusion could be drawn as to the original purpose and the practical application of the detail, in a word, as to its "Sitz im Leben", or place in the stream of life. Adolf Deissmann had already effected something decisive for putting the oldest passages of Christian tradition and of the Gospels themselves into their proper place in a development which was progressing from unliterary writing to popular literature, but which did not reach the level of Belles Lettres. By comparing primitive Christian documents with the unliterary texts of the Papyri he obtained a new understanding which was of immediate importance for interpreting the Pauline letters. The insight into the differences between unliterary writing and popular literature, which he had thereby gained, resulted in new criteria of value for measuring the significance of the Gospel tradition. By putting on one side all evaluations derived from literature proper, and certainly everything from the classics, the way was open for appreciating the language and the style of primitive Christian writing according to its own laws.

The right to read the Gospels from the standpoint of the development of their form is the objective of the present volume. This right is supported in no small degree by the fact that in quick succession several works have been published which showed the necessity for such a research, and they have made a beginning—to some extent from the other side. The solution of the problem offered by "Formgeschichte" was immediately voiced in many different ways, and it was supported by a criticism which began in a vigorous and, for the most part, perspicacious manner. It is due to these facts that the questions which were raised by the first edition of this book, and especially by Rudolf Bultmann (in application to the whole synoptic tradition), were not allowed to rest, but compelled us ever and again to test the methods as well as the individual results.

The method of Form-criticism would be completely misjudged if it were regarded as originating in a flirtation with æsthetic standards. In so doing we should be going back to a way of looking at things which has its justification only in literature proper, where individual ability and inclination shape the style, i.e., where the result requires an æsthetic judgment of a personal and creative character. But the popular writings with which we are concerned have no such an individual source. The style which it is our part to observe is " a sociological result ".

Of course, in saying this, it must be understood that the conception of " style " is not meant in the narrow sense which deals only with vocabulary and construction. Rather under the word " style " must be understood the whole way of speaking which, at least in the case of popular writing, is determinative of its category, for the lowly people who use this style write according to laws which are independent of the individual personality. Hence the style characterizes the category. In certain circumstances also by taking account of the choice of words, the construction of sentences, the wordiness or the brevity, the nature of the description, the introduction, and the peroration, we may tell whether the purpose of the author is to awaken interest or to make converts.

Further, the categories enable us to draw a conclusion as to what is called the " Sitz im Leben ", i.e. the historical and social stratum in which precisely these literary forms were developed. Devotional narratives were required by devotional addresses, but interesting and arresting narratives live and do their work by themselves and require, in certain circumstances, no context.

In these cases our enquiry is not directed towards the personality of the authors, nor towards their literary dexterity; rather the issue is concerned with laws which operate as formative factors in popular tradition. The ultimate origin of the Form is primitive Christian life itself. To understand the categories of popular writings as they developed in the sphere of unliterary people we must enquire into their life and, in our special case, which deals with religious texts, into the customs of their worship. We must ask what categories are possible or probable in this sociological connection.

On the other hand, if it becomes clear that certain categories are contained in the majority of the texts, we must measure them up by those researches and determine whether they reveal relationships to particular modes of life and of worship. That research and this determination together constitute our problem.

CHAPTER II

SERMONS

The researches of half a century have examined the history of the rise of the Gospels from a particular standpoint, and in consequence of their analytic method have worked out a widely recognized Theory of Two Sources which in its main lines is to be regarded as a relatively sure result. This theory holds that Matthew and Luke are both dependent upon Mark and, in addition, upon a source which can be reconstructed out of the text of Matthew and Luke as the postulated collection known as Q. We are able to say now how our Gospels arose from their sources, but we cannot yet say how this whole literature arose. We have some conception how the order, increase, and variation of the materials took place, but not how they came to be handed down and collected. We are acquainted with the events in the later stage of the process without however being able to comprehend its motive forces.

We are not concerned with a purely literary process. For its rise in the first instance was not due to the inclination or the activities of professional writers.

The company of unlettered people which expected the end of the world any day had neither the capacity nor the inclination for the production of books, and we must not predicate a true literary activity in the Christian Church of the first two or three decades. The materials which have been handed down to us in the Gospels lived in these decades an unliterary life or had indeed as yet no life at all. The alternatives show the seriousness of the problem.

The relatively large space of time which lies between the life-time of Jesus, A.D. 30, and the writing of our oldest

Gospel, about A.D. 70, constitutes a problem for literary history. The issue is not only as to the question of what traditions could arise in that period but also the much more decisive question, namely, whether during that time, and among those people, a tradition could have developed. An analytical method which starts from the texts and goes back to the sources and isolated elements of tradition is not satisfactory. Rather one requires a constructive method which attempts to include the conditions and activities of life of the first Christian Churches. If we leave this work on one side, the sources and the small details which are brought forward by the analytical method hang in the air, and their sociological relationships, or " Sitz im Leben ", is not clear. Naturally in each method the independence of their way of thought must be preserved, synthesis and analysis must not so much condition, as meet each other.

We may take it for granted that Jesus' words and the accounts of His life and death were kept alive in the circle of His disciples. But we must ask in what way these reminiscences, found in the oldest Churches, were spread abroad, how they reached a certain fixedness if not of word, yet of outer and inner structure, and, above all, by what interest this process of spreading and fixing was governed. It is of little value to distinguish these processes simply by the index word " oral tradition " and to content oneself with that label, for one cannot see at once why these men, with their conceptions of the future, should spread abroad so zealously their recollections of the immediate past. The future, of which they were certain and which they expected in the immediately coming days, was indeed much more glorious than anything that was past, and it is quite impossible to understand to what extent such a spreading of the gospel could have lead to its fixation. Far rather were it to be supposed that what had been incidentally told would feel tame in the storms of " pneumatic " inspiration and apocalyptic excitement, or that it would have been robbed of its proper meaning by frequent repetition. Fixation is only to be accepted where the handing down takes place either in the regulated activity of teaching and of learning, or under the control of immanent laws. We must, however, assume that fixation has taken place in our process if we really believe that the Gospels or their sources arose within the tradition of the Church. In each case we must inquire (1) as to *the motive* which caused the spreading of the reminiscences, although the feelings and desires of the people were directed towards the future, and (2) as to *the law* which governed their spreading and which helped to form and to preserve what had been said. If there is no such law, then the writing of the Gospels implies not an organic development of the process by means of collecting, trimming, and binding together, but the beginning of a new and purely literary development. If there was no such motive, then it is quite impossible to understand how men who made no pretentions to literature could create a tradition which constituted the first steps of the literary production which was even then coming into being.

But in fact both of these, motive and law, can be discovered in the sources. The author of St. Luke's Gospel points to the first as well as the second when he speaks in his prologue of those eye-witnesses and servants of the word from the beginning, who created the tradition from which the composers of the Gospels drew their material.[1]

We must not empty this reference of significance by some such remark as that it is well known that Luke followed a method common to Greek historical writing. In fact he did follow such a method, and hence we require his assurance that he " had traced all things accurately from the first ", and that " he was writing things in order ", but not as the sign of a work with a specially individual character. Rather we must understand it only as a sign of the care which was laid upon him as a historian, just as is the case in literary histories.

---

[1] Cf. the detailed exegesis of the Lukan prologue by Cadbury, in Jackson and Lake, *The Beginnings of Christianity*, vol. ii, pp. 489–510.

In the same way also, the reference to the "many" predecessors corresponds to convention and so does not prove that there were many, but only that there were several of such texts. As soon as one questions the conventional character of Luke's Prologue, however, then the departures from the usual convention receive greater significance. It is, indeed, customary in such an introduction to mention the eyewitnesses, deny them to the predecessors and to claim them for the author who is now writing. It is by no means usual to support the other works, as well as one's own work in an indirect fashion, by the eyewitness of unnamed persons as Luke does in this case :

"Forasmuch as many have taken in hand to draw up a narrative concerning those matters which have been fulfilled among us, even as they delivered them unto us, which from the beginning were eyewitnesses and ministers of the word, it seemed good to me also, having traced the course of all things accurately from the first, to write unto thee in order, most excellent Theophilus, that thou mightest know the certainty concerning the things wherein thou wast instructed."

It is obviously not the author's purpose, when he uses the phrase "eyewitnesses and ministers of the word", to mention two completely distinct groups, for he unites them by means of the common definite article. But it cannot be his meaning that both groups were identical, for, of course, there had been preachers in growing number who were unable to make the claim of being eyewitnesses. But at the beginning it seemed to the author to be certain that those who had heard the word also preached as ministers of the word. They were the missionaries, preachers, and teachers who carried the gospel of Christ abroad in order to win the world.

Because the eyewitnesses were at the same time preachers, what they had experienced must have come out amongst the people—here we see the reason for the propagation of the gospel. And this propagation remained subject neither to personal taste, nor to the circumstances of the hour, but took place in a regular manner in the service of certain interests and for the purpose of reaching certain goals. This is where we begin to catch sight of the law, according to which the formulation of the tradition was perfected. Our synoptic Gospels themselves fill out and prove these observations. Numerous cases of parallel tradition indicate that the narrative material had not been subject merely to accident, that it had neither fluttered about nor split up, but that it had crystallized out in different places under similar conditions. Even to-day certain narratives and groups of sayings betray the interests which their formulation or their collection was meant to serve. Thereby they show clearly what it was that, more than anything else, led to the handing down of the tradition, viz. *missionary purpose was the cause* and *preaching was the means of spreading abroad that which the disciples of Jesus possessed as recollections.*

This first consequence requires more exact definition. Tradition grows out of what the " eyewitnesses and ministers of the word " say. If what they say were only a matter of reminding one another of things which they had experienced together, there would have been no order in the propagation, no formulation of the material, in short, no tradition.

What those Christians who knew something about Jesus added, in order to shape and pass on what they knew in some regular manner, was not a concern about the future world, for such a concern was foreign to men who lived in expectation of the End itself. Rather what drove them to such a formulation and propagation of the tradition was the work of proselytizing to which they felt themselves bound, i.e. the missionary purpose.

We are concerned, then, not with things remembered complete in themselves, though without form, and thus passed on, but, from the very beginning, with recollections full of emotional power to bring about repentance and to gain believers. Thus the things which were remembered automatically took on a definite form, for it is only when such matters have received a form that they are able to bring about repentance and gain converts.

Whether in making these converts we are dealing with the Jewish or the Gentile mission is not the first question. For this way of stating the question raises a false issue when we are dealing with the progress of the mission where in all probability the most important and the most frequent question was that of winning the proselytes and the " God-fearers ", i.e. men who either altogether or to some extent had passed over from paganism to Judaism. In missionary work Jews, Gentiles, and proselytes, needed some description and application of what was known about Jesus. The same was also necessary when it was a matter of building up and confirming the churches. Moreover in the course of worship " sermons " were delivered to the Christians who had already been won. The letters of Paul are adapted to be read out aloud to the congregation, and so made accessible to all the members. This preaching must have made use from time to time of the tradition. In the churches which had not been founded by Paul and which were more closely bound to the first church as well as to Judaism there was in all probability a more frequent connection between their witness and the tradition than amongst the Christians of Paul's missionary circle. Hence we must assume the presence of tradition operative in both the missionary work and the preaching in the course of worship. Finally, the same must have been the case for those who were becoming Christians ; they required instruction which made them familiar with their new faith, and with the new life which was required of them. It is obvious that this didactic preaching would have to show how faith and life were determined by the words and works of Jesus. If, therefore, I describe preaching as the original seat of all tradition about Jesus, I am thinking of everything which stands behind the expression in Luke i, 4, " that thou mightest know the certainty concerning the things wherein thou wast instructed." This may refer to the preaching to non-Christians and also to a Christian congregation, as well as to the teaching of catechumens. And so if I speak of preaching in this connection, all possible forms of Christian propaganda are included : mission preaching, preaching during worship, and catechumen instruction. The mission of Christendom in the world was the originative cause of all these different activities.

Once more Luke's Prologue indicates the limits of the significance which tradition has for preaching. The author wishes to give to the Theophilus who is mentioned in the dedication a more certain account concerning the things which he had learned from the didactic and missionary preaching. Luke's Gospel contains, not the content of the preaching, but a guarantee for that content. All the observations and conclusions which we can put forward, in fact, prove that the primitive Christian missionaries did not relate the life of Jesus, but proclaimed the salvation which had come about in Jesus Christ. What they narrated was secondary to this proclamation, was intended to confirm it and to found it. We must beware of too mechanical a conception of the nature of the preaching, and of the connection between preaching and tradition. Our purpose is not to reconstruct a special type of sermon within which the whole tradition would find its place ; rather the dependence of the formation of tradition upon the preaching is to be conceived somewhat in this fashion : the material of tradition gave objectivity to the preaching of salvation ; it explained, expanded, and, in accordance therewith, was either introduced into the preaching, or related at its close. The oldest passages of the tradition must have corresponded, in the form they assumed, to this connection with the sermon.

The question arises whether we can recognize enough of the nature of the preaching of those days to enable us to grasp it as a Form-giving principle. At least the primitive Christian sermons which have really been preserved do not come to us out of the first decades. It is of no value to enter into discussion whether anything, and if so, how much, of the speeches in Acts really was spoken or indeed could have been spoken in the then situation. For this question is only raised by anxiety concerning the historicity of special texts. As if something could be saved where nothing can be lost ! Such a concern ignores the fact that the historian of that day— even the Jewish, as Josephus proves—readily interpolated his record with speeches which he himself introduced, speeches which were composed by him in a special interest that frequently arose out of the writing itself.[1] Even when he does use sources which recorded a speech, or at least its theme, an assumption which is in no way proved in Acts, the formulation of the speech which we read to-day is his work. The importance of this is seen by making a comparison between the speeches contained in the *Antiquities* of Josephus and his source in the Old Testament.

It is exactly this understanding which helps us further. If the author of Acts was not bound by the composition of the speeches, but had the right to shape them according to his own ideas, the question arises why he did not exercise this right with more concern about variations. Every reader of Acts knows how very similar are the speeches of Peter and Paul, at least when they each stand before the Jews. On these occasions the author might well have adopted a different style as the speeches before Felix and King Agrippa bear witness. Hence it follows that he does not appear to have tried to give variation in the composition of speeches which were in the nature of sermons ; rather he was content with repetition. That is to be seen clearly in the sermons to the Gentiles (xiv, 15-17; xvii, 22b-31). Both passages preach God as the Creator ; both depict His revelation in nature and amongst men, and both proclaim His will to bring to an end now the age of Gentile error. The other sermons in Acts show such a repetition in a much higher degree ; in the speeches of Peter to the people (Acts ii, iii), and to Cornelius,

---

[1] Cf. Cadbury, *The Making of Luke-Acts*, 1927, pp. 184 ff.

as well as in the sermon of Paul at Antioch, there is an introduction varying somewhat according to the situation. But otherwise there is a similar well-planned outline whose sections are frequently repeated and only accidentally change their order. Thus we have the right to speak of a scheme which the author consciously accepts and which consists of the following: Kerygma or message, scriptural proof, exhortation to repentance. The Kerygma, i.e. the preaching of Jesus Christ, was contained in a few short sentences.[1] What was important was proved out of the Old Testament. Then followed the exhortation to repentance and conversion. It is not the peculiarity of the two Apostles which shows itself in these repetitions, neither is it the literary art of the author that is to be seen here. On the contrary a certain similarity of tone is unmistakable. But this similarity of tone is manifestly intentional, for the author is by no means so unskilled that poverty of sensibility led him to dispense with variations. He does not wish to reveal the variety but the oneness of the Christian preaching. And his concern could be illustrated with the words which St. Paul wrote in regard to his own reproduction of the message handed down to him (1 Cor. xv, 11): "Thus we preach and through such preaching you have become Christians."

These speeches, and above all the message with which we are here specially concerned, represent a certain type, and in particular an ancient type. This is proved by observing the formulation of the pronouncements about Christ as we have often done. Just because the Lucan writings use the title "the Lord" even in narrative, it is striking that in the message (iii, 13, 26) as in the prayer (iv, 27, 30) the terminology employed is God's "Servant Jesus". It is equally remarkable that the Christological outline appears to be "Adoptionist" to the unprejudiced reader, just as if

---

[1] The Kerygma is to be found in Acts ii, 22 ff., iii, 13 ff., x, 37 ff., xiii, 23 ff. (also v, 30 ff. is similar). The scriptural proof ii, 25 ff., iii, 22 ff., x, 43*a*, xiii, 32 ff. (the exhortation to repentance), ii, 38 f., iii, 17 ff., x, 42, 43*b*, xiii, 38 ff.

the man Jesus only became the Messiah at the Ascension. Ascriptions used in worship and dogmatic ideas which were developed very quickly in the Christian Churches had not yet exercised any notable influence upon this conception of Christ. Indeed the very term " Servant (of God) " is honorific, because one is reminded of the Suffering Servant of the Second Isaiah. The term, however, soon fell into the background in the Church because it was offensive. The archaic form of speech here, as in the prayers of the apostolic teaching, proves the antiquity of the tradition.

Alongside of these indirect indications of Acts concerning a primitive Christian message, there comes a further and significant witness. It is significant above all, in that its testimony points to the earliest period, to St. Paul or rather to the tradition which he hands on in 1 Cor. xv. Its value is apparent to anyone who remarks the difference between this passage and the Gospels. There is here as yet not a trace of any attempt at harmonizing. And as far as the form of this passage is concerned,[1] it is my opinion that, at least in verses 3-5, Paul imparts a formula and that he does it word for word. For the first point it is sufficient proof that he wanders so far from his subject. In the context he is really concerned only with the Resurrection, and indeed he begins with the death and burial. In such a quotation we should assume a literal reproduction of the tradition if there were no contrary consideration.[2] Thus we must assume that Paul

---

[1] In the interpretation of the introductory words we must differentiate between the solemn rhetorically coloured proem contained in the three parallel relative clauses, and the connecting remarks. The following is the sense of the proemium : he wishes to proclaim once more to them the gospel " which you have received, in which you stand, through which you are saved ". Behind the word " gospel " in St. Paul we cannot assume a formula, but only the very preaching of salvation. Reference to the formula occurs only in the remarks which follow the proem, and I do not doubt that it is referred to by the word ($\lambda \acute{o} \gamma o s$) which we frequently interpret in this place so meaninglessly. St. Paul said if you still know with what $\lambda \acute{o} \gamma o s$ I preached it to you (but you are certain of that, otherwise you would have become Christians without understanding its earnestness). At this stage he cites the $\lambda \acute{o} \gamma o s$: for I have handed down to you (not " preached "), as among the main things, what I myself received as tradition.

[2] Johannes Weiss says in his Commentary that perhaps it was felt that the doctrine " for our sins " could not be entrusted to the primitive Church and that a Haggadistic

himself had learned a formula in which, amongst others, the following words were to be found :—

He died for our sins according to the Scriptures.

He was buried.

He rose on the third day according to the Scriptures.

He appeared to Cephas, then to the Twelve.

We cannot infer how the formula ended, nor how it began, nor indeed what it said about the life of Jesus. For our problem the mere fact of this witness is far more important than its content, because this passage provides the answer to the other questions with which the speeches of the Acts confronted us, questions concerning the time and place, the form and language of the formulation of the gospel message. From the text of Acts we could only infer a relatively early age, but here we find more. We learn that even Paul himself received this formula possibly when he became a Christian or at latest when he became a missionary, i.e. in the thirties of the first century and in Damascus or in Syrian Antioch. Even these Hellenistic churches apparently handed to their new converts or to the missionaries whom they sent out a short outline or summary of the Christian message, a formula which reminded the young Christian of his faith and which gave a teacher of this faith guidance for his instruction. Further, those speeches of Acts allowed us to infer only one special type of preaching, and in this type the message was to be recognized in its content. We could not penetrate so far as the exact words, and even the question whether there was only a Greek or also an Aramaic tradition had to remain unanswered. In Paul we find quoted a fragment of the evangelical formula, which moreover is in the original

---

expansion of Paul's message had always to be reckoned with. But the researches of the last few years (Heitmüller, *Zeitschr. f. d. neutest. Wissensch.* 1912, S. 320 ff. and Bousset, *Kyrios Christos*) have shown that in the case of what Paul " received " it was not the primitive Church which gave, but rather the circle of Hellenistic churches to which Paul attached himself when he became Christian, and which transmitted to him both the Christian tradition and the call to be a Christian missionary. But that interpretation of the death of Jesus must certainly be ascribed to these Churches since Paul was not the first to deal with this matter.

language. For the passage took its rise in Hellenistic circles whose kernel was constituted by those who formerly belonged to the Jewish Diaspora, and for whom a formulation in Greek sufficed. It does not appear to me to be quite credible that such men in such circumstances would have accepted a translated Aramaic formula. The text was not holy, but only the history to which it bore witness. The content of this history, spread abroad by eyewitnesses and preachers, first in Aramaic and then in Greek, was put together by Greek-speaking churches for missionary purposes in definite words which they themselves formulated. This would of course be in their own (Greek-Christian) language.

Thus they created the formulæ. For there is no question of one and the same message published and received abroad everywhere by tradition. That there were several formulæ is altogether probable because, as we ever more clearly recognize, the foundation and the development of the Church was not carried through by a single will according to a single plan. The primitive church at Jerusalem is by no means the proper mother of all the gentile Christian Churches. The latter are on the one hand incidental foundations due to the fluctuating life of the Roman Empire ; on the other hand, however, they were shaped by one will and according to one plan, but that was the will and plan of Paul, and thus of an outsider who, as he himself says in Gal. i, had very little contact with the primitive Church in Jerusalem in the first few years of his missionary work.

Bi-lingual Antioch on the Orontes was obviously a much more significant starting-point for missionary activities than Jerusalem which was relatively uni-lingual. And further, if the development of the tradition had been so uniform that Christian preaching had everywhere employed the same formulation of the message, we should discover literary traces of this uniformity. Instead of this, however, we meet with significant and striking differences. The message found in 1 Cor. xv regards the appearance of Jesus to Cephas as the first, and as fundamental for the Easter faith. It is this very appearance which, as is well known, is not recorded in the synoptics. The mention of the burial of Jesus (1 Cor. xv) which had already become part of the message, and thereby, so to say, one of the acts of salvation, is lacking in the speeches of Acts, with the exception of Acts xiii. Such discords bear witness to a far-reaching variation in the tradition, not only in the narratives, but also in the short summaries. Hence we must presuppose not merely one, but several types of message. Yet these types of message, introduced into the preaching of salvation, gave the preacher opportunity to guide the thoughts of his hearers to the story of Jesus. Thus, we have here the point of connection for communicating tradition within the borders of preaching either for missionary purposes or for those of worship. The repetition of message in the course of preaching in Acts, and the assurance which Paul gives that he himself had received such a message, show that in the handing down of the message we are dealing with a widespread custom of Christian missionaries and preachers. In this form the events which formed the basis of all preaching for conversion were brought home to the non-Christians. The Christians were in this manner also ever and again reminded of that piece of history which guaranteed their salvation. We have a right to presuppose such a custom both in Aramaic and in Greek-speaking regions, for such a mode of carrying on tradition obviously corresponds to use in Palestinian and Hellenistic Judaism. Paul himself seems to hint at this when in 1 Cor. xv, 1 and 3, and 1 Cor. xi, 23 he obviously uses as technical terms the words "receive" and "handed down", which are the equivalent for the official Jewish terms for the taking over and passing on of tradition.[1] What significance the development of tradition had for Judiasm is well known. Its theological education and its legal praxis rested on tradition, on taking over and developing further. It is certain that the Greek synagogue

---

[1] παραλαμβάνειν corresponds to קִבֵּל, and παραδιδόναι to מָסַר.

also lived according to tradition. Hellenistic Jewish congregations were, however, not only the models for, but
frequently also the nuclei of the Greek Christian Churches,
since many of their members or of their " God-fearers "
constituted the kernel of the new Christian congregations.
Some care for traditional elements must have been found
in the oldest Christian congregations in Palestine as well as
in the " world ".

Convinced in this way of the existence of the message
and of the value of the tradition contained therein, we may
glance at the data which it contains or probably contained.
On comparing the passages already mentioned, we may
begin by making two observations. On the one hand we
find the Passion is dealt with everywhere, and indeed with
remarkable detail. There are differences in individual matters,
but agreement in essentials ; death, resurrection, evidence
for the resurrection. On the other hand, in the mention of
other data out of the life of Jesus which the Pauline text
completely excludes, there is evidently no agreement.
Sometimes the Baptist is mentioned, as in Acts x and xiii ;
sometimes the subject is the deeds of Jesus as in Acts ii
and x. It is precisely this material which offers good
support for the assumption that the passages dealing
with the gospel messages give us contact with the
primitive Christian preaching ; for what we gather from it
we must assume to be, as far as it goes, the oldest message.
It shows an out and out interest in the Passion and in the
Easter story with its attendant circumstances, but, on the
other hand, it deals only incidentally with other data out of
the life of Jesus.

If what was preached was a witness of salvation, then,
among all the materials which were related, only this one,
the Passion, was of real significance in the message. For
what it dealt with was the first act of the end of the world
as then believed and hoped. Here salvation was visible not
only in the person and the word of the Lord, but also in

the succession of a number of events. To set these matters in their connection corresponded to a need, and all the more as only a description of the consequences of the Passion and of Easter resolved the paradox of the Cross, only the organic connection of the events satisfied the need of explanation, and only the binding together of the individual happenings could settle the question of responsibility. Here we meet with the interests of edification, of the most primitive theology, and of the simplest apologetics, which certainly, for the time, tended to the relating of the Passion story in its historical circumstances.

We do not say that this account of the Passion must have occupied the same length of passage as we find to-day in Mark, but it is likely that, in accordance with the interests just mentioned, it showed that the Messiah was sent to the Cross by His own people, that this dreadful and shameful event took place in accordance with God's will, i.e. was prophesied by Scripture, and that God had expressly made Himself known to Jesus in the Resurrection, and had let the Risen Lord appear to His own people. Hence we must presuppose the early existence of a Passion narrative complete in itself since preaching, whether for the purpose of the mission or of worship, required some such a text. We may say at this point that this presupposition is justified by a glance at the tradition which has come down to us. The relatively fixed character of the Passion narrative in the synoptics, and the quite unique agreement between John and the other evangelists in this part of the narrative, show that this material had duly and uniformly reached its definite form.[1] (Cf. Chapter VII.)

---

[1] Also in the newly discovered Berlin fragment of the Acts of Paul, Paul's preaching is founded upon the Kerygma. The apostle begins his sermon by mentioning the kindness of God to Israel, and there follows in the same sermon (after an intermediate passage unknown to us) a description of Jesus' work and preaching, in the course of which we read ἀπολείπετε τὸ σκότος, λάβετε τὸ φῶς, οἱ ἐν σκοτίᾳ θανάτου καθήμενοι, φῶς ἀνέτειλεν ὑμῖν. Then came a description of the deeds, for the following has been preserved: θαυμάσια . . . δώδεκα ἄνδρας . . . νόσους θεραπεύων . . . τυφλοὺς θεραπεύω[ν] . . . [λεπρ]οὺς καθα[ριζαν].

The description of the deeds of Jesus was not governed
by the same interests in the course of preaching. These events
had only an incidental and not an essential significance for
the understanding of salvation. They are not cosmic acts
constituting an introduction to the approaching world change.
Rather they are only signs of what lay in the future because
they constituted the actualizations of the wonderful power
and might of the Messiah. Even if they were related in the
course of preaching they did not require to be reproduced
in their completeness, nor in their context, but only incidentally
for the purpose of illustration and as *examples*. In so doing
no biographical representation of the work of Jesus could
be used which was not in itself a preaching of salvation.
Neither could a detailed description of isolated matters be
used, which by their comprehensive character would only
have disturbed the sequence of the sermon. Hence, we must
presuppose the occasional insertion of narratives from the
life of Jesus into the context of the sermon.

If we were to look for an analogy of such an insertion
we might consider the citation of the story of Cain and Abel
in 1 Clem. This letter is in itself a kind of sermon, for it was
obviously intended for public reading during service in
Corinth, and probably also in Rome. It is only in this way
that the conclusion of the whole by means of a long public
prayer can be explained. Of course, the section about Cain
and Abel, 1 Clem. iv, 1-7, offers only a general example, for
the Roman preacher is an author to a high degree, and, in
addition, makes use not of a recent and still variable tradition,
but of the sacred Scriptures which had been handed down.
Nevertheless it offers a certain analogy. The author,
probably following a Jewish tradition, mentions a number
of illustrations for the wickedness of rivalry and envy. In
his seven "old Examples" (v, 1), he describes sex in a
single sentence and furnishes the example of Moses with a
few words from the Old Testament. But the first and
earliest example, that of Cain and Abel, he illustrates with

the whole story which he reproduces according to the Septuagint, six verses altogether, down to the death of Abel. Then he says: "you see, my brothers, that rivalry and envy led to fratricide." (iv, 7.) And now there follows in a brief sentence the second example of Jacob and Esau. In some such a manner Christian preachers also could have woven an anecdote of the deeds of Jesus into their sermon.

The significance of the speeches in Acts concerning the deeds of Jesus corresponds to these general observations. In regard to both passages which are relevant here, one mentions kind acts and healings (x, 38), the other mentions acts of power, miracles and signs (ii, 22). In spite of appearances we must think of the deeds of Jesus in the broadest sense, i.e. of decisions in disputes, answers to questions and other sayings. His speeches are to be understood as manifestations of the "power" which dwelt in Him (Mk. i, 22). In both those passages of Acts the deeds of Jesus appear as proof that God is with Him. This view sets them in relation to the evangel, and only this view could cause a Christian missionary further to develop the significance of the Kerygma in the way found in Acts ii, 22 and x, 38. For what Acts offers as the content of a speech which was really delivered, is proved by its brevity to be rather the skeleton than the substance of a speech. Therefore the Christian missionaries delivered in their speeches not the bare message, but rather the message as explained, illustrated and supported with references and otherwise developed. That is the case quite especially in regard to the deeds of Jesus, for the "acts of power, miracles, and signs" remain mere words unless they receive life out of the narratives. The hearers must themselves feel the power which went out from Jesus. Therefore, in the narrative, not merely the historical connection, but the individual act must be described to them, and this narrative must not refer to individual things in the style of a chronicle, but, rather in the style of a sermon, must bear witness to what was the principal matter of the utterance, viz. the salvation effected through Jesus Christ. And thus the conclusion that we have already reached from general considerations is also supported here. The narratives of the deeds of Jesus could only be introduced as *examples* in support of the message. But that is as much as to say that very little depended upon order or balance, but only upon individual matters. Further also, within this story itself, the method of the narrative was not intended to satisfy curiosity, to arouse wonder, nor especially to make an impression for its own sake, but was conceived only in connection with preaching, and was intended to support its edifying tendencies. This aim necessarily created the form. It necessarily effected the method of the narration by excluding, by concentrating, and by giving a certain tone. If the custom of the preacher, as we may in all probability conclude, was to illustrate his message by relating examples, and if this constituted the oldest Christian narrative style, we can perhaps best give the name of *paradigm* to this category of narrative.[1] It is an open question how far this category is present in the form of the tradition which has been preserved for us. Naturally the constructive method which I have employed here by further inference from the speeches in Acts, can in the first instance lead to only hypothetical conclusions.

If with these premises we ponder the possibilities of the construction of Form as they would be occasioned by primitive Christian preaching, various developments may be regarded as probable. We may suppose that the manner in which the doings of Jesus was narrated was determined by the requirements of the sermon ; in this way an illustrative style fitted

---

[1] I suggested the name first of all in my publication *Die urchristl. Ueberlieferung von Johannes den Taufer*, S. 5 ; compare also *Zeitschr. f. neutest. Wissenschaft.*, 1915, S. 113, A.1. and Johannes Horst, *Theol. Studien und Kritiken*, 1914, S. 430, A.1. Naturally more depends upon the recognition of the style of category than upon the name. Nevertheless the name " paradigm " appears to me more clearly to express the connection of preaching and style of category than some such a name as " Mission-story " would do. V. Taylor, in *The Formation of the Gospel Tradition*, 1933, p. 30, proposes the name " Pronouncement Stories ".

for missionary work and for worship could arise. The story of the Passion, however, could not have gained its form within the borders of the sermon proper. Its material was too large for such a purpose. Yet it might well have developed in connection with the sermon as an illustration following upon the message properly so-called. This illustration would be in itself a sermon by means of what the story contained and by its method of approach.

We must presuppose the operation of still another law for the handing down of the sayings of Jesus. Here we have to do not with the words of Jesus which constituted either the kernel or the goal of the story, for the tradition of these sayings is closely connected with the handing down of the narratives, but rather we are now dealing with another class, viz. isolated sayings, especially proverbs, metaphors and commandments. As we shall show in Chapter IX, their place is to be found to a large extent in catechetical teaching, and therefore in that kind of preaching which we have already described (cf. p. 14) as the third possible kind of primitive Christian sermon alongside of that specially used for missionary work and in the course of worship.

This instruction would make use to a large extent of hortatory material, i.e. of loosely connected sayings which had been handed down. That there was such a handing down has been evermore recognized as a result of the researches of Alfred Seeberg. In the same way we must establish a stream of tradition whose current is to be differentiated from the development and the spread of other materials, such as the story of the Passion and the narratives. We shall inquire into the nature and laws of this tradition in Chapter IX, but we must establish now the general probability of such a special development. Mark's Gospel made relatively little use of this branch of the tradition. The two larger synoptic Gospels, Matthew and Luke contain a great deal of this material, and to some extent in such an altered formulation that, by means of analytical criticism, a special source of Sayings " Q " could be deduced.   The nature of our Gospel texts thus permits us to suppose that in these Sayings we are dealing with a special development of tradition : *the tradition of narrative and the tradition of words are not subject to the same law.*   This may seem strange to a modern observer, since he, necessarily governed by biographical interests, does not see at once why words and deeds of Jesus are not handed down as a unity, and should not have the same " Sitz im Leben ".   But if one takes account of the amount and the possibility of the tradition in the neighbouring Judaism, every sense of strangeness disappears.   For amongst the Jews there is a common differentiation between the Halakha, or the tradition of rules concerning life and worship, and the Haggada, which is the tradition of historical and theological material.   In the time of Jesus and of Rabbinism it is quite comprehensible that the Halakha should stand in the forefront for Judaism.   It had to be taken much more seriously than the Haggada, because it demanded obedience, whereas the Haggada only required respect and discussion.   Hence the tradition of the Halakha must have been stricter and more regulated than the Haggada, which frequently depended upon accidents and upon the availability of a Haggadic tradition for the Halakha (see Chapter VI). Hence, for a Christian formerly a Jew, the differentiation between the Haggadic and the Halakhic parts of his new Christian tradition would be easy from the very first.   The sayings of Jesus were handed down within the framework of a Christian Halakha, and so it is by no means surprising, but rather in the nature of things, that this tradition arose under other conditions than those of the narrative material.

We   have   now   touched   upon   the   question   as   to which Churches we may ascribe the formulation of the tradition.   The earliest tradition, if it is trustworthy, must somehow be connected with the Palestinian circle of Jesus.   But we know little of the Christian Churches of Palestine, and of their actual tradition nothing at all has been received by us directly, i.e. in Aramaic.   At best, we can only deduce its part in the process of tradition by working backwards, and not forwards. Nor can the essential part of tradition be ascribed to the Pauline Churches, although they come earliest in our literature. If the tradition had gained its normative form in their midst we should have before us more traces of its influence in the Pauline letters. And whatever grounds we may adduce to explain the silence of the Apostle about the earthly life of Jesus, yet the impression cannot be avoided that in the spiritual discussions between Paul and his Churches the data of that life play a strikingly small part.

The hints contained in the Apostle himself suggest another origin of the tradition. The traditions which he adduces in 1 Cor. xi and xv he confesses to have received. According to the evidence of Galatians, Jerusalem, which Paul only rarely and briefly visited as a Christian, may be left out of account as the place where he received this tradition. Hence we have only to do with Churches in which Paul became a Christian or was a missionary, i.e. Damascus and Syrian Antioch. Hence it is the pre-Pauline *Hellenistic Christianity* which at least handed on this tradition and, to the extent that the formulation is Greek, also " formed " it. This Christianity, however, was differentiated from the Pauline Churches by closer proximity to Judaism. These Christian Churches and Greek-speaking regions, for example, Antioch, Damascus (but also Alexandria and Rome) grew out of Jewish Churches without making a logical breach with Judaism. In this way we may explain how this sort of Christianity, which is really Judaism without Jewish national limits, brought over a large amount of liturgy, Jewish prayers, hymns, and exhortations into the Christian Church.[1]

The Christianity of these Churches is not characterized by the consciousness of a new paradoxical revelation of the

---

[1] The following texts, containing Jewish material in a thin Christian covering, exemplify this tradition : The Prayers, Didache, 9, 10, 1 Clem. 59–61, many hymns of the Apocalypse and many Odes of Solomon, the exhortations of James, and Hermas (Mandata).

God worshipped by Judaism, as in the case of Paul, but by the faith that Judaism, properly understood, reached its completion in preaching the coming of the Messiah, Jesus Christ.[1] Thus in preaching about God the Creator, about the moral life required by the law, about the Resurrection and the Last Judgment, they needed only to weave in the message of what had happened in Palestine as the first act of the final End of the World. This Christianity was, therefore, in a special degree interested in the material contained in the tradition of the life of Jesus, but not in the sense that it was necessary to bequeath to a following age a valuable historical recollection—no one counted upon such a following age—but rather, from the standpoint that a long-expected salvation had now been realized in particular events amongst the Jewish people. The great problem with whose solution Paul was concerned in teaching, preaching, and discussing was not felt amongst these Churches in its full weight. The fellowship of Jews and converted Gentiles in the Church offered no fundamental difficulty—even in Antioch meals were held in common (Gal. ii, 12)—for already within the Jewish Churches this question had been brought to a solution in connection with the " God-fearing " Gentiles. Since, in consequence of the fact that proselytes and " God-fearers " had been received into these Churches, the boundary between Gentiles and Jews was not unsurmountable. Thus the chief problem of Paul, the conversion of Gentiles apart from the law, could not be envisaged in full completeness. The question of practical living was regulated in the end by means of Jewish exhortations. If words of Jesus were included in these exhortations, then at least the boundaries of a Christian mode of life were laid down.

In such Churches, therefore, worship, preaching, and teaching were of a Jewish kind although conducted in Greek.

---

[1] It is significant that Acts and the Pastorals also make Paul a preacher of this faith, Acts xxiii, 1, 6 ; xxvi, 2–23 ; 2 Tim. i, 3–5.

It is in this place that we must look for the real home of a
tradition which was passed on to missionaries, preachers,
and teachers. Concern for the tradition arose from this
necessity, and not from literary or biographical requirements.
Concern for tradition, exercised in the manner of the Greek
Judaism with which the Churches were connected, meant its
cultivation. This could prevent the tradition becoming
rank, spoiled by being broken up, robbed of its point, and
rendered un-Christian by the intermingling of ideas foreign
to it. All things of this sort would make the fragments of
tradition unusable for the needs of the missionary, of worship,
and of catechumens. This is not to say that no rankness
of tradition was to be found in these Churches at all. The
point is that the material available for the preacher was not
immediately subject to such accidental tendencies to change,
as popular tradition in the circle of unliterary people is
readily subject. But such a concern could not prevent,
it might indeed even require that the material should be
shaped and directed for the purposes which it should serve,
i.e. definitely sharpened, obscure points made clear, the
material placed in closer connection with the subject of the
sermon, and the actual interests of the life of the Church
introduced. How far the content of the Gospels corresponds
to these propositions is a matter for research. At this place
we can only show what part was played by the process of
tradition in the Churches of the kind we have described,
for they already possessed the tradition which was afterwards
made use of in the Gospels. In its own circle this tradition
had reached a definiteness which permits us to speak of its
Form. This level of the whole process of the tradition is the
earliest which can now be touched by some such a constructive
observation. Here lies the beginning of the history of the
Gospel material on a Greek foundation as still knowable
to us.[1]

---

[1] These arguments meet the objections which have been brought against the
constructive method. We are not dealing with Churches whose unworldliness and

If we were to consider what might have been before this
beginning we should meet with the question of language,
which is particularly important for our present research.
It has been frequently dealt with. It is really to be found
in a problem which we cannot take too seriously, in the fact
that the works of Jesus, according to every hint that may be
gathered from the Gospels, were done in the main on
Aramaic soil, whereas the early tradition of these works now
exists exclusively in Greek.   In the absence of sources this
problem cannot be completely solved, but by means of
a few boundary marks we may help towards its solution.

1. There may have been an Aramaic tradition of Jesus
more or less " formed ".   If so, it was neither of great significance nor of long duration, for it is obvious that the Aramaic-
speaking people of the second century no longer possessed
any special tradition.   The Nazarenes in Syria had by that time
made their own Aramaic Gospel later known to and translated
by Jerome.   The fragments of this Nazarene Gospel which
he and other witnesses, especially the MSS. of the so-called
Zion Gospel edition, hand down,[1] show that we are here
dealing with an expanded Matthew and not with its predecessor
or with some other " Urevangelium ".   Hence, in the second
century a Greek text had to be translated if an Aramaic Gospel
was wanted.   Thus there was no Aramaic source of the life of
Jesus, and since the later Aramaic Evangeliarium calls Jesus
not Jeshua Meshicha, but Jesus Meshicha, the use of the Greek
form of the name seems to show that no independent tradition
had been kept on Palestinian soil.   The cause may be deduced.
The standard formulation was made with the purpose of
converting missionary Churches and of teaching converts.
For this purpose the Greek language was required since

---

sanctity left the picture painted by Luke in Acts i (so Scott Easton, *The Gospel
before the Gospels*, 1928, p. 79 f.). In speaking of a cultivation which protected the
tradition from rank growth, I mean a certain way of handing down, and not ethical
evaluation.   The unworldliness of the preacher shows itself in its ignorance of
literature proper, and not in its ethical quality.

[1] Cf. Dalman, *Jesus-Jeschua*.

the essential direction of the early Christian mission pointed toward the West. Therefore Greek texts in particular were fixated. Missionary work in Aramaic had little scope and little significance in the world. Thus the formulation in Aramaic did not become very firm and was never ready for writing down. Where Aramaic texts existed, they possessed a limited life soon to end. For the purposes of literature, i.e. for the wider world and the future, they were left out of account, even as it appears for the unliterary writings in the sense of the Gospels.

2. Further, the development of the tradition of the Haggadic stories may not have been the same as that of the Halakhic words. All the Aramaic words of Jesus must once have been translated. This touched upon the question of literal reproduction, especially when people wished to live according to these words and to follow their directions. Modification and filling out of the sayings cannot be excluded, but before the correcting or filling out, literal translation had to be undertaken. On the other hand, stories were narrated. But whether this took place on the basis of the Aramaic form, or in some new way, cannot be determined immediately. A literal translation was not required except of the words of Jesus. That such a difference between the tradition of the words and of history existed in the understanding of those who handed it down is shown by the fate of certain well-defined words of Jesus in the source Q. In the record of the messengers of the Baptist (Matt. xi, 2–6, and Luke vii, 18–23) it is striking that question and answer in both passages are given in almost the same words, although the narrative context is completely different. It is the same with the words of the centurion of Capernaum and the answer of Jesus (Matt. viii, 8–10, Luke vii, 9). Introduction and conclusion are completely different, but the kernel is handed down almost as a unity. Thus there must have been in the source either a definite narrative text which was not regarded by one or both of the writers as binding, or else the source contained

no such definitive text at all. In either case the writers clearly differentiated their responsibility toward the text of Jesus's words from their duties as narrators.

3. Moreover the boundaries of language, with whose crossing we are concerned, must not be understood geographically. We must presuppose a wide knowledge of Greek, especially in Northern Palestine, and we must recognize without reserve that, in Syrian towns like Antioch and Damascus, there were bilingual people in all classes of the population. Modern Germans, the majority of whom know nothing of any language but their own, are accustomed to regard facility in other tongues as a sign of a special education. The Dutch and the Swiss should convince them to the contrary. Present day Esthonians and Letts offer perhaps a still better example, since their lingual facility comes not by contact with foreigners, but by the veneering of their own language with those of their erstwhile rulers. We must conceive in a similar fashion the conditions in the Syrian Churches. Jews of those regions who understood Aramaic heard about Jesus among the early Church at Jerusalem, but in their own Syrian home they passed it on in Greek. Or else bilingual Christians from Jerusalem acting as evangelists brought the gospel in Greek to Syria. Acts xi, 19 f., depicts expressly the second manner of its spread, but this does not preclude the first, for what happened in the case of the eunuch of " Queen " Candace, viii, 27–39, could be experienced also by a Jew from Antioch or Damascus.

4. We may attempt in this fashion to reconstruct the passage over from Aramaic to Greek. At the same time we should admit various possibilities from verbal translation (especially of the words of Jesus) to complete new formation (especially of narratives). Nevertheless we must beware of making the Semitisms of the evangelical tradition into criteria of these possibilities. " Semitism " is not an unambiguous scientific term. The proof that an Aramaic original has been translated can only be given by incidental wrong translations ;

possibly such a proof can be made here and there, especially
in the words of Jesus Christ, but it is not a character of the
tradition as a whole. The Semitic colour of speech and
description can be observed much oftener, and is, in fact, much
more significant. But this phenomenon cannot be explained
always in the same way. It may be connected with the
Aramaic original (as is often the case in the words of Jesus),
or it may also be traced to an unconscious dependence upon
the diction of the Septuagint, as would be quite conceivable
in these Churches. Nor, again, can we exclude the possibility
of a conscious imitation of the style found in the sacred
narrative of the Old Testament. This is especially the case in
the peculiar style of Luke, who makes the story of the Baptist
(iii, 2) begin like that of a prophet, " And the word of the
Lord came to John the son of Zacharias in the wilderness."
Finally, we must reckon with a wide dispersion of ordinary
Semitisms, especially in the Greek of born-Jews and, as a
consequence, among the people in whose midst they lived.
Many of the linguistic phenomena which come forward as
" Semitisms " may also be understood in the last analysis
from the history of Greek speech from within. In fact, we
must often admit that the evolution of late Greek was forwarded by Semitic tendencies. Thus it is impossible to solve
the problem of the existence and nature of an Aramaic tradition
by the evidence of Semitisms. In all our researches we must
take account of the above possibilities. Further, however,
we are obliged to admit the formation of a tradition in Greek
within a sphere which was in the closest connection with
Greek-Judaism, which formation of tradition was the normative
prime datum of the process which led to the rise of our
gospels.

The considerations of this chapter show that three of the
elements of the Gospel tradition stand in immediate connection
with Christian preaching (in its widest meaning), the story
of the Passion, Paradigms, words of Jesus with " Halakhic "
content. These categories cannot be analysed without placing

them alongside other types from which they differ. Hence in the sequel the analysis of Tales (Chapter VI) and Legends (Chapter V) is excluded from our treatment of Paradigms (Chapter III). The same holds good for our examination of other forms of narrative common in the surrounding world (Chapter VI). Similarly the other kinds of tradition of Jesus' words are bound up with that of hortatory preaching and the traditions of sayings which it contains (Chapter IX). As is also the case in analysing the Passion narrative (Chapter VII), we must continually raise the question whether, and to what extent, the tradition has been orientated to the needs of preaching.

Chapter III

PARADIGMS

The paradox has become probable to us that unliterary men created a definite style. In so doing they followed, of course, not some need of making an artistic form but a compulsion of their life. It arose out of the only practical activity which these men, who belonged to a new realm in the old world, were really acquainted with, viz. propaganda on behalf of their faith. The words " We cannot but speak the things which we saw and heard " (Acts iv, 20) express the tendency which influenced this unliterary process of development. What arises as a consequence is a style of narrative from which every expression of individual sensibility is absent but which is in a high degree concerned with the matter itself. A protocol or official report constitutes the direct opposite to a record whose style is developed by the necessities of missionary work. For the protocol requires a record of a particular situation in a form which is as far as possible free of tendency and therefore of individuality and colour. In consequence of the familiar passing over from literary to historical criticism, the sources of the synoptics, reconstructed in some form as (Ur-) Mark and Q, have often been dealt with as if they were protocols. The error of such a proceeding is manifest, for if the earliest narrators had been so lacking in definite aim in regard to the presentation of the materials as is the writer of a protocol to the evidence with which he is dealing, they would have completely omitted to make any records at all. They made their records, however, because they had a definite object in view, and it was the same object which was fundamental to their preaching. They desired to win men, and further to convince and confirm those whom they had won. The style which corresponded to this object could be called edificatory, if one may use a most general term.

It is credible that this object operated, however, in the direction of constructing a definite form, but we may doubt whether this construction of form was the same everywhere. Similarity of result must not by any means be assumed in different places and in different circumstances, but rather a certain similarity of development, since the same rule, the missionary objective, determined everywhere the choice and style of the narratives. If a speaker to-day journeys through a region geographically limited, for the purpose not only of arousing certain sentiments but of producing definite practical results, e.g. for political canvassing or founding an organization, he will frequently use the same forms of thought as the representative of the same things in a neighbouring region. The aim, the objective presented by their leader, the historical and statistical material with its outline and its methods, which have been handed to the two speakers, these together condition the similarity. And yet even in this case there will still be a certain amount of variation, because they are men of different inclinations, culture, and education, and also often with a different public. In the case of the primitive Christian propaganda only the last consideration, that in regard to the hearers, can have caused any significant variation. The personal differences of the speakers carried less weight because these unliterary men probably enjoyed insufficient elasticity of speech to enable them to express corresponding variations. To a greater extent than speakers of to-day, they remained bound to what appeared to themselves or to their fore-runners as the form of the narrative which corresponded to their missionary aim, and which was now handed on further from one to another (a precursor of the modern " material for speakers "). This material was relatively fixed, i.e. the type of narrative and the development of the principal points remained unaltered. Considerations having to do with the aim of the sermon, could and must have often brought forth variations. No answer can be given to the question whether the single individual carried his material in writing or in his memory. The retentive power of the individual which, as is well known, should not be under-estimated in the case of these uncultivated men, their amount of practice as writers, together with their personal inclinations and other incidental circumstances, come into consideration. When Paul, in this reference also a missionary like others, and dependent upon his material, says in 1 Cor. vii, 25, " Now concerning virgins I have no directions from the Lord," we do not know whether in this case he speaks of a tradition which has been handed down by his memory, or of words of Jesus which he possessed upon sheets of papyrus. Even when in 1 Cor. xi, 23 he makes use of the tradition of the Lord's Supper, it is by no means certain that he had it at hand written out. The Jew of Rabbinic education had had sufficient mnemonic practice to be able to quote such texts by heart. Thus, it is said of Rabbi Jochanan Zakkai in the Bab. Sukkah 28a, " No one ever saw him sitting silent, but rather sitting and reciting in whispers." People of less education among the preachers must often have relied more upon papyrus than upon memory. In any case the frequent question whether an oral or a written tradition is to be accepted is a problem of secondary significance. A relative fixation which does not exclude variations is possible in the case of either the one or the other mode of handing down.

We must assume unliterary beginnings of a religious unpretentious " literature ". To some extent perhaps it was never written down but passed on from mouth to mouth, or if written down and copied, it was intended not to be read verbatim, but as " material " for the use of the possessor for the time being. Under our modern conditions such writings would be ear-marked " for personal information only ", or " private manuscript ". We should look in vain for analogies in literature proper. Even Justin's naming of the

Gospel [1] should not compel us to make some such comparison, for in this case an apologetic tendency is operative which is lifting up Christendom into the region of culture. By means of the title " Memoirs " the gospel books would be classified as literature proper. Nor are Xenophon's " Memorabilia " really to be compared because they contain too much of the personality of the author, too much pleasure in telling the story for itself, in short, too much literature. Therefore they are probably less reliable than certain strata of the evangelical tradition.[2] In literature proper there is for this reason no real analogy to the Gospels as books, because these " books " have been put together out of different elements to some extent of a pre-literary character. The consciousness that his book contains a selection of narratives is not altogether lacking in the author of the Fourth Gospel.[3] For this reason it is difficult to settle the place of the Gospels in the history of literature. Some collections of stories about the philosophers constitute a formal parallel, but we can only enter into the whole problem of the parallels in Chapter VI.

I have attempted to indicate the conditions under which the evangelical tradition must have been formed if it indeed received any form and therewith life and endurance. By this construction a general sketch can be gained of the development which must have taken place from the time of the first reports of the eyewitnesses to the formation of a narrative type which I call the Paradigm. If we now desire to ask further how these narratives appeared we must turn our attention to the tradition which we have received, and try to discover

---

[1] ἀπομνημονεύματα *Apology*, i, 66, and frequently. The references are printed in Preuschen's *Antilegomena*, 2nd ed., pp. 33 ff.

[2] Cf. Wendland, *Urchristliche Literaturformen*, 2nd ed., p. 266 and footnote 1.

[3] I draw attention to a significant example. It is commonly not sufficiently emphasized that the author of the Fourth Gospel gave his work a conclusion (xx, 30 f.) which really would suit a book belonging to another category, viz. a collection of " signs " of Jesus such as the synoptics describe. The author probably does this in order to let his book appear, like the synoptics, as a Gospel. It was with a conclusion of a similar character that Lucian ended his collection of Chriae from the life of Demonax (67) ταῦτα ὀλίγα πάνυ ἐκ πολλῶν ἀπεμνημόνευσα, καὶ εὔτι ἀπὸ τούτων τοῖς ἀναγινώσκουσι λογίζεσθαι ὁποῖος ἐκεῖνος ἀνὴρ ἐγένετο.

in their witness the most ancient and most valuable type.
We can do this more readily, since the work of literary
criticism in the synoptic Gospels has already come to
conclusions which are of the highest value for answering
our question. *The constructive method* which inferred the
process of the development out of its conditions, and the
analytic method which split up and examined what had been
received, approximate to each other.   The thesis gained
from the constructive method, viz. that the oldest tradition
was formed and fixed for the purpose of preaching
would be finally confirmed only by proving that the
oldest stratum of the synoptic narratives, as the analytic
method is able to separate them out, shows traces of such
a formation and such a growth.   And in fact that is the case.
Since literary criticism learned to employ the help of the
criticism of style and its results, we have become aware of the
difference between two styles of narrative in Mark's Gospel.
This line of thought, initiated with fine artistic sensibility
by Hermann von Soden,[1] has been confirmed and developed
with philological means by Emil Wendling.[2]   Both try to
bring out the oldest stratum of Mark's Gospel, the Ur-Marcus.
Both must, therefore, meet the question in regard to each
section of the Gospel, whether it belongs to the earlier or
to the later group of narratives.   Wendling must decide, in
addition, whether such a paragraph belongs to the editorial
work.   By this method they raise questions also as to the
connection between one section and the next, the relation to
the general aim, and the possibility of reaching the original
report.   If we wish to retain the clearness of a criticism confined
to style, we should do well to omit such arguments.   We can

---

[1] *Die wichtigsten Fragen im Leben Jesu*, 1904, pp. 22 ff., 37 ff. The same author's
monograph may also be compared ; Note A, p. 19.

[2] *Ur-Marcus*, 1905. *Die Entstehung des Marcus Evangeliums*, 1908. I may say
that I by no means agree with the results especially of the second work, which
appears to me to count too much upon literary imitation, and too little upon the
naïve use of current motifs. Nevertheless both books have essentially furthered our
knowledge. Compare also J. Weiss, *Das älteste Evangelium*, and *Theol. Rundschau*,
1913, 183 ff.

do this all the more as we are not concerned with a book, a source, or a number of connected stories, but rather only with the Paradigm as a type in the form in which it may have existed in the earliest stories. The questions of connection are thereby fully excluded, for all these example-narratives, being really Paradigms, originally existed separately. For the recognition of this type, however, the observations of both those investigators are of the highest significance. Both distinguish narratives like the one contained in Mark ii, 1, or iii, 6, from the comprehensive stories of the group in iv, 35—v, 43 " In the former all interest is centred upon the actual words of Jesus. In the latter the process as such is what matters." [1] A rapid glance shows at once that narratives of that first order correspond roughly to our expectations in regard to the Paradigm. We approach them not in order to analyse Mark, but to make ourselves acquainted with the style of the Paradigm. If Paradigms have been preserved they ought to be found here.

Of course we must not forget one thing. When these reports were gathered into a Gospel, then what had hitherto been the " material " of a preacher now became reading-matter for Christians. The development arose which is revealed in Luke's prologue, in that the process of making literature was begun. We must recognize that this process had already affected the purity of the type in Mark, and that the style had become more literary. We shall thus distinguish what is typical among the multitude of witnesses without over-valuing single aberrations. In essence, Mark gives us the material. Certain Lucan stories can be included in the circle of considerations. The two little stories of the two blind men and of the dumb man (Matthew ix, 27 ff.) would be very valuable if we could be certain of their authenticity, but perhaps they are only compilations of the evangelist out of current motifs found in the Paradigms and are thus literary constructions. In all we find about eighteen narratives which

[1] Von Soden, *Die wichtigsten Fragen*, p. 23.

correspond to our expectations although in very different degrees. In order to give an illustration of the style of the Paradigm as clearly as possible, I will first of all enumerate eight stories, which, as far as I can see, represent the type in noteworthy purity.

The Healing of the Paralytic . .	Mark ii, 1 ff.
The Question of Fasting . .	Mark ii, 18 f.
The Rubbing of the Ears of Corn .	Mark ii, 23 ff.
The Healing of the Withered Hand .	Mark iii, 1 ff.
The Relatives of Jesus . . .	Mark iii, 20 f., 30 ff.
Blessing the Children . . .	Mark x, 13 ff.
The Tribute Money . . .	Mark xii, 13 ff.
The Anointing in Bethany . .	Mark xiv, 3 ff.[1]

In addition to these eight typical stories another ten of a less pure type can be regarded as illustrations—and will be so employed in the following research.

The Healing in the Synagogue .	Mark i, 23 ff.
The Call of Levi	Mark ii, 13 ff.
Jesus in Nazareth . . .	Mark vi, 1 ff.
The Rich Young Man . . .	Mark x, 17 ff.
The Sons of Zebedee . . .	Mark x, 35 ff.
The Blind Man of Jericho . .	Mark x, 46 ff.
Cleansing the Temple . .	Mark xi, 15 ff.
The Question of the Sadducees .	Mark xii, 18 ff.
The Inhospitable Samaritans . .	Luke ix, 51 ff.
The Man with the Dropsy . .	Luke xiv, 1 ff.

We commenced with preaching, and we were concerned with the preacher's material which he could draw upon for examples at his own choice in the course of his utterance. We are not going to speak here about the Passion story (*vide* Chapter VII). Hence those passages are not considered which are in that context, such as the scene of the Last Supper, or which perhaps are in connection with it, like the narrative of the Triumphal Entry. In the same way the epiphanies like the Baptism and the Transfiguration cannot properly be regarded as examples of the life and work of Jesus which can be evaluated according to taste (see Chapter X).

[1] This narrative was not an original part of the Passion story, but was at first independent. Cf. Chapter VII *infra*.

The Paradigms existed in *isolation*. Independent life
must, therefore, be noticeable in them even to-day. The
healing of Peter's mother-in-law is narrated in Mark
in the context of the description of a day's work,
and is rounded off neither at the beginning nor the end.
The calling of the disciples constitutes the opening bar
and the point of the narrative is to be found only in the
general healings (Mark i, 32 ff.) and in the wandering
in the neighbourhood occasioned thereby. So also the
confession of Peter in the present text seems to be interwoven with the first prophecy of suffering. Hence we do not
learn how Jesus responded to that confession, nor can we say
which significance of the events was normative for the earliest
narrator, i.e. whether he meant to bring out the act of
confession of the disciple, or to differentiate his worldly
desires from the thoughts of Jesus, or, on the other hand
whether he laid more weight upon the fact that the decisive
Christian confession of the Church had already been expressed
in the life-time of Jesus. Hence we must leave out of account
the narrative of Peter's confession as well as that of Peter's
mother-in-law.

The real characteristic of isolated and independent existence
must be an *external rounding-off*. This shows that originally
a number of independent little elements were in existence
and not a connected biography of Jesus. In fact, we see that
the majority of these stories end with a complete rounding-
off of the event. Either in a word or a deed of Jesus the
action reaches a high point which is never again surpassed,
as in the case of the blessing of the children or the story of
the relatives of Jesus. Otherwise it ends in the approving
words of the people, as in the case of the healing of the lame
man. In the one case, as in the other, the nature of the
conclusion permits us to imagine the transition to preaching,
for both forms characterize the narratives with which they end
as examples of that which Jesus was and brought into being.
Endings which point to a more extended connection no longer

belong to the original form of the Paradigm, hence Mark iii, 6 is an illustrative remark of the evangelist which sets not only the story of the withered hand, but also the whole section ii, 1–iii, 5, in connection with the Passion. It is possible, even probable, that this remark has replaced an original illustrative conclusion of the story. Mark xi, 18, ends the scene of cleansing the Temple with a quite similar illustrative conclusion, but it was obviously intended also to go beyond that moment and point to both the whole of the appearance of Jesus in Jerusalem and to His " teaching ". Hence this verse is foreign to the original section which perhaps concluded with the word of Jesus.[1]

The independent and valuable parallel to this story in John ii, 14–17, a more colourful but by no means more mundane narrative, concludes with the reflection of the disciples that such zeal for the House of the Lord corresponds to Scripture, and is in a higher degree edifying like a sermon (what follows thereon is the Johannine interpretation, having nothing more to do with the pre-Johannine tradition). Here we have to do, in fact, with the rare case that an event has been handed down in two different Paradigms, approximately of a similar kind and value. Perhaps this peculiarity in the handing down of an historical event can be explained by saying that the section once stood in one or in both forms in connection with the story of the Passion : (its place at the beginning of the work of Jesus in the fourth Gospel goes back to the evangelist himself).

In consequence of the pre-eminence of the Passion story in preaching, the narrative continued to be retained in a double form.

---

[1] Difficulties arise only by the question of the connection between this section and that about authority, Mark xi, 27–33, which with the words " by what authority doest thou these things? " appears to require a reference to the cleansing of the Temple omitted by Mark. But perhaps the question of authority deals with a piece of the traditions of the Sayings, for we find a similar undefined ταῦτα (Matthew xi, 25) in a section from the source Q. In this case the historical construction of Mark xi, 27 would be due to the evangelist and the question of authority would be originally handed down with historical occasion.

The fact of an original isolated existence can also be proved by going backwards to the rounding-off. In many cases the introduction of a section still clearly shows its lack of connection. The action begins without any presupposition or even without any detailed introduction. A good example is the story of plucking the ears of corn (Mark ii, 23) " And it came to pass that He was going on the Sabbath day through the corn fields and his disciples . . ." To what extent Mark has preserved the original is shown by a comparison with Luke. The section on the calling of Levi is, in Mark ii, 13, only loosely connected with the story of the Paralytic, " and he went forth again by the seaside and all the multitude resorted unto him, and he taught them." This is the connecting link. But now quite independently and indeed illogically was added the new section, " And as He passed by He saw Levi," whereas really we had already come to deal with the question of teaching. In Luke, on the contrary, we read " And after these things He went forth, and beheld a publican named Levi "—in which case it is impossible to draw a definite boundary between the sections. In the same way at the end of this story there is an entirely new beginning in Mark ii, 18, " And John's disciples and the Pharisees were fasting, and they come and say unto him . . ." Luke, however, remains in the situation of the publican's feast which the Pharisees and Scribes have opposed, and he proceeds, " And they said unto him, The disciples of John fast often . . ." (Luke v, 33).

On the other hand the beginning of the section dealing with the relatives of Jesus requires special consideration. In the first edition of this volume, as also in Bultmann, the narratives about the mother and brothers of Jesus were held to begin at Mark iii, 20 f. His relatives go out in order to bring home their son and brother, who, as it appears, is no longer of sound mind. The defence of Jesus against the aspersion of being in league with the devil (Mark iii, 22), would thus seem to have split the beginning from the rest of the story ; but Mark iii, 31 is itself an independent beginning requiring no introduction " and His mother and His brethren came ". The subject is here mentioned in a different way from that of apparent introduction,[1] and the meaning of the apparent splitting of the introduction from the body of the narrative cannot be rightly understood. But probably everything that first strikes one can be explained by assuming that Mark iii, 20 and 21 was written by the evangelist as an introduction preparatory to the story in iii, 31 ff. Such a practice may perhaps be ascribed to the evangelist who prepared also for the sermon at the lakeside (iv, 1) by the remarks in Mark iii, 9, where Jesus orders a boat to be made ready.[2]

Starting from similar considerations we may perhaps, though with due caution, evaluate the story of the inhospitable Samaritans where both the beginning and the ending have been edited. The beginning of the traditional story can be seen clearly enough in Luke ix, 52a, " and in the course of their journey they came to a Samaritan village ". Neither the conclusion of the journey, nor the sending of the messengers belongs to the original perikope. And the criticism which Jesus makes at the end in regard to the zeal for punishment shown by the disciples, certainly did not conclude with the colourless remark " and he turned and threatened them " (Luke ix, 55). Neither can we say whether the manuscripts D, etc. Lat. and Syr. Cur. contain the original reading when Jesus says, " Do you not know of whose spirit you are ? " The majority of MSS., but not D, add still another real conclusion, " The Son of man did not come to destroy life, but to save." Perhaps these MSS. have interpolated the missing saying in accordance with true expectation. The change of the text probably goes back to the same narrator who gave the names James and John to two disciples who had hitherto been unnamed. Perhaps his purpose was to explain

---

[1] Mark iii, 21, οἱ παρ' αὐτοῦ—Mark iii, 31, ἡ μήτηρ αὐτοῦ καὶ οἱ ἀδελφοὶ αὐτοῦ.
[2] He uses the boat in iv, 1.

the name " Sons of thunder " in Mark iii, 17. He was
concerned not with the scolding but with the zeal. The
story was for him not a testimony to the spirit of Jesus, but to
the holy passion of the sons of Zebedee. Hence he did not
need directly to express denial of this zeal, since it was
sufficient that Jesus had admonished the disciples. If this
change may be regarded as probable, then we may reckon
the narrative in its original form as a Paradigm.

As an example of the rounding-off of a Paradigm we
may with due caution refer to the narrative of the Last Supper
which Paul quotes in 1 Cor. xi, 23. In the main its formulation was probably determined by the cultus. Its beginning
may be regarded as adapted to the purpose of illustration
(since it is without value for the cultus), " The Lord Jesus
in the night in which he was betrayed took bread . . . "
This formulation has no connective, and no presupposition,
giving, as it does, the subject-matter completely, as also the
point of time.

A second characteristic which we must observe is the
brevity and simplicity of the narrative. Only short passages
could be introduced into a sermon. Only a simple description
which was limited to what was most necessary was allowed
to a speaker or a hearer lest his thoughts be distracted from
the sermon. The action of the narrative has no independent
value for the preacher. Thus the telling is not specially
marked by the elements upon which weight would be laid
by a good, educated, and artistic author. The attractive
working out of the details for their own sake, the characterization of persons, the sketching of their surroundings out of
pleasure in the description, all these things Paradigms must
lack, and, in fact, they do so. Of the actual circumstances,
we learn only as much as we must know in order to understand the intervention of Jesus. They bring children to
Him that He may touch them. But the disciples oppose these
people . . . that is all. Where it happened, when, and in
what circumstances is inessential. They come to a Samaritan

village ; He enters a synagogue ; He begins His journey again—but almost nothing is said of more detailed circumstances, the time of the day, the cause, other people—at most only the place.

Pharisees and Herodians wish to trip Him up in His speech, and come to Him with the question of the Tribute Money. This also is very little, " but there may have been more that was worth noting." The paralytic was let down through the roof and the reason thereof had to be told, in order that we may understand the following words, " When Jesus saw their faith " (Mark ii, 5). The Sadducees have to be represented as denying the Resurrection (Mark xii, 18) if the meaning of their question is to be understood. The situation is described with a certain amount of detail in the story of Jesus' relatives, Mark iii, 31. He who hears the Lord's saying about His true relatives will also know how it came about that He had to sacrifice His own home. This was only to be understood from the attitude of His own family.

But it is just in this place that we can see clearly what did not interest the narrator, viz. biographical material. Neither the mother nor the brothers of Jesus are mentioned by name. So also in the story of Nazareth which is concerned with His family connections, and in which, therefore, names should not be lacking, at least the names of the sisters are not mentioned. The oldest tradition has no answer to give to questions about persons belonging to the most intimate circles of Jesus—whether the family *always* hindered Him, whether Simon the Leper in Bethany was a sympathetic friend, or a lurking enemy—to all these questions about persons belonging to Jesus' closest circle during His lifetime the oldest tradition gives no answer. *The lack of portraiture* is a characteristic of the Paradigms. The paralytic and the man with the withered hand, Matthew the publican and the relatives of Jesus, the persons healed in Mark i, 23 ff., and Luke xiv, 1 ff., finally the woman with the alabaster box of whose aim nothing is clearly said—what do we really learn in regard to these people? Nothing except the fact and nature of their contact with Jesus. What we learn and are intended alone to learn is how Jesus acted on these occasions.

There seems, however, to be an exception. The rich man dealt with in Mark x, 17 ff. appears to be an individual sketch, but if we rightly understand the words which depict his approach they are seen to be necessary for the development of the narrative. "A man came running in and fell at His feet and asked Him, Good Master . . ." The denial of the eager homage, and also the love of Jesus to a disciple who appeared so ardent [1]—both motives depend upon this introduction. The whole, however, is related for the sake of the phrase which closes the story, the phrase concerning the rich in the Kingdom of Heaven (x, 25) which in Mark, indeed, together with its tempering interpretation in x, 27, has been worked up into a little dialogue. The story reveals therefore in this original form, not a personal, but a material interest. We never learn what drove the rich man to Jesus, nor even his name. Other traits giving an individual character were added only at the time of a later editing, viz. that he belonged to one of the leaders of the people (Luke), that he was a young man (Matthew), that there were two rich men and that one of them scratched his head thoughtfully at the demand of Jesus (The Gospel of the Nazarenes—in Origen on Matthew xv, 24). The original story, however, is a Paradigm. I should like to pronounce the same judgment, but not with the same certainty, over the narratives which reveal their interest in the people who appear with Jesus by giving their names and mentioning certain characteristics. And in the

---

[1] The words ἠγάπησεν αὐτόν perhaps do not refer to an attitude of mind, for a narrative so terse in all essentials does not describe feelings. Probably some act of petting is meant " and He stroked him ". This would not be a superfluous trait in this context, for it could be suggested in this way that Jesus did not regard the confession in x, 20, as empty flattery, but that He believed in the religiousness of the rich young man and wanted to gain him as a disciple.

story of Zacchæus, Luke xix, 1 ff., the anecdotal traits told in regard to the publican are evidently the main things—his small stature, the way in which he succeeded in seeing Jesus in spite of it, his reward and justification before Jesus. Also the request of the sons of Zebedee, Mark x, 35 ff. contains in the present text an answer which has to do with their personal fate of martyrdom.

It may indeed be asked whether x, 41 or x, 42 ff., which expresses the resentment of the other disciples, or at least the warning of Jesus, originally followed immediately upon the request x, 37. Then the further question arises whether the narrative does not really deal with unnamed disciples concerned about the coming Kingdom of God with an ambitious zeal, and who dared to utter a request for pre-eminence. In this case the story must originally have been a pure illustration or Paradigm, but depending entirely upon the request for eminence, and the answer as to true greatness or eminence. As we have it at present, the passage shows a real interest in the significance of the sons of Zebedee, although this interest is surely foreign to the Paradigm.

The story of Martha and Mary shows the same interest, but here the names of the two women, as well as the description of their personal attitude, are so ineradicably firm in the words of Jesus, that we cannot dream of removing the personal element from the narrative. This is not an example-story which illustrates the gospel with an event taken from the work of Jesus no matter who the protagonists were. Rather we are approaching another type : narratives of famous " religious " men and women, and their more or less " religious " deeds. In short, we are at the beginning of Christian legend, the main principles of which will be discussed in Chapter V.

The story of the blind man in Jericho (Mark x, 46-52) I would not reckon in this group, but among Paradigms of a less pure type. Admittedly he is given the name Bartimæus, a feature which does not appear elsewhere in

the Paradigms with the exception of names of the disciples.
Moreover the point is rather his attitude than what Jesus
did. But the story is not intended to relate some special
matter about the blind man. The fact that he throws his
cloak aside and springs up only shows his readiness and his
confidence, in short, his faith. But all the emphasis lies upon
the compassion of Jesus : the blind man, who cannot push
himself into the procession of the multitude, cries after
Jesus ; many of the people wish him to be silent, but Jesus
calls him. Thereby he is already saved. It is faith which
has helped him for very little more is said about the actual
healing. The name Bartimæus, however, seems to be
connected with the mention of the place as Jericho, for we
have almost the impression that " the son of Timæus,
Bartimæus, a blind beggar (or the blind beggar) " was a
well-known figure in this region. The name of the place,
on the other hand, belongs to the section as such, as is seen
from its very striking and distracting mention on two
occasions [1] : " And they come to Jericho "—a connective
sentence coming from the evangelist—" And as He
went out from Jericho with his disciples "—that is the
beginning of the section. It tells of the healing of a well-
known blind beggar, Bartimæus in Jericho. It would, of
course, be possible that, on occasion, even a Paradigm
would mention a well-known name, but it seems to me to
be more probable that this particular Paradigm originally
told of the compassion of Jesus for a nameless beggar—
a genuine Paradigm without the peculiarities of another
category, i.e. that of the tale without portraiture and without
description of the healing, but solely with emphasis upon
the compassion of Jesus and the faith of the blind man. At
a later date, this nameless unfortunate was identified with
a well-known blind man of Jericho. Matthew and Luke,

---

[1] D and it. smooth the reading, and on the second occasion, Mark x, 46, read
ἐκεῖθεν instead of ἀπὸ ʼΙεριχώ showing that the difficulty was felt at an early
date.

who do not mention the name, prove that it was not felt as essential for the story. The mention of the name in Mark would be less remarkable if we suppose that Bartimæus became a follower of Jesus, and, later, a member of the Church. Perhaps the conclusion points to this, " And he followed Him in the way."

By means of such individual observations the nature of the illustration or Paradigm becomes ever clearer. The Legend introduces individual persons, but the Paradigm only impersonal types in the way we have already discussed. Or else it lets the people speak in chorus, and quite remarkably, almost never one at a time. Especially do the enemies of Jesus appear in large numbers—the call of Levi, the discussion about plucking the ears of corn, and the tribute money are examples. We must also take note of the inhabitants of Nazareth, the disciples (in the incident of the children, originally also in the Samaritan village), finally also unnamed persons (in the question of fasting, in the stories of Jesus' relatives and of the Anointing) come forward in this manner. The dealing with these things collectively cannot be traced back to a conscious artistry of the author, but to a naïve feeling for style which simplifies in this manner the actual event (the speech of a single person, or the different cries of many), because only the content of the words, not the person of the speaker, is important.

Herein we have to do with a mode which is frequently used in popular narratives, but the word " popular " is not a sufficient characteristic, for a popular narrative can be verbose and answer questions raised by curiosity. The concentrated brevity of Paradigms rests upon a concern which makes the material subject to the purpose of the preacher, hinders wandering, and silences the unessential. Even what is only vivid or only arresting cannot be regarded as essential from the standpoint of a sermon.

The simple method of narration is shown also by the representation of the *healings*, especially if we compare other

Christian and non-Christian stories of healing. We see then what sort of motives occur in the traditional style of stories of healing. We get data of the history of the illness, information in regard to the technique of the therapy, proofs of the reality of the recovery. Of all these aspects of a healing we find little or nothing in Paradigms. A word of command of Jesus and its carrying out—that is the whole apparatus. Sometimes, as in the case of the man with the dropsy (Luke xiv, 4), even this is lacking. Where it is different, as in the case of the leper (Mark i, 40 ff.), the story also reveals another character which does not correspond to the style of a Paradigm. Other Form-giving powers are at work here than reside in a sermon. On account of this difference I am not able, like Bultmann, to ascribe almost all the healings in the Gospels to the same large group, viz. Bultmann's group of miracle stories. Such a classification can only appeal at bottom to the criterion of content, viz. that in both cases a miracle of healing is taking place. From the point of view of criticism of style four stories of healing stand out which I classify as Paradigms, and not as stories of healing with a definite subject of healing (as in the " Tales " about healing, *vide* Chapter IV). The healing of the lame man in Mark ii is characterized as a special case, since its middle point is not the healing, but the forgiveness. [1] The healing, when at last completed, shows to everyone the right of Jesus to forgive sins. The healing in the synagogue, Mark i, 23–7, has for its central point Jesus' meeting the demoniac " we (belonging to the spiritual world) know who you are, you Holy One of God ". We must not put this on the same level as the cry of the demented man in the other narrative of healing a demoniac, Mark v, 7, " Jesus, thou Son of the Most High God." Interest in this case is directed to the point that the demon on foreign soil recognizes the envoy of the true God and begs Him for mercy. Both stories have the same significance for Mark in the sense of his theory of

---

[1] For the relation of the forgiveness to the healing, see below, p. 66.

a Messianic secret, i.e. the demons sense Him whom men mistake. The interests of the first narrators, as expressed in the form of the stories, are different. In Mark i, it is confirmation of Messiahship, in Mark v, it is a miracle on foreign soil.

Hence in the former case the healing is the main subject, but in the latter case, in the synagogue, only a sentence is devoted to it. Finally, the healings of the withered hand and of the man with the dropsy, the third and fourth stories of healing of an illustrative character, presuppose already that Jesus can heal. What they mean to give is the outcome of the question of the Sabbath. The concluding word in Luke xiv, 4, says that clearly enough. As already mentioned, the original ending in Mark iii, 6, is concealed. But the indignant question in Mark iii, 4, shows what is the point of the narrative; it proclaims the new righteousness under whose rule there is no limitation for doing good. We cannot really prove that the two narratives are actual doublets. The observation that Luke gives both forms makes us pause about such an identification, for we may notice that he recognized and, therefore, omitted the anointing by the woman who was a sinner and the fishing of Peter as being doublets. Thus we have no reason for regarding the two healings on the Sabbath, Mark iii and Luke xiv, in the same way. Rather we must recognize that we have two different events narrated in this simple manner of the Paradigm.

The self-limitation of the Paradigm on stylistic grounds must be understood in the case of healings in the same manner as in those which we have already analysed. No question is raised about the technique of the miracle, and none about the technical skill of the miracle-worker. The only important points are that Jesus healed, and in what way He revealed the meaning and purpose of His work in a brief word to the man who had been healed and to the witnesses. Those are motives which have immediate significance for preaching, and thereby we pass over from the negative to the positive characteristics of a paradigmatic style. We can most suitably call this style edificatory (see pp. 37 f.).

The third essential characteristic of the paradigm following upon the rounding-off and the brevity is the *colouring of the narrative in a thoroughly religious, i.e. realistic unworldly manner.* Even there it can be established that expressions drawn from biblical language and the early Christian mission are used in their technical sense : " He preached the word to them," Mark ii, 2, " being grieved at the hardening of their heart," Mark iii, 5 ; " they were offended in him, Mark vi, 3, perhaps " he blessed them " in the story of the children, Mark x, 16. That in cleansing the Temple Jesus should not fling a threat at the multitude, " but taught them and said," Mark xi, 17, is contrary to the requirements of the art of realistic narrative to the same extent as it satisfies the needs of the sermon.

The didactic style of the Paradigm causes the words of Jesus to stand out clearly, but this means that we must note a fourth characteristic of the category Paradigm. We do not learn what the companions of Jesus say to the parents of the children or to the woman with the alabaster box, but rather how Jesus dealt with such harsh repulses. *Many a Paradigm reaches its point in, and at the same time concludes with, a word of Jesus.*

This is the case with the Sick of the Dropsy (Luke xiv, 5), with the Rich Man (if Mark x, 25 is a conclusion), with the Sons of Zebedee (if Mark x, 42–5 is a conclusion), in any case with the Tribute Money and the Sadducean Question, as well as with the Alabaster Box—if we delete the pragmatic ending (Mark xiv, 8 f.). Everywhere it is evident that what Jesus said possesses somehow a *general significance*, and, as a regulation for faith or life, gives the whole story an immediate relation with the hearer. It is no wonder then that we find this true of many Paradigms if by means of such sayings the story could be woven into the preaching. It is another question whether Jesus Himself was accustomed to employ such a word in order to crown some deed, be it healing or the decision of a disputed question, and thus make the individual case appear only as an example, i.e. a Paradigm of general rules or regulations. It is thus a question whether He was not content to say of His hearers, " These are my mother and my brothers " (Mark iii, 54), and whether the continuation, " for whoever does the will of God, he is my brother and sister and mother " comes rather from the preachers who made Paradigms from cases isolated in the tradition.

We shall have to deal with this question later. At the moment still another characteristic of Paradigms interests us : the conclusion of those narratives which do not close with a saying (or with the development of what was said, as in the story of the children). I have already mentioned this other characteristic when I showed the independence of Paradigms from the context. For there are stories which conclude with a choral ending expressing wonder and praise at what has happened. " We have never seen such things," we read after the healing of the paralytic ; " Never have such things taken place in Israel " at the end of the story of the dumb man,[1] and similar exclamations of wonder conclude the narrative of the demoniac at Capernaum, Mark i, 27, although the present text has perhaps been worked over by the evangelist.[2] Even in this instance the relation to preaching is clear. Choruses, as naïve stylistically as Paradigms in general, point with their " never yet " to the greatness of the deed and the significance of the doer, and it is precisely with this significance that preaching is concerned.

In this way a fifth characteristic must be added to those

---

[1] Mt. ix, 33. The story is, as I suggested on p. 42, perhaps not a Paradigm but a composition of the evangelist. In any case, however, it depends upon paradigmatic motives and may therefore be cited here.

[2] It is remarkable that several unclean spirits are spoken of as if Jesus had already affected many cures in front of this public. But that is doubtless a generalization of the evangelist and like the following verse (i, 28) is of pragmatic tendency. But since the astonishment in i, 27 is a stylistic expression of success we may claim one of the acclamations as a Paradigm originally independently current.

already mentioned in connection with the category
Paradigms, rounding-off at beginning and end, brevity,
edificatory style, emphasis upon the words of Jesus. The
next is that *the narrative should end in a thought useful for
preaching purposes*, whether it be in a general phrase or in
exemplary act of Jesus, or, finally, in an exclamation of the
onlookers praising the act.[1] It is no objection to this last
characteristic that similar choruses may also be found in
another category of Gospel narratives, in the " Tales " with
which we shall deal in Chapter IV. That is indeed the case.
In the former, as in the latter, miracle stories conclude with
acclamations, for acclamation is a characteristic of miracle
stories, even in the surrounding " world ". Hence in this
kind of conclusion we must establish an element of style
which does not differentiate, but bind the two groups. The
motive arising in " the world " has been developed in the
miracle story as well as in certain Paradigms. The reason
for this common property is plain : both the miracle stories
of the surrounding world, and the primitive Christian
" Tales " which end with such an exclamation have a
missionary purpose ; to labour either for the God or the
man of whom they report. The difference is that their
propaganda is not connected with preaching, but operates
independently. This common feature, therefore, does not
set aside the difference of the categories. Certainly it does not
give the exegete the right to classify all the Gospel miracle
stories in one group, and thereby overlook the far-reaching
differences between the categories.

Above all it is not the quality of this characterization of
Paradigm simply to mention landmarks which probably
do not occur elsewhere, so that the category can be considered
valid. The categories will be described by us with a *number*

---

[1] To what degree the total impression of the passages is determined by these
endings can be seen in the healing of the ten lepers, Luke xvii, 11-19, Here such
an ending is lacking along with other marks of the Paradigm, and as a consequence,
the story offers no point of contact with missionary preaching or that of public
worship.

of landmarks whose totality makes clear their nature. This
differentiation of categories is not made for its own sake,
but in order to assist our understanding the history of
tradition. It puts forward a working hypothesis intended
to clarify the process of tradition, hence every sign of the
category must be mentioned which is of importance for this
process, even if one of these signs should also be found in
the analysis of another category.

So far I have passed over a certain question because otherwise the deduction of the laws of tradition simply from
the form of what had been handed down would have
been disturbed by considerations of a different nature. But
now at the end of our inquiry into the Paradigm this
question about the *historical trustworthiness of the Paradigms*
presses to the front.

The question of historicity is, in the first instance, restricted
by us to the Paradigms. In so doing, the statement of the
problem changes from what was customary for a long time in
scientific criticism. Inquiry into the historicity of the Gospels
used to be made dependent upon the solution of the
question of authenticity, and so attempted to establish the
relation of the authors to the eyewitnesses in order to prove
how much the evangelists could have known or learned
of the real course of things. These inquiries would have led
on to a wrong road, even if they had not been burdened with
the old question of uncertain authorship, for the very statement of the question upon which they stand is too much of
a literary and personal character. The authors of the Gospels,
at least of the synoptics are not " authors " in the literary
sense, but collectors. We are not, therefore, concerned
first of all with their knowledge of the subject matters, but
with the knowledge of those who gave the tradition its
form, and this taking form was not mediated by authors
but by preachers. Thus it came about not according to
personal desires or powers, but in accordance with the
necessities of the sermon, i.e. according to laws independent

of the individual, and growing out of the very life of the first
Christian Churches.   The point of view of Formgeschichte,
therefore, includes a sociological issue.   This immediately
implies that we must inquire into the question of the formation
of tradition, in the first place, and then, in the second place
and to a limited degree, into the historicity of this tradition.
If, then, we raise the question of trustworthiness in the
case of Paradigms, we must recognize that it can only receive
an indirect answer by the means at the disposal of Formgeschichte, and then only if we go forward from the isolated
observations regarding form to general considerations.

In a few places, by using pure stylistic criticism, we can
proceed from the present text of the narratives to an earlier,
i.e. from a Paradigm which has been worked over by the
evangelist, and which in some degree is already literary, to
the pure form in which it could serve the missionaries as an
illustration in the course of preaching.   That is naturally
a step from less to greater historical trustworthiness.   I have
already ventured the supposition that in the story of the sons
of Zebedee the part x, 38–40 originally was lacking.   Because
it is interested in persons and their fate, it offers an example of
what I have differentiated from Paradigms as the beginnings
of legend.   This purely formal criticism is now supported
also by historical considerations.   Mark x, 38–40 is evidently
a *vaticinium ex eventu*, which is bound up with the pericope
for the purpose of glorifying the martyrdom of the two
brothers that had already taken place.   The incident of the
alabaster box offers a similar case.   The word of Jesus
whereby He praises one woman's deed as a " good work "
as over against the original good work of giving alms, is
the summit of the Paradigm, and indeed also its conclusion.
Hitherto the narrative had no relation to the Passion story.
This relation enters only with the following words.   But
now the woman's action is understood as a prophetic sign
of the burial (although thereby the incident ceases to be an
example) and upon the basis of this significance the fame of

the woman appears so great that it is connected with the world mission, although words offering praise to a secondary person are completely foreign to Paradigms. Thus, even in this case, on stylistic grounds we must infer a shorter form of the Paradigm, and we shall also thereby meet what is historically more credible, if only because these words evidently contain a *vaticinium ex eventu*.

But these are mere relative results. In this way we reach greater historicity, but the question remains as to the final trustworthiness of the Paradigms. If it may be regarded as proved that it was only in connection with preaching that traditions about the story of Jesus could have been preserved among those unliterary men waiting for the end of the world, we have at the same time obtained a criterion of historicity ; the nearer a narrative stands to the sermon the less is it questionable, or likely to have been changed by romantic, legendary, or literary influences. The category of the Paradigm is very close to that of the sermon, and is especially guided by the interests of the carrying of the message, but is cold toward the infiltration of tendencies of another nature. Thus we have a sound preliminary decision in favour of the unspoiled character of paradigmatic tradition. The connection between the Paradigm and the sermon points to the early rise of this category. The narrative-technique of the time was not yet master of its material. The customary motives found in legends and the completely extra-Christian traits of the anecdote had not yet penetrated any significant degree. The narrators did not yet understand, and probably never consciously tried to discover, the relations between what they told and events in the larger " world ". The " world " had as yet so little to do with this tradition that we can only imagine the rise of such traditions in the first decades after the death of Jesus. At that time eyewitnesses of the events were still alive. This is proved by Luke's Prologue which classes together the " eye-witnesses " and the " ministers of the word ", without emphasizing the fact of a difference of

a generation between them.   Thus it is probable that these
stories rose amongst the eyewitnesses, both in a temporal
and a spatial sense, as is emphasized on p. 34.   Because the
eyewitnesses could control and correct, a relative trustworthiness of the Paradigms is guaranteed.

Nevertheless it is only a relative trustworthiness, for just
because they serve the purpose of preaching, these stories
could not be told in a neutral fashion ; they must meet the
requirements of the hearer, support and prove the message.
Thus they were introduced with an underlying motive and
intended for a definite purpose.   The narrator himself is
concerned as strongly as possible ; his desire is to relate the
events which for his own faith make the commencement of
the eschatological era of salvation certain.   Having this
knowledge, we have placed no weight upon literal authenticity in the sense of a judiciary pronouncement, or a police
notice.   Those who, on religious or scientific grounds, hold
to the idea that every secondary circumstance must have taken
place exactly as it stands either in Mark, or in Mark as critically
edited, will regard this omission as an injury.   But whoever
holds this opinion is really applying the old conception
of inspiration about the Holy Scriptures, in all its narrowness,
to an original germ which has been reached by criticism.
He is also deceiving himself in regard to the application of
this omission.   He is wrong when he regards the disinterested,
colourless, much-corrected, description of a process, i.e.
when he regards the records in all circumstances as the ideal
of a historical pronouncement.   For misunderstandings
arise not by introducing an interest which is too much alive,
but by excluding every form of personal interest.   The
very style which, in accordance with edificatory preaching,
excludes complete objectivity shows that we have to do with
an old and relatively good tradition.   Colourless records,
if we had them, would be altogether doubtful.   Finally one
must not underestimate the effect of this narrative style
upon the next age.   The historical significance of these

Paradigms depended, of course, not upon the reliability of every word but, just by virtue of this interested mode of reporting, it handed down an impressive picture of the person and work of Jesus. Without this interested impressiveness faith would not have reached what it had to achieve, viz. to bear witness to the revelation of God. Without this abbreviating, style-giving, concentrating, and interpreting kind of narrative as found in the Paradigms, the very picture of Jesus would have been possessed only by the educated, and not as is the case a human possession accessible to all, making His words come to life in a most powerful fashion. If we can only perceive this special quality of those stories, we shall see how the first Christians spoke in this manner, and only in this manner, of what Jesus did. The relative dependability of the Paradigms rests upon the fact that they belong to the same sociological stratum as the earliest preaching. The right to test the narrative critically comes from seeing that that very sociological condition excludes an exact description in the manner of an official report.

Therefore it should cause no surprise if in the Paradigms we were to come across sentences or at least words of Jesus of whose historical reliability there is doubt. They are not proved to be genuine by the fact of relatively primitive tradition, and on the other hand the paradigmatic nature of the matter is not spoiled by such unhistoric traits. For both aspects belong together. Tradition of this nature, the oldest anywhere to be found among Christians, conditions unhistorical changes of the words of Jesus. In the example of the relatives of Jesus I have already shown the simplest case. What Jesus answered in Mark iii, 34 would be sufficient for that situation, " Behold, my mother and my brothers." But for the purposes of preaching it was necessary to deduce a general principle out of this isolated situation. That was done when the glance and gesture of Jesus, whose significance was clear only to the eyewitnesses, were described unmistakably to the hearers of the story by the words: " whoever does the will of God the same is my brother and sister and mother." In the same way the conclusion of the story of Levi (Mark ii, 17) may have come into being. Jesus justifies the calling [1] of the tax-gatherer with the words, " They that are whole have no need of a physician, but they that are sick . . . " But the tradition enshrined in the preaching obtains from this saying " a doctrine "—that Jesus has come to call sinners and not the righteous—and this teaching is placed in the mouth of Jesus Himself.

These are small instances only worth while discussing on methodological grounds. Methodological knowledge, however, is important. For even here we must beware of the temptation to employ literary criticism and to delete " additions " for the purpose of reaching a historical and completely purified original-original form from the original form found in the Paradigm. Such an original-original form never existed, or at least not in the region of the missionary tradition in Greek. When this tradition was created it was for the purpose of preaching, and that preaching required those sayings of a general character which are probably unhistorical.

Of great importance is the problem of these *sayings out of sermons* for the understanding of the matter of the Ears of Corn. Here Jesus justifies His disciples by saying, " The Sabbath was made for man, not man for the Sabbath." But the following words, " and so the Son of Man is Lord also of the Sabbath," can only be understood in this context if the implication referred to men, not to the Son of Man. Wellhausen had therefore the right feeling when he held that " Son of Man " originally had none of the solemn technical

---

[1] The calling—and not the subsequent feast. For in my view Mark added this. The recognized difficulties in Mk. ii, 15, 16a ($\mathring{\eta}\sigma\alpha\nu\ \gamma\grave{\alpha}\rho\ \pi o\lambda\lambda o\acute{\iota}$) may best be explained by assuming that these words were added by Mark. The opposition, as expressed, was concerned with the association of Jesus with publicans. Instead of "associate" they say in references to the laws of cleanliness "eat". To act as background to that, Mark supposes a meal and weaves into it the pragmatic remark which the followers of Jesus have accepted. "There were many, and they followed Him." But Jesus' word, Mk. ii, 17, refers not to the meal, but to the call.

sense, but, like the original Aramaic, meant "human being". In this case, the saying would speak of the lordship of man over the Sabbath. But it is nevertheless very questionable whether the preacher who exercised great caution in regard to matters of worship, as is shown by the question of fasting, would have spread such a word of Jesus without limitation or explanation. The problem is solved much more simply if we see even in the final words a *saying from a sermon*, i.e. the congregation is referred to the answer of Jesus, and thereby its hearers could see that the Son of Man, this Jesus, is also Lord of the Sabbath (cf. also Mark x, 45).

These thoughts show that the writers had small share in the inner freedom of Jesus, but made an energetic and, historically, a very significant attempt to fix the practical value and relevance of the evangelical tradition. The dealing with the question of fasting in the tradition of preaching shows the same spirit, apart from the problem whether the preaching, or whether only the evangelist, introduced the saying of Mark ii, 21 f., which is really independent, at the end of the section. Without it the story still concludes with a justification of fasting. Its real content (Mark ii, 18 f.) however is decidedly the defence of a mode of life without fasting. This latter was the mind of Jesus, the former that of the Churches which had introduced fasting. It has long been recognized that that conclusion contains a *vaticinium ex eventu* which presupposes the sufferings of Jesus and which, in the words "In that day shall they fast", appears to touch upon the Friday-fasting of Christians. But the consequence of this recognition is commonly a literary operation which deletes Mark ii, 19*b*, 20.

Of course by this route we come nearer to what Jesus really said. Nevertheless the short form of the story never existed in the actual tradition, i.e. by the time that the narrative had been reduced to a fixed form for the purpose of preaching, its reference was understood to be to the custom of fasting which had arisen in between. We may accept this view because Mark ii, 19a is anything rather than a paradigmatic conclusion, whereas Mark ii, 20 is a typical Paradigm ending. By just such an example we may recognize the good quality of the tradition, and its conservative character. Although the need was felt of justifying fasting, it was preserved in a saying of Jesus really of a contrary tendency.

In the examination of the conversation dealing with fasting and the story of the Ears of Corn, a light falls upon the first part of this group, the story of the Paralytic. The special difficulty is well-known. The first issue, forgiveness of sins, or healing, is crossed by a second: Who can forgive sins? The first issue conditions the process of the action. That Jesus should, by the healing, confirm the forgiveness of sins, corresponds to Jewish views of the connection between sin and illness. The issue is only the reality of the forgiveness, not the right of Jesus to do it. This latter consideration is emphasized by the middle part of the story (Mark ii, 6–10): Scribes, whose presence has not hitherto been mentioned, murmur inwardly at Jesus' attitude. He blasphemes God since none other than God can forgive sins. Jesus takes up these unuttered thoughts of which He is nevertheless aware, and puts the question, " Which is easier, to forgive sins or to heal?" This is a teasing question. The opponents must be refused an answer. Their ill-will would have made them reply that forgiveness was easier, for they had looked for healing, and are displeased that He heals only with words and not with acts. But their piety must forbid this answer, for they, and they especially, could not grant that the physical God-forsakenness of the illness was worse than the moral God-forsakenness of sin. In this way Jesus disarmed their ill-will—and then came the healing. Thus what these verses ii, 6–10 contain is not an actual, but only a fictitious conversation, for the opponents say nothing. Within the limits of the incident the verses only serve the purpose of passing over from the forgiveness to the healing. But in the context of a sermon they mean more, for Christ is proclaimed here. If now in this connection we read the word Son of Man, then a mere reference to the Ears of Corn shows that the same solution is helpful in this case also. It is not Jesus who speaks in the sentence concerning the Son of Man, nor his historical opponents in the reproach. The narrator, who is however the preacher, composed this middle piece for the sake of the point which was to him the principle thing, and whose proof was found in the healing. It took place " in order that you might know that the Son of Man has power to forgive sins ". In any case we may guess the actual proceedings. After the word of Jesus which assured forgiveness, there was perhaps a protest from the others that Jesus " only " forgave sins, and then perhaps the enigmatic word of Jesus about hard and easy (ii, 9), intended to bring those who protested to a right appreciation of the circumstances. Finally came the healing. But we cannot lay bare an original Paradigm which reproduces only this proceeding because it cannot be reached by mere elision, nor may we do it, because such a primitive report never existed.

Preaching insisted out and out that the question of forgiveness and of healing should give way to that in regard to the right of forgiveness, for this was a question of the worth of Jesus and therefore more important than the other for preaching. That in this case also only a change and a trimming but not a complete inversion of the actual event took place, may be seen from the innocuous, but quite " un-Christological " concluding chorus, " We never saw it on this fashion," which sounds as if the narrative dealt only with a miracle and not with the worth of the miracle-worker.

This analysis of the story of the lame man shows also that such passages cannot be described as disputes. If it were a genuine dispute, that i.e. actually held or even thought out, but real, it would contain, in argument and counter-

argument, a subject which was being developed and dealt
with. In this story, on the other hand, and most of the
other Paradigms, the objector has no independent significance.
In this case his only purpose is to bring out the decisive
act of Jesus, or, in the case of the anointing, his only purpose
is to deny, in order that Jesus can answer him. Neither
the Sabbath commandment, nor Cæsar's claim to the tax is
discussed in the give and take of a debate. Hence one is not
justified in describing the circumstances as a dispute; it is
all the same whether the other parties remain in gloomy
silence (Mark iii, 2) or silently make reproaches (Mark ii, 6 f.),
or show their opposition in general phraseology (Mark
x, 13), or in express words (Mark xiv, 4 and 5). Hence the
fact of a dispute is not characteristic for a category. The
occasional occurrence of a long dialectic discussion as in
the story of the Rich Man, Mark x, 17 ff. cannot affect this
general result. The main interest is not the dispute, but
what Jesus said or did, and hence the story of the children,
as well as that of the rich man, or the lame man, belong to
this group, and this in spite of the fact that elements of
dialogue as found in these Paradigms sometimes do not
occur at all, or sometimes occur in a different way. Neither
have we the right, on the basis of the element of dialogue
to deduce the " Sitz im Leben ", and therefore to regard the
sections as coming from discussions of the Church. Hence
we cannot explain, as Bultmann does, that, in Mark ii, 5b–10,
the Palestinian Church intended to prove its right to forgive
sins by its power of healing by miracle. In the first place
it is very doubtful whether there were any discussions of
this kind in the Christian Church in the years A.D. 50–70.
A comparison with Jewish methods of writing which we
shall offer in Chapter V will show the great sociological
difference which existed between these Christians and the
Rabbis disputing in the schools. But if so, then the elements
of dialogue found in the Paradigms are, as I have shown,
not so essential that we may deduce from them the main

interest of the section, and thereby also the " Sitz im Leben ". The nature of " real " discussions can be seen in the Rabbinic texts. In these texts we can see their rise in just such discussions ; but the parties to the discussion and the course of the dialogue receive here a very much greater significance than in the Paradigms of the Gospels.

In this way the individual observations converge and support what we might expect of the Paradigm. The Paradigm reveals itself in fact as the narrative form whose use we could assume in the preachers of the Gospel. It is the only form in which the tradition of Jesus could be preserved at a time when a yearning for the end and a consciousness of estrangement from the world would still entirely prevent concern for a historical tradition or the development of a literature in the technical sense of the world. What " literature " and what " history " was present in the Churches lived only within the sermon and by means of preaching. The preacher is he who both hands down and reports. Therefore in Paradigms the objectivity of a protocol and the richness of colour of tales is lacking, but therefore also recruiting and edifying power is proper to them.

CHAPTER IV

TALES

In the sermon the elements of the future Christian
literature lay side by side as in a mother cell. The more
Christianity reached out into the world, and the more the
separate needs were distinguished, then the more the various
means were separated from each other with which these
needs were met in the Churches. For the further development
of evangelical tradition the *story-teller* and the *teacher* appear
to have been of special significance. We can gain some idea
of the activity of the teachers by certain notices found in
primitive Christian literature. Their influence upon the
evangelical tradition will occupy us later. The sources have
nothing to say of the tellers of tales. Nevertheless there
were such, who could relate stories out of the life of Jesus
broadly, with colour, and not without art, as we may conclude
with every certainty from the existence of such stories.
We are concerned now with a number of narratives which
I excluded from observation in the preceding Chapter. Their
formulation shows clearly that they were not created for
the aims of preaching, and that they were not repeated as
examples as opportunity arose in the course of preaching.
There is found here exactly that descriptiveness which we
missed in the Paradigms ; that breadth, which a paradigmatic
application makes impossible ; that technique, which reveals
a certain pleasure in the narrative itself ; and that topical
character, which brings these narratives nearer to the corresponding categories as they were to be found in the world
outside Christianity. Descriptions of the illness and of the
healing (or of the miraculous events) belong to this subject,
as also the proof of its success—all this differentiates Tales

from Paradigms. But we find also the chorus of acclamation for the miracle-worker at the conclusion, just as in the case of certain Paradigms (see p. 58). Nevertheless such choruses must be regarded as in accordance with the style of this category in a conclusion. In contradiction to the first (German) edition of this volume, this must be asserted, for the same thing is to be found in miracle stories beyond Judaism and Christianity. Apart from this characteristic, common to both categories, the differences of style can easily be shown. If we understand the peculiar quality of Paradigms, we shall also be clear about this second category, because we shall have learned how to differentiate the one from the other. In order to describe this second category, we may best use the term " Tale " (Novelle). For a literary name is in place here. The category which it is meant to describe is more " worldly " and has more of its literary forms than the Paradigm. It is true that we know nothing of those who put together these Christian tales, but we can describe the characteristics of their creations.

Almost more clearly than the Paradigms, these Tales stand out from the text of Mark's Gospel. That is not surprising. The simpler category, when worked over, can be more easily defaced, more easily befogged in the purity of its type, than the richer and more developed form whose stately nature cannot be completely robbed of characteristics even by being worked over. Especially in Mark a number of narratives show the unmistakable signs of this category, so that we may recognize the following nine as Tales :—

The Leper : Mark i, 40–5.
The Storm : Mark iv, 35–41.
The Demons and the Swine : Mark v, 1–20.
The Daughter of Jairus and the Woman with the Issue : Mark v, 21–43.
The Feeding of the Five Thousand : Mark vi, 35–44.
The Walking on the Sea : Mark vi, 45–52.

The Man, Deaf and Dumb : Mark vii, 32–37.
The Blind Man of Bethsaida : Mark viii, 22–6.
The Epileptic Boy : Mark ix, 14–29.

To these must be added the long miracle stories of the
Fourth Gospel which undoubtedly originated as Tales. They
show unmistakable marks of the Tale style, even if they have
been more or less edited by the evangelist :—

The Marriage at Cana : John ii, 1 ff.
The Son of the Royal Official : John iv, 46 ff.
The Lame Man at Bethzatha : John v, 1 ff.
The Man Born Blind : John ix, 1 ff.
The Raising of Lazarus : John xi, 1 ff.

It would seem also that though edited by the author, the
following is really of similar character :—

The Raising of the Widow's Son at Nain : Luke vii, 11 ff.

In this case also we are concerned with _individual stories
complete in themselves_. Where there are connective links
we shall have to examine carefully whether they originate in
the evangelist, and whether their deletion makes the narrative
completely independent and so quite comprehensible. Only
in one case may we not attempt such a separation of the
material, for the Healing of the Woman with the Issue and
the Raising from the Dead in the house of Jairus are
inseparably bound together. The anxious father calls Jesus
to a person who is only sick. While they go to her the
people crowd round and in the confusion of the multitude
a woman who is ill makes her way to Him whose miraculous
power heals her. Thereby Jesus is delayed and meanwhile
the daughter of Jairus dies. He who was called to heal
must now raise from the dead. In this way the first operation
is bedded into the other and forms an artistic whole. The
attempt to separate them would completely destroy the
structure of the main, together with the subsidiary narrative.

On the other hand, however, the story of Jairus is not

indissolubly connected with that of the man possessed by "Legion". And this latter is connected with the Stilling of the Storm only in so far as it takes place on the further coast and in the neighbourhood of the lake,[1] which Jesus therefore had to cross. The narratives of Mark iv, 35–v, 43 constitute, as it were, a cycle. But the cycle was not necessarily created by the first narrator. Further the connection of the Tales of the Feeding the Five Thousand and the Walking on the Sea, is not necessarily original, although it is very difficult to be certain on the point.

In other passages, with a little labour we can see that the evangelist included the Tales in his writing with *remarks of a pragmatic character*. Above all, the stereotyped prohibitions to publish what had happened can be easily freed from the narratives, as at the end of the stories of the blind man and of the deaf and dumb man respectively. Both these stories have already reached their conclusion, which, as we shall see, is characteristic of the category. Thereby it is true we must distinguish between the secret nature of the miraculous process and the keeping the healing secret. Whereas the former is not surprising (cf. Acts ix, 40) the latter is in practice impossible, for the man who had been hitherto blind, could not live in hiding in the future. That the healing was to be kept secret must therefore be a theory of the evangelist. It is the well-known conception of the Messianic Secret. The prohibition at the end of the Jairus incident is also impossible to carry out as the girl brought back to life cannot remain hidden. So also we may suppose Mark v, 43*a* is a pragmatic remark of the evangelist. On the other hand I do not think that a stereotyped prohibition is to be found in Mark i, 43 f. The sick man is healed of a

---

[1] Perhaps the textual and topographical problem whether originally the matter dealt with the land of the Gerasenes, Gadarenes, or Geregesenes, is explained in the simplest way by supposing that the story first of all gave no indication of the place. Then quite generally and somewhat superficially it was localized in the region of the well-known Gerasa, without the town of Geresa itself (Mk. v, 14) necessarily being mentioned. The effort to identify this town led to the conjecture of the place-name at the beginning of the story.

disease which forbade any intercourse with others. The healing therefore only holds good when the legal verdict has been pronounced, when the sick man is described clean by the priestly supervisor and by sacrifices of purification, "as a witness to them (i.e. to men)." Hence Jesus forbids him to speak now of his cure, and hence He threatens him [1] and sends him away (not only from Himself, but also from all human intercourse). True, Mark understands all this in the sense of this theory of a secret. His view is shown by verse i, 45, which was added by him after the Tale had already reached its conclusion with the command of Jesus i, 44. Something similar is said by the verse which the evangelist placed at the end of the Tale about the deaf and dumb man, vii, 36: Jesus desires His success to remain secret, but the people carry the news of it far and wide against His will. In this way the evangelist develops out of the narrative of individual cases, a description of the immense success of Jesus which survives in completely primitive character. Much the same holds of the conclusion of the tale of the demoniac, Mark v, 18–20. Jesus refuses to accept, amongst His disciples, this witness of His healing power. Rather He sends him home. But the man who has been healed does not act in accordance with the command of Jesus. On the contrary he moves to and fro in Decapolis as a herald of the miracle of Jesus. Here also there has already been reached a characteristic conclusion of the narrative in the genuine style of a Tale.

The beginnings of the Tales are relatively untouched and almost without traces of the editorial or combining work of the evangelist. Only Mark iv, 36 reveals such signs as Wellhausen has shown. The words, " They take Him with them even as He was in the boat," are related to the sermon which has just been delivered in the boat. So also in front of

---

[1] This appears to me to be the very simple meaning of the much disputed expression ἐμβριμησάμενος αὐτῷ, and this meaning can be illustrated without difficulty by Mk. xiv, 5, and lexicologically also by Mk. ix, 30.

the story of the Feeding of the Five Thousand there stands an editorial addition by the evangelist (Mark vi, 30 ff.). The threads of the Tale can be followed with certainty only from vi, 35.

When we have once learned to reckon with the intervention of the evangelist, we shall also number amongst the Tales, the story of the widow's son at Nain. What appears above all to be the contribution of Luke, the evangelist who depicts feelings and who readily mentions women, is the verse (Luke vii, 13), "And when the Lord saw her, He had compassion on her and said unto her, Weep not." If we separate this sentence and perhaps also the mention of another in verse 15*b*,[1] we obtain a closer and better connection. The mother is named only at the beginning and her presence is perhaps not even assumed. The touching of the bier which brings the procession to a stand-still is more immediately effective if Jesus never even spoke. The story then mentions in genuine Tale-fashion the unmistakable signs of returning life: the restored man begins to speak. Finally the Tale concludes with the acclamation of the crowd which has a special significance, since it deals not with the spectators (usually tacitly assumed), but with the funeral procession which had already been mentioned in chapter vii, 12, as a necessary part of the description. In these words, which remind one of the language of the Septuagint, "A great prophet is arisen amongst us and God hath visited his people," we have one of those choruses, common to both the categories of Paradigm and Tale (cf. pp. 58, 71) but which have a different significance. A cry of such a nature always betrays an interest in the use for propaganda purposes of the incident narrated. But such a unique event as the raising of the young man at Nain was not preserved in tradition in order

---

[1] "And He gave him back to his mother," corresponds to the sentence ix, 42, "And He gave him back to his father," which Luke had also added, for it is lacking in the synoptic parallels. There is also a parallel in Lk. viii, 52, to "Do not weep," where Luke has softened down the words to the mourners "Why make ye a tumult and weep?" (Mk. v, 39), to "Do not weep".

to serve as an illustration in a sermon. The narrative is too sorrowful for that, and again, by its very nature it attracts the attention of the hearers to itself. Rather the narrative was intended to do missionary work by its content. To some extent it is a substitute for a sermon among hearers already accustomed to miraculous acts of gods and prophets. That this kind of conclusion to a narrative rarely occurs in the New Testament shows that the New Testament tradition was still shy of this kind of propaganda which is really of a literary nature.

In the Tale of the widow's son the acclamation constitutes the significant conclusion, for the following verse Luke vii, 17 describes in the pragmatic fashion known to us from Mark how this deed helped in furthering the knowledge of Jesus in the whole countryside. This verse originated with the evangelist; the chorus belongs to the Tale. In the story of the Deaf and Dumb Man, on the contrary, the acclamation is not original. This Tale reaches its conclusion, in accordance with its style with the confirmation of the cure (Mark vii, 35). Verse 36, as already shown, serves the pragmatic objective of the evangelist. The wording of the acclamation proves perfectly that vii, 37 did not belong to the corpus of the Tale, since the words, " He hath done all things well; He maketh even the deaf to hear and the dumb to speak " are rather the conclusion of a number of stories than the acclamation of the people to Jesus who is just passing by.

Therefore we may say that the majority of the Tales stand complete in themselves as the Paradigms do, although they have a totally different character. Even a hasty comparison with the Paradigms shows the relative length of the Tales. Above all else the latter rest upon the *breadth* of the description which sometimes reminds one of parallels in the Old Testament and makes one think of writers who understand their art and who love to exercise it : " Then arose a great wind and the waves beat upon the ship so that the ship was ready to sink," or of the demoniac, " He had his dwelling

in the tombs : and no man could anymore bind him, no, not
with a chain ; because that he had been often bound with
fetter and chains, and the chains had been rent asunder by him,
and the fetters broken in pieces ; and no man had strength
to tame him. And always night and day, in the tombs and
in the mountains, he was crying out, and cutting himself
with stones." Or in the case of Jairus : " And he suffered
no man to follow with him, save Peter, and James, and John
the brother of James. And they come to the house of the
ruler of the synagogue ; and he beholdeth a tumult and
many weeping and wailing greatly. And when he was
entered in, he saith unto them, Why make ye a tumult, and
weep ? The child is not dead, but sleepeth. And they
laughed him to scorn. But he, having put them all forth,
taketh the father of the child and her mother and them that
were with him, and goeth in where the child was."

Thus in Tales we learn far more of the secondary circumstances than in the Paradigms, far more indeed than we have
need to know. In the feeding of the 5,000, the seated multitude
and the praying Saviour are depicted ; this presents a scene
which possibly may be traced back to the primitive Christian
congregational meal, and the mention of the very purpose of
Jesus when walking on the sea : " He wished to pass them
by," is perhaps connected with a special " mythological "
meaning of the record. But it is nevertheless doubtful
whether the given numbers, the twelve-year-old girl ; the
twelve-year-long illness of the woman ; the 2,000 swine ;
5,000 men, 5 loaves, 2 fishes, 12 baskets, bread worth
200 denarii ; the fourth watch in the case of walking upon
the sea, can all be characterized as " temperamental ", i.e.
as of mythological or other significance. In any case no
secret allegorical significance is to be found in the cushion in
the stern which Jesus used when asleep, nor in the detailed
descriptions to which we have just referred.

I have attempted to sketch the condition which determines the breadth and the brevity in the case of the

Paradigm. Only what is useful for preaching, or what prepares for, conditions, or supports the desired aim of the sermon—only this is told with somewhat more detail; all the rest is dealt with in a few short strokes. The breadth of the style of the Tale on the contrary is in no wise " didactic " or otherwise conditioned in some way by the praxis of preaching. On the contrary the living realism of the narrative loves *secular motives*. The coloration is not toned down by reference to some sacred style which must be preserved, the vividness of the language is not restricted by an effort to derive teaching or doctrine from the material. That is seen particularly in the description of the disciples. Especially when we compare the text in Matthew do we see how secular its relationship is, as Matthew has recast such passages together with the secular reference of the tales into something didactic or at least inoffensive. Thus the disciples awaken Jesus with the cry " Rabbi, carest thou not that we perish " (Mt. " Lord save, we perish "). They put Him right openly when they say " Thou seest the multitude thronging thee and sayest thou, Who touched me ? " (lacking in Matthew). They know better than Jesus when, to His command to feed the 5,000, they answer, " Shall we go and buy bread for 200 pence in order to give them to eat ? " (Mt. " We have only 5 loaves and 2 small fishes"). This description does not arise from a religious tendency or theory but from joy in lively and graphic description. And those who prefer, throughout the last passage, the theory of misunderstanding well-known in John, will find equally clear an unmistakable indication of the broad narrative style of a Tale, for the disciples must first have counted the loaves and fishes before they could tell Jesus how many they had.[1]

---

[1] The story of the feeding of the 4,000, Mk. viii, 1–9, is completely lacking in such marks of a story-teller's gift or pleasure. But this short record is neither didactically nor even paradigmatically conceived so as to furnish a motive for preaching. Therefore the shortness must be understood as a shortening. In addition to this, dependence of this form of the narrative upon the Tale of the feeding of the 5,000 is probable.

If we have reached some understanding of this realistic and therefore relatively secular character of the Tales, *then the lack of devotional motives and the gradual retreat of any words of Jesus of general value,* are no longer surprising. Didactic applications altogether fail. For we can with certainty reckon as a Tale what is said about the sheep without shepherd (before the miracle of the 5,000, vi, 34), because the connection introducing the miracle is the work of the evangelist. As words of Jesus we can only take into account the recognized sayings about faith " Fear not, only believe," as addressed to Jairus ; " All is possible to him who believes," as addressed to the father of the epileptic boy. But these words do not mean the faith which the missionaries preach to the Churches, but belief in the power of the miracle-worker. The content of faith in such a connection is not the conviction that through Christ God's call has gone out to all mankind, but the confidence that Jesus, the great miracle-worker, excelled all other thaumaturges. In order to estimate the difference one needs only to compare the story of the palsied man. There the faith of the bearers—also pure faith in miracle—meets not only with the expected cure, but also with the quite unexpected forgiveness of sin. In the story of Jairus on the other hand, faith in One who can help the sick was meant to grow into faith in One who raises the dead. Faith in the Saviour who " could do something " (Mk. ix, 22), was meant to help the father of the epileptic boy in spite of the failure of the disciples who could not heal. We are not dealing here with saving faith but with the experience of miracle, and hence these Tale-like stories had something to say to Churches which believed in and continually experienced miracles. Therein we come upon the kernel of the whole

Wendling, *Entstehung des Markus Evangeliums*, p. 68–75, gives the proof in all detail. It is also quite possible that the evangelist himself, finding that different numbers in regard to the miracle were in circulation, put together a second form of the story in order to include the numbers. The compound passage, Mk. viii, 14–21, is intended to do justice to both narratives. In any case the story of the 4,000 belongs neither to the Paradigms nor to the Tales.

problem. It is not Jesus as the herald of the Kingdom of God
with His signs, demands, threats and promises, who stands
in the centre of these stories, but Jesus the miracle-worker.
The Tales deal with Jesus the thaumaturge. Only a few
miracles are related in the Paradigms and even then only from
a definite, practical point of view. What, in the Paradigms,
is an opportunity for Jesus to state His requirements or to
pronounce His message, is, in the Tales, an end in itself
which stands in the centre of the picture and dominates
everything, viz. miracle.

The *conclusions* also are here most apt. They contain
nothing of practical usefulness for preaching such as we find
in Paradigms. They furnish no didactic motives. The
story of Jairus concludes without didactic : " He said, Give
her to eat." The story of the 5,000 similarly, " There were
5,000 men who had eaten." *But in this way the reality of the
miracle is proved,*[1] and if this is not immediately apparent in the
case of other Tales, the reason is to be found in the pragmatic
conclusions supplied by the evangelist. We have already
taken them away, and we now find that the healing of the
deaf and dumb man concludes, " He spoke properly " ; the
healing of the blind man, " He could see everything clearly " ;
the widow's son at Nain (probably), " The dead man sat
up and began to speak ". What we read at the end of other
Tales bears witness to the same interest in the fact of miracle.
The narrative of the epileptic boy ends in the words of Jesus
to His disciples, " This kind goeth out only by prayer and
fasting," which is a recipe for the repetition of such a healing
miracle. After the healing of the demoniac, the inhabitants
of the district, gripped by fear, begged the miracle worker to

---

[1] An analogy from the present day testifies to the constancy of such forms which
is founded not on literary borrowing but on the thing itself. Two cases of healing
were known in the sixtieth national pilgrimage to Lourdes in 1932. The newspaper
L'Écho de Paris of 23rd August, 1932, concludes its account of the second case (Sœur
Marie-Françoise de la congrégation des Pauvres Filles de Jésus, 31, consumption of
the lungs and heart-disease) with the words : " On l'a conduite devant la grotte,
où un bien-être mystérieux l'envahit aussitôt. Elle est guerie et, de retour à l'hôpital,
demande à manger." In this case also ability to eat testifies to the recovered vitality.

leave their neighbourhood. The story of the walking on
the sea, is concluded with a representation of similar anxiety
amongst the disciples.[1] The second story dealing with the
sea ends, it is true, in a chorus and could appear at first sight
like a paradigmatic conclusion. But the content of this
chorus is not at all paradigmatic, " Who is this that the wind
and sea obey Him ? " We see that the interest is fixed upon
His identity as a thaumaturge.

That in the Tales Jesus is purely and simply the great
miracle worker, can be clearly observed elsewhere, and
perhaps best in the story of the epileptic boy. The disciples
could not heal him but Jesus comes exactly at the right moment.
The people are astounded, not however at a reflexion of the
Transfiguration, of which nothing is said, but like the populace
staring at a celebrated man, and running up to greet him.
Mysterious magic surrounds the figure of the miracle worker.
While some are repelled by Him, others run to Him, like the
suffering woman who had heard of the " fame of Jesus ".
He compels the demoniac to fall upon his knees ; and as soon
as the wonder worker touches the bier of the young man,
the bearers come to a stand.

Most clearly of all, the interest of the Tales is concentrated
upon the thaumaturge when His acts are described. So much
detail is given that even the question " Why " is in some
degree answered, and we obtain a peep into the *technique of
the miracle*. That is a point about which the Paradigm is
almost silent, and it is precisely this silence which differentiates it from miracle literature proper. The Tales, however,
are more secularly conceived in that they stand noticeably
nearer to that literature, for they not only speak of the
thaumaturge's art, but also bear witness to another feature

---

[1] The parallel traditions show once more in this case that such conclusions were
felt to be too secular. Matthew, or the Church of which he is the spokesman, introduces in this place the greeting of Jesus as the Son of God which is quite in harmony
with the Epiphany character of the Tale, but which does not correspond to the
continuation of the history of Jesus and in particular with the Messianic confession
of Peter. The need for edification was stronger than the historical sense.

which must not be lacking in miracle literature, i.e. *Literary style in reporting miracles*,[1] a feature which we missed on the whole from Paradigms, but which appears in the Tales with a certain regularity.

From the ancient stories of healing up to modern reports of similar miracles, as in Lourdes, it is one of the favourite practices in such narratives to depict the dangerous character of the suffering and the failure of all attempts to cure. Naturally this is done in order to increase the worth of the miracle. *The history of the illness*, which we have in such detail in the case of the epileptic boy is to be understood in this sense, as also, in broad outline, in the case of the demoniac, and briefly but significantly in the case of the woman with the issue of blood, and in that of the lame man of Bethzatha (in John's Gospel). If we are told here of unsuccessful cures we must remember that there are many analogies in other records of healing. In the same sense we are told that Jesus was laughed at by the multitude (before the raising of Jairus' daughter), a motif which occurs also elsewhere in a similar connexion, e.g. in the Epidauros cures. The severity of the evil is emphasized by the fact that the disciples of the master cannot cure it. Analogous cases are known. Thus in Lucian's *Philopseudes* 36, Eucrates, the original of Goethe's student of magic, cannot change back the pestle which has once been changed, and thus also the priests of Asclepius [2] are not in a position to put back the head of a woman patient, cut off for the purposes of an operation. The greatness of the disease is also brought out in the stories of raising the dead in the Gospels. The few data about the dead young man serve this purpose, and still more the details about the situation into which Jesus enters : the mourning ceremonies for the girl have already begun, the young man is already

---

[1] Compare Weinreich, *Antike Heilungswunder*, especially pp. 195 ff. ; Fiebig, *Jüdische Wundergeschichten des neutestamentlichen Zeitalters*, and both pamphlets published by Fiebig in Lietzmann's collection *Kleine Texte für Vorlesungen und Uebungen*, No. 78, *Rabbinische Wundergeschichten*, No. 79, *Antike Wundergeschichten*.

[2] Cf. Aelian, *De natura animalium*, ix, 33.

being buried,[1] and Lazarus (in John's Gospel) had been in the
grave four days already—leaving no doubt that they were all
really dead.

What is recorded concerning the *technique of miracle*,[2]
permits a similar judgment. It is significant that Jairus asks
the miracle worker expressly to lay his hand upon the patient;
similarly the persons conducting the deaf and dumb man and
the blind man, and also the woman with the issue, who sets
out with the intention of touching His garment. One sees
how these technical matters, which were never touched in the
Paradigms, here become centres of interest. The notices of
the methods and means of the miracle worker are manifold.
Jesus asks the demon for his *name*, because to know the name
gives *power* over the spirits. Almost without exception are the
miracles of healing and of raising performed with the aid
of a miracle-working formula. Jesus says to the leper, " I will;
be thou clean." In driving out the legion (Mark v, 8), the
formula is, " Thou unclean spirit, depart from this man."
But in this instance it is introduced too late, for the demon,
affrighted by the approach of Jesus, had already prayed:
" I adjure you by God not to trouble me." Perhaps Mark,
(or some earlier, but nevertheless secondary narrator)
introduced the formula, because he missed it from the text.
This in itself would be a proof that it belonged to the technical
therapeutic.

In two cases, the daughter of Jairus and the deaf and
dumb man, the formula is given in the Aramaic original:

---

[1] The same trait is to be found in a case of raising from the dead at a funeral in
the story of Asclepius in *Apulius Florida* 19, and in the narrative of Apollonius of
Tyana, Philostratus, *Vita Ap.*, iv, 45.

[2] The records of healing at the Temple of Asclepius in Epidauros in *Inscr. Graec.*,
iv, 951 f., very often reproduce the technique of the divine therapy. Cf. also *Inscr.*,
iv, 915; xiv, 960. Josephus in *Antiquities*, viii, ii, 5, tells of the exorcism of a demon
in the presence of Vespasian, and gives the technique of the cure; also the instance
of the driving out of the demons by Apollonius of Tyana (Philostratus, *Vita Ap.*,
420) belongs here. The Talmud also gives notices of the technique of miracle workers,
e.g. the prayers of Rabbi Chanina Ben Dosa in Berakhoth 34*b*; the declaration with
which Rabbi Gamliel stills the storm, Baba mezia, 59*b* (cf. the healing in the name of
Jesus, *Tosephta Chullin*, ii, 21–3). A noteworthy reflection on the simplicity of the
technique of healing is to be found in 2 Kings v, 11 ff.

"Talitha cum" (Wellhausen conjectures: "Rabitha cumi"), and "ephphatha". It is certain that the use of the foreign word gives the process an esoteric cast, and the secret strengthens faith in the power of the miracle worker. But perhaps that was not the only reason why the composer of the Tale gave the word in the original meaning, for when a magic word is passed on, would not a practical objective be operative? We have observed that the Tale of the epileptic boy concludes with a prescription for working the miracle. Hence the repetition of such a miracle in the Church was reckoned upon. By giving a detailed description of the technique of the case, especially by handing on the very formula, particularly in a foreign tongue, the narrators obviously wish to help Christians to whom the gift of healing was entrusted (1 Cor. xii, 28, 30). Josephus depicts, quite in this sense, the magic art which was ascribed by Jewish tradition to King Solomon (*Ant.* viii, 2^5): "God granted him to learn the exorcism of demons in order to help and to cure mankind. By means of the magic formulæ which he understood, and with which he healed diseases, he passed down to us methods of exorcism by which demons could be bound and hunted out till they never returned. And this art of healing still retains its power among us." Then follows an account of healing a demoniac by the Jew Eleazer by means of Solomon's formula (see p. 83, note 2). Hence when the Christian narrator lays value upon giving the formulæ in the original, a practical purpose is obvious. The wider "world" is exercising a definite influence in this instance, since the employment of formulæ in foreign languages was usual on the part of contemporary miracle-workers.[1]

Alongside of, or as in the case of the blind man, in place

---

[1] In Lucian, *Philopseudes*, 9, the belief is discussed that fevers and tumours fear either magic formulæ or foreign words (ἢ ὄνομα θεσπέσιον ἢ ῥῆσιν βαρβαρικήν). Among the formulæ preserved in the Babylonian Talmud Sabbath, *67a*, are some (against curses and against ghosts) containing foreign and incomprehensible names. Cf. also Origen, *Contra Celsum*, i, 24, v, 45, *re* the power of names and formulæ in the original language.

of the usual formula, a certain *action* serves to explicate the
miracle. Such traits were not altogether lacking in the
Paradigm, but in this case we had to do with motive only
incidentally. In the Tales, on the contrary, this side of things
is developed as in the miracle literature of the period.[1] The
significance of the act in our Tales is found above all in
the two little healing narratives of the deaf and dumb, and the
blind man. The healing of the blind man is effected by the
laying on of hands. In the case of the deaf and dumb, a
reference is made to touching his ears and to a glance towards
heaven, in addition to the sigh of Jesus which is very thoroughly
explained in the commentaries. The mention of this sign
in between the two moments of the glance which sought and
obtained power on the one hand, and the formula "ephphatha"
on the other hand, makes me feel certain that the sigh also is
a medium in the cure. I am thinking now of all sorts of magic
formulæ which prescribe to the miracle worker what technique
he should apply. In the great Parisian Magic Papyrus
(Preisendanz, *Papyri magicæ*, 1928, p. 150) line 2492 says
at the end of a magic prayer: "Throw smoke-making
material into the fire, sigh and step away backwards (from the
roof), and she will come immediately." In the Leyden
Papyrus W. (Dieterich, *Abraxas* 202, 15 f.) we find words of
a similar kind, "Enter, act with your eyes shut, bellow as
much as you can, then take in your breath with a sigh, and
let it out again with a whistle." In Dieterich's so-called
"*Mithrasliturgie*" we find, in a similar connection the words
(page 64), "Breathe the radiance in, three times, as strongly
as you can," [2] and again (page 10, 23), "Draw in the spirit-

---

[1] Compare Weinreich, *Antike Heilungswunder*, Kap. i, θεοῦ χείρ, especially
pp. 18 ff., but also the act of prayer mentioned in footnote 2 (p. 83, *supra*) belongs
here. For the literary character of the miracle records compare Weinreich, p. 7,
footnote 5, etc.

[2] In the *Harvard Theol. Review*, 1927, pp. 171 ff., under the title "Traces of
Thaumaturgic Technique in the Miracles", Campbell Bonner, referring to my
deductions, proves: "That the action denoted by them (the words στενάζω and
ἀναστενάζω) may be considered as a conventional feature of the wonder-worker's
behaviour." For this reason, as also proved by the parallels, ἀναστενάξας in the
Parisian Magic Papyrus should be translated "sigh" and not "cry out" as
Preisendanz holds.

breath to yourself while looking away from the deity."
From such passages we may conclude that the " sigh " belongs
to the technique of mystical magic. The look and the strong
breathing (called " sighing " popularly) are healing media.

Taking by the hand is also a miracle-working gesture.
By this means the epileptic boy lying there as if dead is
restored, and the daughter of Jairus brought back to life.
In the case of the widow of Nain, the touching of the bier
upon which the corpse lies prepares for the miracle and
obviously possesses a power-dispensing significance. The
woman with the issue is healed by touching Jesus. In this
case a transfer of power is quite clearly described ; we might
almost call it an electric contact set up by the fingers which
touch Jesus' garment. Jesus does not feel the contact but
rather the outflow of the dynamic current.

The two short Tales of the deaf and dumb man and of the
blind man agree also in that, beside the miracle-working
gesture, a healing medium is employed, i.e. the spittle.[1]
This plays a part in folk-medicine and folk-beliefs, and
is mentioned again in the New Testament in the case of the
healing of the man born blind. Similar media of folk-healing
are made use of elsewhere in miracle stories. In the gospel
Tales we must recognize a certain shyness towards such
practices. But thereby we have the greater need to ask what
made their occasional occurrence possible. It cannot be the
desire to glorify the miracle or the miracle worker, for the
miracle is, to some extent, rationalized and made human.
Nor may we guess some specially developed pleasure in telling
the story, since, on account of their brevity, neither of the Tales
in Mark mentioning spittle suggests this motive. Rather here,
as in the cases of formula and gesture, there is probably
another reason, viz. to give guidance to Christians gifted
with healing powers. This object may have arisen as a
principle interest in cases where the healing is described in

---

[1] Vespasian healed with spittle; cf. Tacitus, *Hist.*, iv, 81. Sueton, *Vesp.* 7. Cf.
also Strack-Billerbeck, *Kommentar*, ii, 15 ff.

stages. When the epileptic first falls into a death-like state, or when the eyes of the blind man are only opened to see indistinctly, then Christian miracle workers would know what to do in similar circumstances.

The last-mentioned trait of gradual healing may also be regarded as one of the features which establish the *success of the miraculous act*. We have already said that several Tales end with a proof of the reality of the miracle, e.g. the lepers must show themselves to the priests, or the girl who has been restored to life must eat. We see the difference from Paradigms quite clearly in the conclusion of the two narratives about the blind man. In Mark x, 51 f. the healing, told in the manner of a Paradigm, reaches its high point in the proof and the consequence of faith, whereas in Mark viii, 24 ff. the Tale reaches that point in describing the gradual healing and in proving perfect sight. Of course even in Paradigms an element is incidentally mentioned which proves the success (e.g. the lame man shows himself healed by carrying his bed, Mark ii, 12). But this is not the heart of the story, and the trait does not draw attention to itself. Rather the narrator's main interest is devotional and didactic above all else. On the other hand, in the case of the Tales, we see, in the fact that the proof of the miracle is put with emphasis at the end of the story, that this feature was of special importance.

The conclusion of the long story of healing in Mark v, 1–17, gives the most striking, but also the strangest, instance (*re* the second ending v, 18–20, due to Mark, see p. 74). The miracle is proved by the fact that the people find the former invalid now " sitting properly clothed and in his right mind ". (Luke adds the edificatory phrase " at Jesus' feet ".) They then become fearful and ask Jesus to leave their neighbourhood. Jesus is represented not as the benign Saviour who helps, but as the strange miracle man who terrifies. Perhaps the bewitching of the herd of swine is to be understood in the sense of this motive, i.e. confirming the reality of the miracle.

Of course other explanations have been put forward which
would ascribe an independent meaning to the event. The
best known is the view that here we have a fable of a devil
which had been outwitted. The demons would gladly have
remained in the neighbourhood and they choose a herd of
swine for their home, but it is just in that fact that they are
cheated of a lodging and can see their real case. But it is
questionable whether really in this instance a joke is related
for the pleasure of it. We can sense that the narrator had no
sympathy with the animals or with their owners, yet we do
not feel that he told the conclusion with pleasure. And
further, if this conception of things were right, he would
have omitted the essential point, viz: that the demons
were without home and that they were destroyed. The
subject is the swine, not the spirits, whose fate, therefore,
is not the point. Hence the view has been put forward that
the demons and the swine go to Hades, because the swine
have a special relationship to Hades. Hence it were possible
to think of the ætiological Saga of the Thesmophorian
festival in Athens which Clement of Alexandria mentions
(*Protreptikos* ii, 17[1]) as also a scholion on Lucian (*Dial.
meretr.* 2, 1). It was to the effect that at the rape of Persephone,
Eubouleus, a swineherd of the neighbourhood, together
with his swine was swallowed by the earth along with the
goddess. But a reference to the underworld stands only in
the text of Luke, according to whom the demons beg their
exorcist not to condemn them to the abyss (Luke viii, 31).
Moreover the whole Tale is lacking in the feeling with which
such a mythological journey to Hades must have been related.
Thus this interpretation, like the first, can only be due to
a complete transformation of its real motif. We ought,
however, to ask whether the story cannot be understood from
its own self, and so not be as a story about Jesus. For the
interpretation that the demons wished to make Jesus equally
responsible for the destruction of the herd so that He should
thereby be driven from the district contradicts the wording

of the Tale. The point is not at all the mischief which had been done, nor the responsibility laid upon Jesus; for the people wish a miracle-worker, not a harm-doer, to depart from the land, and it is fear, not wrath, which disturbs their minds. But it seems to me that the solution of the problem lies in the name and the nature of the demon: he calls himself Legion, "for we are many." The magnitude of the miracle is seen in the number of the demons, just as with Mary Magdalene (Mark xvi, 9). If this is to be described, then the multiplicity must be seen in the exorcism; it corresponds to the nature of such stories of exorcism that the manifestation of the exorcised spirit takes place in a visible phenomenon or even in some mischief which he causes: "I myself saw one go out black and like smoke," says Ion in Lucian's *Philopseudes* 16. The demon which Apollonius of Tyana cast out upsets a statue (iv, 20). The one cast out by Peter in Rome damages a statue of the Emperor (*Actus Petri cum Simone*, ii). The spirits driven out by the Jew, Eleazar, used to upset basins or jugs of water (Jos. *Ant*. viii, 2^5). In the same way the demon Legion in Mark searches out a collective object which he makes use of for his mischief. If this story were originally related of a Jewish exorcist in a Gentile country, and only afterwards ascribed to Jesus, it would contain nothing surprising. That a great number of unclean animals was the proper subject would be clear in itself, as also that the narrator betrays no sympathy either with these animals or with their Gentile owners. It is a narrative full of secular motives, and, it must be admitted, of secular Jewish origin in the last analysis. Only its striking opposition to every kind of evangelical ethos differentiates it from the other Tales.

The relationship of non-Christian miracle-stories with the Gospel Tales in the very proof of the result exists also elsewhere. At the conclusion of the story of the healing of Midas, (Lucian, *Philopseudes* ii) we read that he carried his bed and could walk. At the raising of the maiden by Apollonius, Philostratus says explicitly (*Vita Ap*. iv, 45) that she let her voice be heard and returned to her father's house. The story had already dealt with the question about the name of the girl, the touching of the corpse and the speaking unintelligible words. In the narratives of healing from Epidauros this motif of proof occurs in various forms: either the health is proved, or the reality of a successful intervention when the patient, waking up from a trance, discovers traces of the work during the night. We shall speak of this subject further in Chapter VI.

So far I have brought out the typical traits of the Tale mostly from stories of healing or raising of the dead; other Tales such as those of the nature-miracles also possess the specific character of this category. In the calming of the storm a formula is employed.[1] With the words " He rebuked the wind " a definite act [2] is also pictured. In the case of the feeding of the 5,000 the glance towards heaven and the blessing are miraculous media, and the success is confirmed not only directly by " They were filled ", but also indirectly by the notice that twelve baskets were necessary in order to contain the remains. In the story of the walking on the sea the reality of the phenomenon is proved in that the apparent spirit speaks to the disciples and embarks with them in the boat. In addition the wind is calmed now that Jesus is present.

At the conclusion of this inquiry into the motifs characteristic of the Tale we must consider the miracle-stories of John's gospel in this context, although we have already mentioned isolated traits. They have been preserved of course only in an edited form, and the person who gave them their present shape was an evangelist working with initiative and, in a certain sense, in a literary manner. He interwove some of these miracle-stories directly into dialectical

---

[1] πεφίμωσο at least need not refer to the alarm, but may be a formula for binding the spirit as in magic. Compare the references for φιμωτικόν = κατάδεσμος *Rohde Psyche*, ii, 5, 6, 424.

[2] Compare the act of a god on the lake in Aristides' Λαλιὰ εἰς 'Ασκληπιόν, (§ 10 (II, S. 337, Keil) ὡς αὐτοῖς πλέουσι καὶ θορυβουμένοις φανεὶς ὁ θεὸς χεῖρα ὤρεξεν.

scenes which express his ideas, e.g. the narratives of the man born blind and of Lazarus. In other cases, e.g. the healing of the lame man and the feeding of the 5,000, the scenes follow. Again in the cases of the miracles which are given only as plain records, e.g. the marriage at Cana, the healing of the officer's son, the walking on the sea, we must ask whether he gave his own emphasis to the traditional record and erected his own guiding lights. A detailed analysis is not in place here but it would bring to light "Johannine" material. But numerous Tale-like traits prove that these stories were originally Tales and that John cannot be the narrator to whom they owe their original form for the style and technique of the Tale-writer are the very opposites of his own. The original form of these narratives lay before the evangelist just as in all probability the old form of the stories about the work of Apollonius of Tyana lay before Philostratus. In this place we must deal only with the Tale-motifs proper.

The " secular " character of the entire narrative is specially remarkable in the story of a marriage at Cana (John ii, 1 ff.). Its Johannine sense does not touch us but rather the confirmation of the miracle, given attractively but indirectly. It is not said how the water became wine, nor how the wine pleased the guests. It is only recorded that the governor of the feast reproaches the bridegroom because he has not passed round *this* wine earlier. Confirmation of success has a definite place also in the story of the healing of the nobleman's son. The point characteristic of the Tale is that the word of Jesus and the recovery of the sick man took place at the same time. This is also a typical trait of miracle-stories.[1] The sick man at the pool of Bethesda (John v, 1 ff.) is described with artistic pleasure. His circumstances, the long illness, the many vain attempts at healing, are all mentioned, and, as a sign of recovery, " he took up his bed and walked." The

---

[1] Cf. the same proof of simultaneity of miraculous word and result in the case of healings at a distance by Rabbi Chanina ben Dosa, Berakhoth, 34*b*.

miracle of the feeding, obviously dependent upon Mark, is accentuated as over against the older record. According to John vi, 7, two hundred pennyworth of bread would not be sufficient for the multitude, according to Mark vi, 37, so much bread would be enough. In John an acclamation constitutes the conclusion of the miracle ; so also in the story of walking on the sea, and indeed at its end, there is a trait which signifies an increase of the miraculous, and not some sort of rational explanation. In Mark, whose account in this case also seems to be at the basis, the miracle ends with the calming of the wind, which promises a safe return. But in John we read, " they wished to take Him into the ship, and immediately the ship came to land and they could disembark." That does not mean to say that the event took place in shallow water near the shore, for the walking on the sea would then have been no miracle. Rather the rapid journey must be added to the miracle of the walking on the sea. As soon as Jesus was nigh they reached firm land. The blind man of John ix was originally not depicted as blind from birth, if we may deduce anything from the introductory speech about the question of guilt. Hence we are dealing with the healing of a blind man described in genuine Tale-fashion. The poor fellow is healed by means of clay made from spittle and earth, together with washing in the pool of Siloam. We have already drawn attention to the proof of the result. Many neighbours did not recognize him when he could see, but considered him a twin. The story of Lazarus (John xi, 1 ff.) lays special value upon the confirmation of the death. Already visitors have come to comfort the sisters. Lazarus is already in the grave. By the opening of the grave already the smell is feared. Jesus raises the dead man by an order given in a loud voice, and the confirmation of the success constitutes the conclusion. Lazarus is able to move himself in spite of the fact that he is bound in grave-clothes. Jesus orders him to be unbound and allowed to walk.

It has become ever more clear in our description of Tale-

style to what degree the edificatory style is lacking, and
to what degree a multitude of secular motifs is proper to such
Tales. Obviously they are not conditioned by the thoughts
found in the preaching of salvation and so do not touch the
question of the relationship of man to God, or what man
enters the Kingdom of Heaven and what is God's real requirement of man. Rather they are dominated by the effort to
make plain the greatness of a miracle, to show the impossibility
of human aid, and to depict the nature of Jesus' intervention.
The process of the event draws our attention to itself, and the
question of its meaning in connection with the sending of
Jesus into the world falls into the background. But when
I characterize this attitude of the Tales as secular, I do not
mean that the material itself is of non-Christian origin.
Yet there is a certain *relationship of kind between the Gospel
Tales and the non-Christian miracle stories*, and thus a certain
approximation to the literature of " the world ", not, of course,
to fine literature, but to popular literature and indeed to the
writing of the people. In face of these facts, the first question
that arises is in regard to the religious significance of the
Tales within the borders of the gospels.

The present-day reader, on reading the Tales, is conscious
of the narrator's interest in the technique of the miracle and
in the miracle-worker. He will perhaps hold that a religious
note is by no means germane to such stories. That, however,
would be a misjudgment, for men of the ancient world
traced the operation of God or of divine messengers more
directly in miracles than modern readers are accustomed
to do, and the Tale-writers have given indications of it.
When Jesus took only three intimates with Him at the raising
of Jairus's daughter, when before healing the deaf and dumb
man He withdrew from the multitude, or when, in healing the
blind man, He left the village, it was not because He desired to
conceal His Messiahship, for the question of the Messiahship
was never raised in this case. Mark had it in mind only in
those concluding remarks which I have differentiated and

separated from the body of the Tale. The idea of a Messianic
secret moreover is not in place in an isolated individual
story. Indeed, it can only be conceived and applied by one
who is describing the whole work of Jesus, and who desires
to answer the question why the Messiahship of Jesus, in spite
of His fame, was not widely known. It is so to speak a
biographical motif. We are on a different footing in regard
to the secret which surrounds the action of Jesus in these
three Tales. The miracle worker avoids the public because
He is not a magician with a propaganda, but an envoy and
revealer of God, who does not allow his action, i.e. God's
action, to be seen by profane eyes. As a sort of *deus praesens*
He shows Himself to only a select group. One has to do then
with *Epiphanies* in which the divine power of the divine
wonder-worker becomes manifest. The vision of God, however, is not granted to the majority. The power continues to
live only within the narrow circle of the disciples, and, therefore, the recipe against the demon of epilepsy is only passed
on esoterically.

With such an orientation of the Tales it may be quite taken
for granted that miracle, and, indeed, as a rule, the great
miracle " impossible " among men is the real subject of the
Tale. Its part is not, as in the Paradigm, to show what the
will of God is, which came to expression in the words and
works of Jesus, even in the miraculous healing acts. Rather,
the miracle is told as an epiphany of the divine on earth,
and this epiphany in the miracle is for its own sake.[1] Thus
the miracle of calming the storm ends with the exclamation,
" Who is this, that the winds and the sea obey him ? " and

---

[1] The word ἐπιφάνειαι may mean definitely the miraculous acts of a god. In
the temple-chronicle of Lindus, the second narrative part is entitled ἐπιφάνειαι
(Blenkenberg, *Die lindische Tempelchronik*, Kl. Texte 131, 34 D 1), whereas the totality
of revelations is ἐπιφάνεια in the singular (ib. 4 A 3). Cf. also my *Kommentar zu den
Pastoralbriefen*, 2nd edition, Excursus ἐπιφάνεια, pp. 63 ff. The title ἀρεταί for
miraculous acts is also old, and ἀρετάλογος means one who announces or explains
visions and dreams (Reitzenstein, *Hellenist. Wundererzählungen* 9 f.). On the other
hand the term θαύματα seems to be found first in Christian collections of miracles.
Cf. on this point and for the whole of Herzog, *Die Wunderheilungen von Epidauros*.

thereby presupposes that the hearers or readers themselves
give the answer that he who commands the waves is the
visible epiphany of God on earth. The Feeding of the Five
Thousand also contains an epiphany, not, of course, to the
5,000, but to the Christian readers. Again, without reference to
the origin of the material, we may sense the deeper meaning of
the picture as painted by the writer : " He looked up to heaven,
blessed and brake the loaves, and gave to the disciples."
It is the Saviour who dispenses the Lord's Supper. Thus, in
Luke, He appears to the disciples at Emmaus; thus the church
which is celebrating the Lord's Supper knows that He is
present imparting His blessings in their midst ; thus do they see
Him in this story of the feeding, which seems to the unbeliever
to be only a great miracle, but to eyes that have been
opened to be a trustworthy picture with soteriological
meaning. I believe that an epiphany is intended also in the
walking on the sea, for, according to Mark vi, 48, Jesus
does not wish to enter the boat, but by walking on the sea
to reveal His nature to them. The words " He would have
passed them by ", strange enough, in this context have no other
meaning. The Christian reader would look for help, and not
for a terrifying appearance, and so this very object, i.e. the
epiphany as such, is diagnostic for the narrative. It is only
the fear and confusion of the disciples which causes Jesus
to enter the boat. A divine epiphany which will be only for
a brief earthly period is also intended in the case of the cure
of the epileptic boy, as is proved by Jesus's reproach, " O
unbelieving generation, how long shall I be with you ? How
long shall I bear with you ? " (Mark ix, 19). From such
considerations we may gather the significance of the Tales
for the first Christian narrators and their hearers. They
were partly too long and partly too secular to be introduced
into sermons as illustrations. They were intended to prove
the miracle-worker was an epiphany of God, and this was
done by the Tale as such apart from inclusion in a sermon.

From this point of view we can see what significance must

be ascribed to these secularly-formed narratives within the bounds of the primitive Christian mission. By them neither the preaching of salvation could be explained nor the knowledge of salvation increased. But by telling such Tales, the pre-eminence of the " Lord Jesus " could be demonstrated and all other rival gods who were worshipped driven from the field. We can see the significance of primitive Christian Tales if we notice two processes within Hellenistic religious history : (*a*) the incidental *replacement of Myths by stories of miracles*, and (*b*) *the disappearance of the boundaries between God and the God-sent man*.

Even as early as the cult of Asclepius, we can see that the sparing mythical element retreats before the multitude of healings. We are not so much concerned whether Asclepius is really the son of Apollo and the grandson of Zeus, if we can speak of his miracles.[1] The cult of Serapis offers a still clearer example, for there is neither a myth nor a genealogy of this god. But myth is replaced by aretalogy, or the description of the miraculous deeds of the god in the life of men—because myths are lacking, miracles are reported. " Sacred cupboards full of sacred books contain numberless examples. Market-places, harbours, and the big squares of the towns are full of such stories.[2] Whoever wished to spread the cult of Serapis told such stories, and thus miracle-stories became instruments of the mission. The New Testament Tales are to be understood as stories of this kind, useful in spreading the new cult. No real myths, but only His works can be told about Jesus (see Chapter X). Preaching saved men and illustrated its points by Paradigms. But the Tales, told by the churches, revealed self-convincing power. Both types gained believers in Jesus " the Lord ". Hence it was in accordance with his purpose that Mark included both Paradigms and Tales in his Gospel.

Against comparison with the deeds of Asclepius and

---

[1] Aelius Aristides, in *Aesculapium*, 4 ff., ii, 335, Keil.
[2] Aelius, in *Serapium*, 29 f., ii, 361, Keil.

Serapis we cannot raise the objection that in their case gods
are acting, but in that of Jesus it is an envoy of God sent
in human form. For the same era which honoured Asclepius
for his deeds ascribed similar deeds to Apollonius of Tyana,
Alexander of Abonuteichus, and many magi and thaumaturges.
Thus it is possible to relate such deeds of a human being
as a proof that he was really a divine being. The faith which
the miracle-story arouses begins with the " astonishment "
or " amazement " proper to the miracle, i.e. with being over-
powered by the miracle. It does not begin with a Christological dogma. The Tales are meant to show Jesus as the
Lord of divine powers, and they effect this object by a
narrative style which does not despise colourful, or even
" secular ", means.

Now at last we can deal with the question of the *origin of
the Tales*. We have seen how this richer and more secular
narrative style serves Christian ends, how epiphanies of
Jesus can be seen in them, how His miracle technique is
described and, occasionally, recommended to Christian
brethren as worthy of imitation. At the same time, we have
hinted at the possibility that occasionally Paradigms may
have been transformed with this tendency. Thus hybrid
forms would arise, the best example of which is the story of
the woman with the infirmity (Luke xiii, 10–17). In the end
this story goes back to the same or similar material as its
two parallels, the healing of the withered hand (Mark iii, 1–5)
and the man with the dropsy (Luke xiv, 2–6), leaving open
the question of the inter-relation of these two Paradigms.
The synagogue is common to the hybrid form and to Mark's
Paradigm. The saying which follows the healing, both
in the Man with the Dropsy, and the Woman with the
Infirmity, refers to the care of animals on the Sabbath, but in
the latter case the saying retains a less Jewish form. The point
of the comparison is not the rescue of animal and man, but,
in more literary fashion, the freeing of the animal from the
stall and of the man from his illness. Nevertheless this

conclusion gives the event an edificatory conclusion, paradigm-like, although the brevity of the Paradigm is lost. The action is cast into dialogue by introducing the words of the ruler of the synagogue, and the whole ends with the shame of the opponents and the joy of the people. The healing itself, however, is unquestionably Tale-styled. Whereas Mark iii, 5, has only a bare command and Luke xiv, 5, has almost no " trait ", in Luke xiii, 10–17, the story of the suffering, the solemn command, the laying on of hands, and the proof of the healing in the praise given by the sufferer to God, offer a vari-coloured picture. The style of dialogue and of Tale show the narrators' tendency for painting in. Christians are becoming at home in a world where such kinds of narratives are usual.

The text of the story of the woman taken in adultery is also to be explained by such tendencies, although it is by no means handed down along one line of tradition. The story is found in John vii, 53–viii, 11, in the Byzantine and in part of the Western text. Its form is hybrid. It represents a sermon-head, Jesus's criticism of the woman's judges, of whom not one was without sin. But the narrative is wordy. Twice is the guilt of the woman mentioned, twice does Jesus bow down and write in the sand in order to show that neither the question nor the questioners really concern Him. The accusation is given at length, and even the concluding dialogue between Jesus and the woman has not the brevity of the Paradigm, and in the variant readings it goes on growing. This last fact is very instructive. Obviously we have here a Paradigm which had been handed on and filled out independently of the discipline of preaching and the fixation of the text by the Gospels. Perhaps in this special case it was also edited in literary interests (cf. Chapter VI). Many examples show that we must presuppose a process of " free handing down ", especially at the time when preaching could depend upon a literary fixation of tradition.

As examples of such a development which necessarily

have lent tale-like colours to paradigmatic narratives, thus creating hybrid forms, certain fragments preserved from the Gospel to the Nazarenes may be of value. Here the man with the withered hand is a mason; he begs Jesus to deliver him from the shame of begging and make him able to work. We have already mentioned the transformation of the story of the rich young man. The Nazarene Gospel makes the interrogators obviously appear as two persons, one of whom doubtfully scratches his head at Jesus's answer. Related to that is the extension of the dialogue. Jesus shows this rich man that in his attitude toward the poor he has not fulfilled the law and the prophets.

By such examples, the possibility of the rise of Tales is clear: the further development of short Paradigms to long narratives by the introduction of a richer miracle content and of other usual narrative elements, for example, that of the dialogue. This process does not mean, or not always means, a literary procedure. Rather the enrichment of the original stories could take place automatically, if once they were set free from their context in a sermon, if they were handed on as independent Tales, if they were handed on by men who were accustomed to narrate according to the plan of the usual miracle-stories or in the style of current anecdotes. This further development is really self-apparent. What may be regarded as astonishing is much rather the fact that in the Gospel-paradigms a number of stories are preserved which have not gone through this process. This fact constitutes a strong proof of the actual linking of Paradigms with preaching, without whose protection they, like many of their relatives, would have been seized by that tendency toward the Tale-form which would necessarily have had its effect. This Tale-making often, but not always, means a degeneration of the tradition, removing it ever further from the historical reality. The degeneration is present to the extent that the Tale-style here and there puts the usual thing in the place of the unique thing. But if it develops a brief Paradigm by the introduction of the ordinary it also enriches the elements which frequently possess a certain probability in themselves, for the scheme followed by the reports of miracles would surely not have arisen at all if the thaumaturge had not once and again employed this praxis (of asking the name, laying on his hand) and if the sufferers had not frequently behaved in this wise.

From this standpoint there comes to light another way in which Tales could have arisen. When once the need for extending the brief paradigmatic narratives had arisen, motives, whether proper or strange to it, could be employed for filling it out. The story of Jesus walking on the sea can conceivably have arisen in such a manner. A primitive Christian narrative of Jesus intervening helpfully in a difficulty caused by winds and waves would then be extended by the motif, "He wished to pass them by." Thus an epiphany motif was introduced into the scene which could be applied in a Christian sense, but which on account of its air, quite unlike that of the Gospels, must be traced back to some non-Christian influence. Naturally these considerations are only possibilities, and not certainties. But the possibilities exist; indeed alongside of them we must reckon with a third type of Tale-formation: the taking over and transformation of non-Christian stories as wholes. The possibility of such a transference is given by the consideration that two different tendencies meet there. The desire of Christians to relate many great deeds of their Saviour which would proclaim His epiphany; and the tendency of folk-tradition to narrate current stories as if they were about some well-known and famous "hero". Such a transference may at times have taken place as an unconscious process. Jewish-Christian narrators would make Jesus the hero of well-known legends of prophets or rabbis. Gentile-Christian narrators would hand on stories of gods, saviours, and miracle workers, re-cast as applying to the Christian Saviour.

That such a probability became actuality is proved by at

least two of the Gospel narratives. We have already proved
in the case of the healing of the demoniac (Mark v, 1–17, S.
84 ff.) that it not only lacks the Gospel ethos, but at its conclusion is also contrary to the mission of Jesus. The indifference
of the narrator to the harm which had been done, and to the
wish of the people that Jesus should leave their district shows
that the narrator is only interested in the greatness of the
actual miracle, not in the benefit to the sufferer and other
help for the people. We have already indicated that all the
problems of the story can be solved if we suppose that
originally it was told about a Jewish exorcist. There would
then be no need for further concern about the owner of the
swine, for he is a Gentile ; nor to ask about the further lot
of the demons. The fact that they had entered despised
animals and these rushed into the lake is a satisfactory
conclusion for a Jewish narrator.

The second story which clearly points to an extra-Christian
origin is the Tale of the miracle at Cana. Every Bible reader
is struck by the fact that Jesus does not bring aid in a case of
stress, but helps them out of a quandary ; moreover this
help is by no means necessary and may even be doubtful, for
it has nothing at all to do with the Gospel ethos. The over-
whelming amount of wine, between five and seven hundred
quarts, may illustrate the greatness of the miracle, but in no
way does it fit in with the special quality of the Gospel. We
have already drawn attention to the delightful way in which
the change of the water to the wine is demonstrated. It is
particularly obvious that a jocular note marks the scene
between the bridegroom and the ruler of the feast, if we compare the interpretation given by the evangelist in John ii, 11,
to " feel " of which contrasts so strangely with that note.
The reference to the " hour " which is " not yet come "
is certainly due to John's own construction of the story, as
perhaps also is something of what is said about the mother
and the servants. But in this reconstruction there was preserved
more or less fragmentarily a narrative which originally told

of a divine, or half-divine miracle-doer, and of a wine-miracle characteristic of his epiphany : we may think of Dionysius or some similar god.   This story would be transferred to Jesus, and thus would arise a Jesus Tale, which the evangelist edited and made to serve his ideas.

Judgment as to the *historical value* of a Tale depends upon the answer to the question—in which of these three ways it arose.   We can see at once how many possibilities there are, from spinning out an old paradigmatic narrative of reliable tradition to the borrowing of a foreign divine myth. The question cannot be decided in general, and we may only say that Tales, in accordance with their own nature are, at best, further removed from the historical text than the Paradigms.   The judgment often expressed, that vivid narratives could not have been invented, depends upon a substitution of realism for faithfulness to actuality.   The vivid realism of the Tales corresponds not to the requirements of preaching, but to the expectations of men who were accustomed to similar stories of miracle-workers, prophets and preachers.   Hence this type, as a whole, is less historical than the Paradigm.   Nevertheless, historical foundations or commencements may be presupposed when a Paradigm is the basis of a Tale ; and only when a non-Christian story seems to be probable as the original of a Christian Tale is the reliability of the Christian narrative really brought into question.

But historical significance is proper to the Tales in so far as they are to be understood as witnesses to a Christian development.   The Tale-tellers have taken over foreign traits or actions and have Christianized them, and this Christianization was not accomplished by merely linking them to Jesus, but also by a much more intensive means. Here I must mention the other interest which we noticed in the Tales alongside of the pleasure in narration : the effort to give Christian miracle-workers example and leading. What Jesus did would remind them of what was now taking place in the Churches, and the attempt was made so to depict the former that the latter were helped. The Tales placed before the eyes of Christians an example of miracle-working and examples of belief in miracles. And *vice versa*, the eyes of the church passed from what was believed about Christ, or addressed in prayer to Christ, to these stories, and saw in them, even though secretly and only unveiled to believers, the portrait of the Lord as He came near to all Christians in worship. In this way we could explain the epiphany-traits which we have suggested in isolated Tales. These also, like the technique of healing and all else of the sort, bear witness to the Christianization of the Tale-material or Tale-motif.

Thus these narratives did not arise uninfluenced by faith and public worship. Nevertheless they were not formed for public worship, for their typical traits contradict its conditions. If to-day one were to read one of the Tales liturgically in divine service we should perceive, if we had any feeling for style, the contradiction between the relatively secular description in the Tales and the style proper to public worship. Even the processes which we are compelled to deduce for the rise and development of the Tale are not thinkable within the borders of public worship: e.g. the spoiling of the stories which had been handed down ; the filling out of the blanks, the introduction of foreign motifs and material. Many things, such as the interweaving of the story of Jairus with that of the woman with the issue, and the use made of foreign examples, might suggest that some of the Tales were soon put down in writing. In any case Tales belong to higher grade of literature than paradigms.

With the motifs proper to tales a bit of " the world " presses into primitive Christian life. By the Christianization of this bit of " the world " which was carried out more energetically than in the later Christian literature written for its own sake, the interest was given which these tale-like narratives still exercise to-day upon the reader.

CHAPTER V

LEGENDS

In fixing the two categories, Paradigms and Tales, we have not exhausted the New Testament content of narratives as such. We must still consider a category which is to be differentiated from the obvious antithesis between Paradigms and Tales. The former represented a category with its own Christian formulation in an edifying style. In the Tales the technique was developed after the manner of the surrounding world, and correspondingly the diction was here and there altogether secular. But there is a category of narratives to be found in the Gospels as well as in the popular literature of the surrounding world whose method of speaking is not altogether secular, but is more explicitly edifying. Here we have to do with " religious " stories as they are known and loved in the world, so loved, indeed, that the name Legend, which applies to their category, has become the typical designation of a religious story.

According to the usage of the Middle Ages the word legend means a story of the " vita et obitus confessorum " to be read on the feast day of a saint.[1] Thus Legends are religious narratives of a saintly man in whose works and fate interest is taken. An ætiological interest is to be found alongside of the biographical ; the endeavour is to give grounds for the significance of the saint's day by such narratives. Thus we may differentiate between *ætiological legends* proper to the *cultus* and the *personal legends*. Of course we must not forget that personal legends in the end serve ætiology because they are intended to give a basis for honouring the saint.

---

[1] Cf. Johannes Beleth, *Rationale divinorum officiorum* ; " at vero legendarius appellatur liber, qui vitas et obitus tradit confessorum," Migne, *Patrologia latina* 202, 69.

The Passion-story of Jesus is really a cultus-legend in this
ætiological sense. It was meant to represent the disgraceful
events of the condemnation and execution of Jesus, so that
the hearer or the reader would recognize therein the expression
of the Divine Will, which would mean that the Christians
had a right to honour this suffering. The Passion-story
gradually, and especially in Luke, developed in the direction
of a personal Legend. We shall speak of this later. At this
point we shall not deal with the Passion-story as such, because
in essence it does not consist of small details, but constitutes
a large connected piece. Pure personal Legends only occupy
a relatively small space in the material of the synoptic Gospels,
and it is important for the understanding of the Gospel
tradition to trace out this fact and its causes. The deeds
and experiences of a man, who for his piety and sanctity is
honoured by God with a special fate, stand as the middle
point of a typical personal legend. He works miracles,
reconciles enemies, tames animals ; distress and danger
lead him to salvation, and even as a martyr he is surrounded
by signs of divine grace. The greatest part of the narrative
Gospel material handed down does not show this tendency.
The narrators do not attempt to depict the holy quality of
Jesus, His piety, or His virtue, but rather the divine message
which He preaches, and the divine epiphany which He
represents. But the other persons of the Gospel-story who
could be regarded as heroes of legends, claim at first no
independent interest. We have already shewn the lack of
portraiture at least in the Paradigms, and even in the Tales
the interest is directed more to the details of the action than
to the peculiarities of the persons. From this we may explain
how the typical narrative motive of Legends is quite in the
background of the Gospels. Legends deal with the human
though, of course, with the human as continually marked
out by God. Paradigms and Tales, on the other hand,
even if in different forms, deal with the divine which
has become human. Thus the most striking thing is

that the typical legendary motif, that of miraculous self-deliverance, plays a very small part in the synoptic tradition. In Thomas' Gospel of the Childhood the dead playmate of Jesus comes to life again in order to witness to Jesus. The boy Jesus also carries water in His garment to His mother (Ps. Thomas 9 and 11). In the Apocryphal Acts of the Apostles, Peter makes a dog talk and a smoked fish swim (*Actus Petri cum Simone* 12 and 13), John destroys the temple of Artemis (Acts of John 38 ff), lions bite themselves to death instead of hurting Thecla, (Acts of Paul 33). In the synoptic Gospels, however, there are only three similar passages; the escape of Jesus in Nazareth (Luke iv, 29 f.); the cursing of the fig-tree which gives no fruit (Mark xi, 14 and 21); and the miracle of the coin in the fish's mouth, related only as a command (Matt. xvii, 27). Of these passages, only the first is an independent Legend, for Matthew xvii, 27, is not a story, and the cursing of the fig-tree perhaps grew from a parable and, in any case, is not a narrative typical of the Gospel. The Gospel tradition, as a whole, was obviously very shy of the invasion of legendary tendencies.

The story of Jesus whose quality shows most clearly the marks of Legend is the *story of Jesus twelve years old* (Luke ii, 41 ff. Its conclusion is in the word of Jesus, ii, 49). The record about the return to Nazareth is no necessary part of the Legend. The words about the mother who treasures all things imitate verse ii, 19, where they have their true place. The clause about the parents' lack of understanding belongs to the context of the life of Jesus, and would be disturbing in a legend which ends with a happy conclusion. The whole event is related to Jewish religion: the pilgrimage of the parents to the Passover feast and Jesus learning from the teachers of the law. And this religion is not, as it were, attacked by the Legend so much as depicted with full agreement, except that the religion of the others is exceeded by that of Jesus who knows Himself as belonging to and at home in the house of God, His Father.[1] We must avoid reading in a tragic note or any hint of a real conflict. The listeners to the discussion become beside themselves with joy, and the fear of the parents is only about the attitude which the boy as an unprepared and obtrusive scholar takes up to the teachers of the law. We must imagine with what respect even a growing scholar learning the law stood before his teacher. The alarm is only human; the parents have been anxious, and have sorrowfully sought the son. Even now when they find Him they have no suspicion of what keeps Him here.

The trait of the precocity of a hero, a wise man, or a saint, who even in youth shows the promise of his later calling, and thereby shames, or at least astonishes his elders, is naturally widespread. But all parallel texts of that sort must be tested upon their own foundation. We must ask what quality of the hero is honoured and whether it corresponds to his future work. Only if it should appear that the youthful trait does not correspond to the traditional picture of the adult, but comes from another world, may we deduce with certainty some borrowing. Similarity in the secondary motives can often be understood from the law of legend-formation. That holds good also of the age given to the young hero which is often twelve years (Buddha, Si Usire, Jesus), although this only represents a sacred number beloved by legends and is biologically suitable. At bottom the most important narratives and those nearest to the legend of Jesus may be understood from their immediate surroundings. Si Usire in Egypt, at twelve years old can read the magic books.[2] The Bodhisattva in India, sitting under the Jambu-tree, falls into various stages of trance. The Jew Josephus at fourteen is visited by

---

[1] The scene is obviously a hall in the Temple forecourt where the rabbis discuss matters. Jesus does not teach but takes part by listening, questioning, objecting (these are the ἀποκρίσεις "Rabbi, I would like to say something to you," *Tosephta Chullin*, ii, 24). In this case ἐν τοῖς τοῦ πατρός μου would refer to the Temple, and not to the law, for this reference could be valid of any synagogue.

[2] Cf. the Demotic Papyrus. *Vide* Griffith, *Stories of the High Priests of Memphis*, 1900, 41 ff.

high priests and eminent persons desiring to hear his exegesis
of the law,[1] and Rabbi Eleazar ben Hyrkanos was found
in the school by his father who meant to disinherit him.[2]
The Legend of Jesus, moreover, points in no way to anything
beyond itself. As the future teacher of the people Jesus even
in youth can take part in the discussions of the rabbis, and,
as the future Messiah, He knows Himself to be at home in the
Temple as the house of His Father. The Legend obviously
arose in regions where Jesus was both teacher and Messiah,
and where not the supersession, but the preservation and
completion of the Temple cultus and the Halakha were the
the common tradition in the gospel. We scarcely need to say
that these were Jewish-Christians, but we cannot determine
whether they were Aramaic- or Greek-speaking.

The question of the historicity can be fundamentally
discussed in this very beautiful example of a Jesus-legend.
The figure of his hero is given to the narrator of such a
personal Legend ; he regards it as historical, and does not
reflect further over the possibility of its existence. The
essential interest is not directed toward the greatness of a more
or less miraculous fact, as in the case of Tales, but to the
edifying character of the whole. But it is not the message by
word or by deed which is intended to be edifying, as in the
Paradigms, so much as the religiousness and sanctity of the
hero together with the protection granted him by God. This
dominant interest may, and in many cases does, lead to an
unhistorical accentuation of the miraculous, to a glorifying
of the hero and to a transfiguration of his life. Simple events
are surrounded with a heavenly light, or elements from other
Legends are transferred to the hero in order to show the
connection of his life with the divine world. But above all,
his life is decorated with characters and scenes which
correspond to the very nature of legendary biography. We
could almost speak *of a law of biographical analogy* which is

---

[1] Josephus, *Vita*, § 9.
[2] Geneses rabba 42 in xiv, 1. Nathans Aboth, vi, 5. Pirqe of R. Eliezer, i, 2.

to be seen here. At bottom is to be found a fixed idea of the life of a holy man : such a man may neither be born nor die without the significance of the event being proclaimed from heaven. His future calling is announced even in his youth, and in the same way his end throws its shadows in advance. Divine powers are always ready to help him in stress and to proclaim his merits. Many points of agreement between Buddha-legends and the Jesus-legends, as well as between Christian Apostle- and saint-legends arise, not from borrowing, but from this law of biographical analogy leading to formulations constantly renewed.

On the other hand it would be wrong on the ground of this understanding to deny historical content to every Legend. A narrator of legends is certainly not interested in historical confirmation, nor does he offer any opposition to increasing the material by analogies. But how much historical tradition he hands on in a legend depends on the character of his tradition only. Historical events in the life of a holy man which from the beginning have been the objects of pious meditation and edifying recollection will live on particularly, perhaps altogether only, in the guise of legend. A legendary form as such is in any case no decisive objection against the historicity of the hero, or even of an event, although again it is no guarantee for the faithfulness of the record to the truth. Rather the contrary, for it offers an argument for historical criticism of details.

The legendary form is also applied to such narratives as had their original formulation under other laws of style. This may be shown in a few passages handed down in different forms : the story of Jesus in Nazareth, of the anointing, and of calling the disciples. In all three cases Luke gives a description which is to be designated as legend, or as narrative transformed from legend.

In Mark vi, 1–6, the *Nazareth passage* is a Paradigm which in the usual edifying terminology relates that the fellow-countrymen of Jesus in His own time took " offence " at

Him. Originally the narrative perhaps ended in a saying of Jesus which consisted of parallel lines, like the word which is preserved by P. Oxy. i, 1, "A prophet is not acceptable in his own country, and a doctor makes no cures amongst his acquaintances." The last half of this saying would then have been changed by tradition into the corresponding event perhaps in order to prepare for the passage about the sending out of the disciples : "And he could there do no mighty work, save that he laid his hands upon a few sick folk and healed them. And he marvelled because of their unbelief." I no longer believe that the whole passage had been developed out of this saying. There is too much special material in the brief story for it to be possible as a mere filling out : the note that Jesus Himself was a carpenter, the naming of His brothers and the mention of His sisters. But we are driven to the conclusion that Mark transformed the end of a Paradigm which originally concluded with a saying of Jesus.

In Luke iv, 16–30, on the other hand, the story has been given quite another conclusion. Here the annoyance that Jesus causes leads to the angry attack of the multitude upon Him, but in a miraculous manner He escapes His persecutors, although He has been dragged to the top of the mountain to be thrown down. The genuine legendary trait of miraculous self-help is here seen in its proper shape. The whole narrative, however, is by no means new as a Legend, but is only filled out by Luke or some older narrator. The traits of Mark's narrative still constitute the skeleton, viz. the amazement, the offence, and the saying about the despised prophet. This last is placed in the middle, as it would not correspond with the violent conclusion of the action. It is also contained here in another recension more closely related to the form of the Oxyrhynchus saying, and of such a kind that the connection with the picture of the doctor is still clear : "physician, heal thyself !" (Luke iv, 23). The "taking offence" leading to anger and action now constitutes the conclusion : the object of this Legend is to give the human grounds. The same is the case with the

sayings about the widow of Sarepta and Naaman the Syrian.
The hardening of the Nazarenes stands only in a quite
conditioned opposition to the blessing of the widow and the
Syrian. We see that the sayings have been interpolated into
this context. Their original intent seems to refer to the
hidden gracious choice of God, and thus, as examples of
blessing, would correspond to the example of anger (Luke xiii,
1–4). The first trait of the Marcan narrative, Jesus' fellow-
countrymen's astonishment at Him, must have the same
basis. Really an example of the preaching of Jesus had to
justify the astonishment of the Nazarenes. But in this case
the author of Luke did not possess the author's freedom
which, in Acts, helped him in the composition of the speeches.
He dare not put such a " speech " into the mouth of Jesus.
Either he, or the Legend he passes on, in the strained circumstances makes Jesus add to the passage read aloud only one
sentence : " To-day hath this scripture been fulfilled in your
ears." In order to justify the strained attention and the
astonishment we must suppose Jesus did not say this, but
gave detailed proof—but this is not recorded. Thus the
narrative in Luke is at bottom only the old narrative filled
out with various materials,[1] but ending in a typical Legend-
conclusion.

A comparison of the Lucan text with the parallels in
Matthew and Mark leads to another result in the story of the
calling of the disciples. What Mark i, 16–20, records of the
calling of both pairs of brothers is not a narrative at all,
for all the conditions of making a plot, whose unravelling
would constitute the " point ", are lacking. Something of the
sort would be dealt with if anyone of the acquaintance of the
disciples had objected to the word of Jesus and Jesus had
rejected the protest. The only thing handed down was
obviously the word about the fishers of men together with the

---

[1] The name $Na\zeta a\rho\acute{a}$ belongs to this material, for its mention satisfies pious
curiosity about " human " data in the life of the hero ; on the other hand, the
formulation of the question " Is this not Joseph's son " corresponds to the conception
expressed in Luke iii, 23.

names of the men addressed. Since Mark related this and no more, and, from the tradition of the disciples' names, added the calling of the second pair of brothers, though without mentioning the words Jesus used in the second call, he must have invented the scene of calling the disciples. Its brevity is scarcely altered by Matthew. This brevity is thus to be explained by the history of the tradition, and not historically by supposing a previous story which justifies the brevity, nor psychologically by supposing some suggestive influence. Nothing more was known than the word with which Jesus called the fishermen to the other kind of fishing.

It is not remarkable that there was a desire to know more. But before we test whether more *could* be known, we must ask what sort of curiosity was in fact satisfied by the narrative preserved in Luke v, 1–11. The mention of the sons of Zebedee does not belong to this narrative, for they appear without any introduction, and the word of Jesus, v, 10b, is addressed only to one disciple, Simon Peter. But the sons of Zebedee have been brought into the text in order to make it a worthy substitute for the Marcan parallel. It was surely Luke himself who added their names.[1] The same hand, however, interpolated, at the beginning, and for the same purpose, the washing of the nets (and probably also the preaching from the boat), for we are reminded of Mark i, 16, and Mark iv, 1. The real event began with the command to push out, Luke v, 4, and what then follows is in no way an extension of the Marcan record, but an independent narrative ; a miracle, not mere help in distress but the unhoped-for success of Simon ; his confession, and this not on account of the preaching of Jesus but of his own unworthiness before the miracle-worker ; the call by Jesus, directed, however,

---

[1] As also in Acts, so often in Mark, the D-text shows that roughness or inequalities existed in the common text, and were not first felt by us. Thus D deletes the mention of the others who were present, a passage which, in fact, does not fit in between the confession of Peter and the answer of Jesus. Again D develops the all too sparing mention of the sons of Zebedee, so that Jesus' call applies once more to all, and hence D transformed the call on the Marcan model.

only to the same Simon, as the real hero of the story. The character of the miracle and the independent significance of Simon in the whole passage differentiate this story fundamentally from the Paradigms and Tales, and characterize it as a Legend. The whole picture shows that it does not depend upon an editing of the Marcan text, for the miracle is here the beginning of the action and the basis of the narrative, and not as in Nazareth an appended conclusion. Moreover, the Legend does not offer the word about fishers of men in the Marcan form, but in quite a different redaction of the same sense. The diagnostic interest of the Legend is, however, not to show how Jesus won disciples, but to tell something out of the life of Simon : his pardon and his pious humility. It deals with the typical interest of Legend in the lot of pious men, and these, in the Gospels, are the persons second to Jesus.

By settling this point, however, we have not determined the historical value of this self-dependent Legend. The question would receive a negative answer, it is true, if the secondary character of the Lucan-legend could be proved by a comparison of Luke v with John xxi, and shown to be originally an Easter-story which had been erroneously placed at the beginning of Jesus' ministry. In this case Peter's confession, " I am a sinful man," would have to refer to Peter's denial of Jesus. But this interpretation appears to me to mistake the sense of this element. It does not say, " I have sinned against thee." On the contrary the unhoped-for blessing calls forth the consciousness of his own unworthiness, for the Galilean fisherman is a " sinner " in the sense of the Pharisees, even without feeling guilty of any great transgression. Hence we must assume that the Easter-stories derive from an incident in the life of Jesus, rather than vice versa. This incident itself could possibly indeed be regarded as a fiction of the church, which longed to know more about Simon than was found in Mark i, 16–20. The occasion of his call and the miraculous catch followed without more ado from the call of Simon and the word used by Jesus. But we must also recognize the posssibility that the connection of the catch with the call was a historical fact, and that knowledge of it had been preserved, though not in the record of Mark—Matthew, which was not interested in the secondary persons of Jesus' life-time. In this case a historical reminiscence would be preserved in the guise of a Legend. But even then we should not have to change our proof for a complete and genuine Legend-form.

The story of the anointing in Luke vii, 36–50, shows still another relationship to the parallels in Mark and Matthew. Here also the interest dominating the whole is plain : more knowledge of the anointing woman is wanted than can be learned from Mark and Matthew. Therefore she is put forward as a well-known sinner. Corresponding to this, her act is changed, and it is no longer a matter of anointing the King or the Messiah, but of a penitent humbly honouring Jesus. Finally the ending does not direct attention to Jesus, but to the woman's lot, showing that the anointing woman is the centre of the narrative. The interest typical of Legend in pious secondary persons proves the narrative to be a Legend. But over and above this, the interpretation is burdened by the question whether the parable of the two debtors, which at present stands in the middle of the passage is constitutive for the whole. If so, the mark of the woman's love would be a sign that she had received forgiveness. There is, however, still the possibility that the parable is foreign to this context, in which case the anointing, independent of the parable, would mean that the woman received forgiveness for the sake of her proofs of affection. But no matter how the question be decided, the legendary character of the narrative cannot be disputed.

The same tendency, leading in this case to a characterization of the anointing woman, has changed the unknown into known persons. We have already shown that the two stories of the sons of Zebedee, that about their request for pre-eminence and that about their zeal against the inhospitable Samaritans, perhaps originally dealt with anonymous disciples and only at a later date were filled out with the persons of the sons of Zebedee. Indeed Mark x, 39, records the prophecy of their marytrdom (cf. pp. 51 and 60 *supra*). The same supposition seems in place in the story of blind Bartimæus (cf. pp. 51 f. *supra*). In all these cases a narrative of legendary character has grown out of a Paradigm.

Hence the Legends found among the Gospel narratives were intended to satisfy a double need : (1) the wish to know something of the holy men and women in Jesus' surroundings, their virtues and also their lot ; (2) the desire which gradually came in, to know Jesus Himself in this way. While this last requirement was still only to be seen in the story of Jesus at twelve years of age, and to some extent in the story of Jesus at Nazareth, " legendary " interests in disciples and adherents of Jesus can be proved in a number of cases. But first we must extend the scope of these Legends with further examples.

It is conceivable that the church recounted more about Peter, the best-known disciple, than only the story of his call. But the best-known Peter passages, his confession of the Messiah and his denial, cannot be regarded forthwith as Legends of Peter. In Matthew, the story of Peter's confession has become a typical Legend, name-giving and *vaticinium ex eventu* included. But we cannot deduce from the Marcan text (viii, 27–30) in what way Jesus received the confession. There is really no mention of any honorification of Peter, nor of any prophecy about him. The prophecy of suffering introduced by Mark viii, 31, has obviously covered over the old conclusion of the passage. Again, the story of the denial is so closely bound up with the whole of the Passion-story that it cannot be dealt with as an isolated section. It is in the closest relationship with the prophecy of Mark xiv, 26–31, which constitutes an essential part of the Passion-story. Even in Mark the denial is not really told in legendary style. Luke xxii, 61, introducing the glance which Jesus directed to Peter, gives a distinct legendary turn, but this very fact shows that the section does not exclusively serve legendary interests (cf. Chapter VII).

But we must mention the story of *Peter's walking on the sea* (Matthew xiv, 28–33) as a kind of Peter Legend. Admittedly it is interpolated as an episode into the narrative of Jesus' walking on the sea which was conceived as an epiphany, but it possesses its own attraction and its own importance. The disciple who walks upon the water by the power of his own faith and who, as he becomes aware of danger, begins to sink, occurs also, as is well-known, in Buddhist tradition (Jataka 190). This Buddhist disciple, who in trance crosses the river Aciravati, could be regarded (i) as the original of the Christian story, because this miracle is specially significant for the miraculous power of the trance, whereas the Peter Legend mentions no reason for Peter's cry to the Master. But we must also admit (ii) the possibility of connections with a Christ-myth, and hence the possibility of an autochthonous rise of the Legend from among Christian ideas (cf. *infra*, p. 175, n. 5).

Christian Legends, and particularly such a characteristic story as that of his escape from prison, told of Peter as the miracle-working apostle. But of Peter the disciple very little of this sort of thing was recorded. This is as striking as it is characteristic for the Gospel tradition. We should have expected that much would have been recorded or at least invented about the leader of the disciples. If this did not happen, it shows us afresh how that the Gospel tradition, along with its eschatological faith, was concerned with and, indeed, concentrated upon the salvation given in Christ.

In accordance with this condition the real growth of Legend took place in the New Testament only as it were by footnotes. In this connection the story of the *end of Judas*, which is really a Place-legend, must be specially mentioned (Matthew xxvii, 3–8). That the " field of blood " was connected with Judas is proved by the narrative (Acts i, 18 f.), which is both formally and materially of another sort. We can see clearly that an interest rules here which is otherwise strange to the New Testament. Matthew xxvii, 19, is most strikingly characteristic of the rise of Christian legends as joined on to events in the Gospel history. This verse mentions the *wife of Pilate*. The Christians certainly did not speak in this allusive manner of the significant dream of this woman which makes her into the defendant of Jesus. The man who first told this undoubtedly gave the content of the dream and perhaps also its reference to Jesus. In this verse the evangelist shows where, in the Passion narrative, legends known to him and to many of his readers had their place. Again, it is indicative of the concern felt for this Gospel itself that its author did not accept this Legend. Perhaps it contained something exceptionable, or perhaps it appeared to him too peripheral.

I think that in John i, 45–51, with the incident of Nathanael, I can detect some suggestion of a Legend. The call of Nathanael is the crowning conclusion of the Johannine stories of calling the disciples. It is told here because it sets aside the mere faith in signs which the book rejects to its last word (xx, 29). It sets it aside with the promise which this book of the epiphany of God in Jesus suitably introduces : " you will see greater things than these." The sign with which Jesus stirs Nathanael has no significance for the evangelist; indeed it is only mentioned in order to be excelled. We learn in an allusive manner in what it consists : "When thou wast under the fig-tree I saw thee." Possibly here also a Legend is in the background to the effect that under the fig-tree Nathanael had preserved the qualities on acount of which Jesus had described him as an Israelite without guile. The Legend told the event and the evangelist obviously knew the Legend. If this is the case then it is impossible to find in Nathanael simply a symbolic figure. Tradition preserved a Nathanael-legend. Thus it was known apart from John's Gospel that a man of this name had belonged to Jesus' circle (cf. also John xxi, 2).

It is no objection that he is not mentioned in the Synoptics. It is quite possible that a Legend is at the basis of the conversation of Jesus with the Samaritan woman (John iv, 1–42). In this Legend the meeting at the well and the clairvoyant-knowledge of Jesus about her five husbands would play a part.

The occasional naming of a man as the hero of a Legend does not make doubtful the historicity of the figure, even if it cannot be guaranteed in this way. This is true also of the story of Zacchaeus (Luke xix, 1–10), a genuine personal-legend fully told. We can see that it is so by comparing this narrative with its neighbour and parallel, the story of Bartimaeus (Mark x, 46–52).[1] Every blind beggar might experience the same thing as Bartimaeus. The experience of the publican Zacchaeus, on the other hand, in the course of which Jesus miraculously notices him and graciously shares his hospitality, accords with the individual traits of the man, with his short stature and his relative religiosity in spite of his objectionable calling. In the former story the interest is in what the blind man received; but in the latter in what the man of despised status does with religious zeal. The very mention of his small stature is diagnostic of the interest in human things, i.e. of a typical legendary interest.

In the passage about Martha and Mary (Luke x, 38–42) this interest cannot be demonstrated with the same certainty. We have already shown (p. 51) that the names of the two sisters cannot be separated from what Jesus says. The saying is, therefore, neither an isolated Logion, nor a concluding sermon-aphorism of general content. On the other hand, it must be granted that the persons and their differentiating attitudes are brought out. But such individual peculiarities as the shortness of Zacchaeus, or the martyrdom of the sons of Zebedee are not told about the two women. Their very

---

[1] The parallel is based upon locality, both narratives dealing with Jericho. Hence Luke, who alone records both, makes the healing of the blind man take place on the road to Jericho.

attitude is so typical that one could almost understand them as symbolic figures.[1] The point of the narrative, however, is not in differentiating between active and contemplative attitudes, but in Jesus' critique of Martha's protest. As is shown by textual criticism the early Church obviously understood this critique far and wide in an ascetic sense. But it should be understood eschatologically. It is altogether probable since Jesus does not give regulations about meals but presses home commands concerning the coming of the kingdom (the same is true of Luke xiv, 7–11, since this rule about meals is a parable). But on the grounds of textual criticism it is probable that the saying which, as is well known, is found in many different forms is so phrased that it must be understood eschatologically. "Martha, Martha, thou art anxious and troubled about many things, but one thing is needful; Mary hath chosen the good part which shall not be taken from her."[2] And this reading must be evaluated by a critique of its Form. The rejected word "many" strictly requires the antithesis of "one thing is necessary", and not the colourless "few things" (and certainly not the ambiguous "few or one"). If the story concluded with the saying but "only one thing is necessary", we could regard the whole as a Paradigm, which exceptionally had preserved the names of the actors. But now there follows the saying that the good part in the Kingdom of God is promised to Mary because she obeys the requirement that "one thing is necessary". The conclusion, and thereby the whole, is thus dominated by the interest in this person and the promise made to her. Hence

[1] Loisy, *L'Évangile selon Luc*, supposes that the evangelist related the two women to Jewish- and Gentile-Christendom, and perhaps shaped the story from this standpoint. But this understanding misses the point of Jesus' saying which is essential to the narrative, as we have shown above.

[2] A decision on textual grounds is made harder by the fact that the best Egyptian MSS. have a mixed text: ὀλίγων δέ ἐστιν χρέια ἢ ἑνός—which would be naturally expounded as "few things are necessary, one for salvation—which is impossible". But this text is a conflatim of the text which read only ὀλίγων (as still found in 38, Syr^pal arm), and which contained a moderate requirement, and of the other which read only ἑνός (like C. Koine, Vulg. and Syr^c) and implied the eschatological requirement of repentance.

the narrative must be regarded as a Legend. The first to tell
it doubtless knew more about this woman.

When we have become clear about the existence of
personal Legends in these examples of persons from Jesus'
environment, we must ask whether there are also Legends of
Jesus Himself in the Gospels in addition to the narratives
already analysed ; religious stories in which Jesus brings to
light His purity, wisdom, and virtue, or in which the Divine
protection and care of Jesus are revealed. Apart from the
legend of Jesus as twelve years old, only the narrative of the
thankful Samaritan (Luke xvii, 12–19) tells of any such active
bearing of Jesus. This is not a Paradigm concluding with
a general saying which can be used by the Church, or with
a chorus, for any expression is lacking which would give
exemplary significance to the thankfulness of this single person.
Nor is the story a Tale, for there is no interest which dominates
the description of the miracle. Nor is it a Legend of a Samaritan,
for it is not he but Jesus who stands in the centre. It is a narrative of the recognition by Jesus of a Samaritan and his religiousness. It is formulated from this standpoint, as Chapter
xvii, 18 proves, with its reference to the " stranger ". That
it has been preserved by Luke from this standpoint is shown
by his insertion of it and introduction to it.[1] It is impossible
for us to describe the rise of this Legend, or estimate its
historical value. Naturally we compare the tale of the leper
(Mark i, 40–45), but the single point of similarity, the
command to visit the priest, belongs to the nature of the case,
and everything otherwise characteristic of that Tale is lacking
in our Legend, viz. the word of healing, the gesture of healing,
the prohibition about meeting anyone before the priest had

---

[1] Luke makes Jesus move through (or between) Samaria and Galilee (xvii, 11). He
used a Samaritan story for his " Journey narrative "—and set value upon our
Legend in this sense. This explains the precedence of Samaria. Really the text of
the story suggests that Jesus was in Judæa or Galilee when a Samaritan appears as
a " stranger " together with nine others standing nearer to Jesus as Galileans or
Judæans. The priests normative for these nine are in accessible proximity. We must
not ask whether the Samaritan, if he is now in Judæa, goes to a Jewish priest. Cf.
K. L. Schmidt, *Der Rahmen der Geschichte Jesu,* 261 ff.

confirmed the cure. The fact that it contains much less
material than the Tale can be explained variously : we may
suppose that the first story was denuded of its pecularities
in order to make it a Samaritan story. But we may also
suppose that here is preserved a tradition interested in the
attitude of Jesus to the Samaritans. In consequence of the
lack of detail and of special quality, we cannot say anything
about the soundness of this tradition. The Legend of Martha
and Mary already analysed, offers an antithesis, for in this
case every sentence contains something special, the narrative
is detailed throughout, though not with secondary things
about time, place, home-circumstances, but with a decisive
question which altogether dominates it. In spite of the fact
that this Legend of the two sisters ends with the honorification of a secondary person, it must be regarded as historically
valuable on account of its detail and its definiteness.

We must still take account of two similar Legends in the
Gospel records about Jesus' work, viz. the *finding of the room*
for the Last Supper (Mark xiv, 12–16, and parallels) and the
finding of the ass for the Triumphal Entry (Mark xi, 1–7, and
parallels). The former narrative is very closely bound up
with the story of the Last Supper, without which it has no
independent life. It tells of the miracle by which Jesus and
His disciples found the room for the Passover. It also gives
to the description of the following meal the character of
a Passover-meal. This is striking since the narrative itself
does not suggest this character. Thus in the passage as a
whole we are dealing with a Legend of the cultus. The scene of
the meal shows how Jesus Himself had celebrated the meal
which the Christians observed. The introduction emphasizes
that the Christian meal is a continuation of the Passover-
meal. The extraneous elements about the prophesied meeting
with the man and the miraculous direction are well-known
in legends and in fairy tales. Their employment here shows
the legendary character of the narrative, for divine pre-vision
takes care that the cultus is rightly carried out.

These motives of prophesied meeting and of miraculous direction connect the section of the Passover-room with the story of *finding the ass*. Obviously the presupposition of this is that the animal has some special singificance. Hence it can only be found by means of divine guidance, and it bears otherwise signs of something special, e.g. it has never been ridden, and it is standing tied up in the street as if made ready for the disciples. This animal bears significance because its use enables the prophecy of Zechariah ix, 9, to be fulfilled. This raises the question as to how far the prophecy had formed or transformed the narrative of the triumphal entry. The section about the Last Supper does not raise the same question. For at least in Mark and Matthew it lacks the characteristics which emphasize the Passover character of the meal, i.e. which would correspond to the introductory Legend of the finding. The passage, therefore, stands in a strained relationship to the Legend of the finding, while the triumphant entry constitutes the direct continuation of its own legendary finding. In the former case the fulfilment of the prophecy of Zechariah is prepared for in advance. And it is recorded without any definition, so that the whole of Mark xi, 1–10, must be pronounced a homogenous Legend. Indeed it is a cultus-legend, since it is not the holy Person of Jesus but the holy word of the Old Testament, read aloud in the cultus, which determines the whole. But here we see most clearly how Legends are incomprehensible to historical criticism. For if a critic would hold Jesus' claim to Messiahship as an idea of the Church, he can, of course, point out among other things that only in the Legend do we hear anything of Messianic worship by the disciples or pilgrims to the feast. It could be objected that the existence of this Legend would be comprehensible most easily if Jesus Himself had given cause for it, though it must remain uncertain how far it took place with conscious reference to the prophecy of Zechariah. But it is in no way surprising, and so cannot be raised as an objection against the historicity of the event

that a matter of Messianic significance should be told in
Christian Churches, not as a story from the life of Jesus
(i.e. as a Paradigm, Tale, or personal Legend), but composed
at the same time with reference to its Christological significance.   Hence the event was told as an example of salvation
completed according to God's plan, i.e. according to the
Scripture, in other words, from the same standpoint as that
which led to the formulation of the Passion-story ; in fact,
we may ask whether this Cult-legend, orientated in the
Old Testament, did not belong in some way to the content
of the earliest Passion-story.

A problem of quite another character is raised by the
Legends of the *birth of Jesus* in its two forms in Luke and
Matthew. They stand in the closest connection and seem to
be antithetic to the Passion-story.   But in reality, unlike
this latter, they do not belong to the common ancient treasure
of tradition of the Church.   The lack of the whole matter
in Mark proves this at once.   The different quality of the
birth stories, again, in Luke and Matthew, shows that an early
tradition was not at hand, and finally, John felt himself
bound to retain the process of the Passion-story and bring out
the significance of the Baptist at the beginning of the New
Testament record of salvation.   But not to take notice of
any tradition of Jesus' birth, the content of both birth-
stories is made up of traditions which grew apart from the
body of tradition common to the first generation of Christians,
but whether they were historical or unhistorical, we cannot
say. As is also the case of the Legend of Judas and with the
notice of Pilate's wife we are here approaching the traditions
of the church which later fed the apocryphal literature.
These ideas have no fundamental significance for the Formgeschichte of the Gospel, because they are subject to other
laws than the mass of Gospel tradition. Thus we shall only
deal with them in this place sketchily.

Luke's Gospel of the Childhood, apart from the Legend of the
twelve-year-old Jesus, consists of four independent Legends.

I have elsewhere attempted to show that their analysis is relatively simple if we elide the connective additions of the evangelist and the links which he himself has added. It would then appear that the Legend of the Baptist's birth (i, 5–25) is only interrupted by the story of the annunciation, and is only ended materially and stylistically in Luke i, 57–66, for it is only when the new-born child receives its name that the curse is broken which had been imposed upon Zacharias in the Temple, and thus the strained relationship with the first part of the Legend is broken. This Legend of John is a unity and in its nature Jewish not Christian.

For what the Christians were accustomed to say about the Baptist is not mentioned here at all, viz. his place as the forerunner, for his subordination to Jesus plays no part; on the contrary, in i, 15, John is as unconditionally called " great " as later, in i, 32, is Jesus Himself. Thus the Legend comes from the worshippers of John, i.e. from the sphere of the Baptist movement itself.

Alongside of this stands the Legend of the Virgin (Luke i, 26–38). Since the first annunciation of the birth (i, 31) depends verbally on Isaiah vii, 14, and this passage itself, at any rate in Greek Judaism, was understood to refer to a virgin's son, the prophecy of a virgin birth in i, 34, 35, must be regarded as an essential element of the whole Legend, and not as a sort of later addition. The well-known difficulty that Mary was affianced and, therefore, could not have been astonished at the promise of a son, disappears when we see that her future husband Joseph does not belong to this Legend, but has been interpolated into the beginning of the Legend (i, 27) by the evangelist, who wished to make a connection with the Nativity story.[1]

The announcement of the birth to the shepherds (ii, 1–19)

[1] The interpolation into Luke i, 26 f., which we have supposed, is supported by its consequences. Only when we delete the words ἐμνηστευμένην ἀνδρὶ ᾧ ὄνομα Ιωσήφ is the overloaded sentence relieved, and the relationship of ἐξ οἴκου Δαυίδ made unambiguously certain : the Davidic descent is then asserted of Mary and not Joseph, and this is, in fact, all that concerns the narrative of a Virgin Birth.

is the centre of the third Legend. Here, as in the Legend of Mary, we are not dealing essentially with the birth, but with the heavenly proclamation of the nature and purpose of the new-born child. Since the announcement in i, 32 f., and ii, 10 f., are of different kinds, however, it follows that the Shepherd-legend was not originally the continuation of that of Mary but its independent contemporary. Hence it is not remarkable that the Shepherd-legend is unaware of a virgin-birth, but speaks of Jesus as the son of Joseph and Mary, born in Bethlehem in a house which the travellers use as a shelter. There the child is laid in a manger fixed for the cattle, since there was nothing else available. Many traits of this Legend, it must be admitted, have been obscured by the fact that the evangelist introduced the motif of the general census as the reason for the journey; otherwise perhaps the relation which to-day we can only guess between the shepherds and the manger would be apparent : probably the shepherds were the owners of the house, and, therefore, they look for the child announced to them in their own manger. Luke has introduced still other fragments into the whole composition, as, for example, the two hymns of older origin (i, 46–55, and i, 68–79), as well as the scene in which Elizabeth and Mary meet (i, 39 ff.). In content this story is not one about the Baptist, for his inferiority is put forward. On the other hand, in style it is not an independent story of Jesus, for it alludes to more than it narrates : for example, it omits the name of the town in which Elizabeth lives in spite of the geographical details of its situation, and it omits the wording of Mary's greeting in spite of its miraculous effect upon the unborn John.

In the fourth of these Legends in Luke's account we have the story of Simeon and Anna (Luke ii, 22–38). Admittedly it seems to have been much edited, since it exhibits one difficulty after another. First, the double motivation of the event in the Temple does not differentiate between the two causes; the churching of the mother, and the redemption of the first-born,[1] and yet gives no satisfactory reason for the scene, for the churching does not require the presence of the child, nor the redemption that of the Temple. Perhaps Simeon originally met the Holy Child somewhere in the countryside, and Luke transposed the scene into the Temple in order to make a parallel to chapter i, 5 ff., and also in order to bring Jesus, like the Baptist beforehand, into connection with the religious centre.

A second difficulty is the appearance of the prophetess Anna, of whom many things are said in ii, 36–37 (much more than of Simeon), although she herself has nothing to say. Measured by everything else already said, the note "she praised God" appears to be very little, and if she spoke about the child to all those who awaited salvation, yet it would appear that what the note hints at did not happen at that moment. Obviously some recollection of the prophetess, known otherwise, had been added to the Simeon-legend when the scene was transferred to the Temple, although no prophecy about Jesus uttered by her was known.

The third difficulty is the multiplication of Simeon's sayings ; the first saying (ii, 29–32) announces the Saviour, and is very closely bound up with the narrative ; the second (ii, 34 f.) speaks of the point of decision to which Jesus would bring Israel. In between, i.e. between two parts of a sentence, we have the notorious word about the sword (ii, 35), a suggestion that even the mother would experience pain through her son. It would be quite in accordance with true Legend that the Passion of the Son should, at an early date, be prophesied to the mother, but the place of this prophecy in the midst of that about the crisis of the people is hard to understand. Perhaps the very same evangelist who composed the scene of the meeting of the mothers also introduced at this place the

---

[1] In ii, 22, Luke characterizes both causes as καθαρισμός and hence writes αὐτῶν (of the mother and of the child. The reading αὐτῆς which is materially correct is only weakly supported, and the Western αὐτοῦ is no help). Then in ii, 23, he gives the ground for the obligation *re* the first-born, or in ii, 24, the purificatory sacrifice.

idea of the maternal suffering.[1] That the two sayings of
Simeon (ii, 29–32, and ii, 34 f.) should stand side by side
may be early, in any case earlier than the addition of Anna,
for it is striking that neither of these prophecies is put into
her mouth, although in the first part of the story we may
remark almost an excess of prophetic sayings. This first part
(ii, 25–35) possesses as its kernel a Simeon-legend which
originally was isolated, according to which a religious old
man surprised the parents of the child with prophecies of its
future. Hence neither the words of the angel to the mother
(Luke i, 30–33) nor the words to the shepherds (ii, 17) are
presupposed. Even if the Simeon-legend is separated from the
chronology of its introduction (ii, 22–24) it appears as
another contemporary beside the Legends of Mary and the
shepherds. It need cause no surprise if the essential element
of the Simeon-legend had a parallel in at least *one* other
legendary sphere, namely in that of the Buddha. For the law
of biographical analogy which causes many lives of saints
to be composed in a similar manner (cf. pp. 108 f. *supra*)
is obviously active when a holy man, while still a child, is
recognized by an aged seer. Thus Asita, according to several
sources, spoke a prophecy about the child which later became
the Buddha, according to which this child would bring wisdom
and light and destroy the darkness of ignorance. The idea
is too widespread to justify a theory of direct dependence.
Since Asita is brought by magic power into the palace and
Simeon is driven by the Spirit into the Temple, since Asita
takes the child to his bosom and Simeon takes it into his
arms, and since Asita bewails his approaching end and
Simeon prepares himself now willingly for death, it appears
to me that these related traits make literary interdependence
possible but do not prove it. Much more probable is the

---

[1] There are only two possibilities, as Loisy in particular clearly saw (*L'Évangile
selon Luc ad. loc.*) ; either the saying about the sword belongs to the whole, in
which case it implies some opposition of the mother to the son ; or else the saying
was introduced by Luke, in which case, and this seems to me more credible, it refers
to the mother's agony about the Passion.

supposition that the development of the Legend followed
the same law in the former as in the latter case. The same
holds good also of other analogies of less importance, such as
the prophecies about Augustus.[1]

The principal moment of the " Introduction " to Matthew's
Gospel is the narrative in Matthew ii which at first appears
to be a unity. It passes from the journey of the Magi from
the east to the slaughter of the children in Bethlehem and the
return of the child Jesus with his parents from Egypt. What
stands previously in Matthew i is the genealogy and the
narrative (Matthew i, 18–25), which can in no way be called
a Legend, although legendary elements are not lacking.[2]
The supernatural procreation of Jesus is neither told nor
hinted at, but is assumed, and the mother defended against
the reproach of illegitimate conception. Hence, in contradiction
to the entire legendary style, the whole secret which the angel
was to reveal to Joseph is revealed in advance : " she was found
with child of the Holy Ghost (i, 18)." It is not the miracle
but its defence which is the centre, and since the decisive
proof-passage from the Old Testament about the virgin who
should become a mother (Isaiah vii, 14) is not interwoven
into the speech of the angel but given as a meditative quotation,
we can trace the customary style of the evangelist who,
in this manner, gives foundation to his description of Jesus'
life, and we must suppose that the entire apologetic section
is the work of this evangelist.

Obviously the unified formulation of chapter ii goes
back to him, for it is scarcely credible that the story of the
Magi was already current in association with the slaughter
of the children and the flight to Egypt. Its high point is the
worship of the child, and it tolerates no bloody epilogue.
Its introduction (Matthew ii, 1) proves it to be independent
as over against the earlier chapter. Another circumstance

---

[1] Cf. Suetonius *De vita Caesarum* II, Augustus, 94.

[2] We may think of the appearance of the angel in a dream—the explanation of the
name Jesus—yet a translation of the name is lacking. Cf. my monograph, *Jungfrauensohn und Krippenkind*, 25 f.

appears to me to demonstrate its independence in the opposite direction. Joseph does not occur at all in the real Magi story (Matthew ii, 1–13); he is conceived as absent, or as already dead since the birth of Jesus. The Magi find only " the child with Mary, His mother " (ii, 11). Nevertheless from ii, 12, Joseph takes over the leading part in the action as far as the child Jesus is concerned, and retains it till ii, 23.

Hence we may suppose that the story of the Magi existed separately as a genuine personal Legend which already at an early date honours the future hero. Its connection with what follows is only in the circumstance that the Herod questioned in Jerusalem by the Magi, is the same as then sought the life of the child. But surely the Magi scarcely required the theologians of Herod's court. They went, as is understandable, first to the royal city and were then led by their miraculous star to Bethlehem. This Legend does not reproduce the echo of a historical event so much as historize a mythical conception of the appearance of a new star among the old ones whose radiance it excels. This conception was actually applied to Jesus, as the passage in Ignatius, Ephesians xix, 2, most clearly shows. But this passage in Ignatius does not seem to be dependent upon the Magi-legend. Rather it reproduces a myth which the Christians have claimed for themselves.

The other part of Matthew ii, now set free from the Magi-legend, does not really require this connection. Its only presupposition is that somehow and at some time Herod came to believe in the imminent fulfilment of Micah's prophecy about Bethlehem. The slaughter of the children is the centre of this section, the opening bar is the flight to Egypt, and the conclusion is the return (as far as ii, 21, for the content of ii, 22 f., does not belong to the legend[1]). The twofold appearance of the angels is now told in some detail, and thus the protection

---

[1] Otherwise we should have to ask why the angel said nothing of the renewed danger, or why Joseph under such an openly proclaimed divine protection, gave hearing to the voice of human fear. Thus the verses, ii, 22 f., are remarks of the evangelist who wishes to introduce Nazareth as Jesus' home.

of the child stands in the forefront. It cannot but be striking
how tersely and how little legendarily the flight into Egypt
is narrated. No mention is made of stress or danger on the
road, or of divine protection of the child during the journey.
The motif of threatening and saving the miracle-child is
extraordinarily widespread, and so in this case one might
refer to the law of biographical analogy and, therefore, in
this case, be doubtful of literary dependence, since the narrative
has so few details. It almost seems as if only the general
scheme had been brought over into the biography of Jesus
and varied with the words of the angel.

But just here the question arises, What cause was there
for this transference? In this connection we may remember
that Josephus (*Jewish War* i, par. 659 f., and *Ant.* xvii, par.
174 ff.) records a plan of wild cruelty which Herod had
conceived shortly before his death. He ordered the leading
men of every place in Judæa to the race-course in Jericho,
and required his sister Salome and her husband, after his
own death, to kill the whole of the imprisoned multitude.
Thus every tribe in Judæa would have cause to mourn the
king's death. Granted that Salome did not carry out this order
it would be possible that this was an old Jewish narrative
really about the death of King Alexander Jannaeus,[1] but
transferred later to Herod. It was, however, not altogether
impossible that the tradition about Herod was dated back
to Alexander Jannaeus, in order to get an older authority for
a fastless day (see footnote). In any case the narrative shows
what sort of thing was expected of Herod, and such a king
could easily have been brought into connection with the
idea of threatening and sparing the life of a miracle-child.
It is usual to cite as the best proof of this idea at the time, the
tradition which Suetonius ascribes to Julius Marathus about
the birth of Augustus (*Vita Caes.* ii, Augustus xciv, 3). The

---

[1] It is contained in the gloss on *Megilloth Taanith*, xi, § 25 ; cf. Zeitlin, *Jewish
Quarterly Review*, New Series, 10 (1919–1920), pp. 237 ff. There the command refers
to seventy elders, and the king's wife Shalminin prevents its being carried out.

senate would appear to have been terror-struck by an oracle
about the birth of a king and to have ordered that "no child
born that year should be reared", but apparently the order
was not obeyed. The question has, however, been raised
whether the Herod story is not older than this parallel case.[1]
If so, Matthew's narrative would only be a reproduction of an
earlier Legend.

Our analysis of the Legends found in the gospels has
shown a relatively large number of narratives which in their
present, or in a still recognizable earlier form, must be called
Legends. But we must recognize a limitation of this result,
for it is easy to see that these Legends are not portions of the
gospel important from either the material or the literary
point of view.

In the case of Paradigms, preaching whether for missionary
purposes or in public worship, could, just because of its
direct significance, be regarded as their home or "Sitz im
Leben". In the sermon everything was linked up with the
eschatological message of salvation.

By the source of their material, Tales are seen to be of
quite a different nature. What gave them, however, their
place in the New Testament was the relationship to Christology
which was proper to the Tales, or which was ascribed to
them by the Church. Everything they said was understood
as an epiphany of the Christ, and in this way the most
secular content was related to the faith of the church.

A few of the Legends have a slight direct relation to preaching. We can imagine that the Zacchaeus-legends, like that
of the woman who was a sinner, were used in sermons as
examples of forgiveness, just as were Paradigms, although,
as the style shows, they were not made for this purpose.

[1] An apothegma of Augustus, preserved in Macrolius, *Saturnalia*, ii, 4[11], shows
in a remarkable way a connection between Augustus and the misdeeds of Herod :
cum audisset inter pueros quos in Syria Herodes rex Iudaeorum intra bimatum
jusset interfici filium quoque eius occisum ait : mallem Herodis porcus esse quam
filius (ῦς—υίός). Against the contention that this pun rests upon a Christian
invention *vide* Erdmann *Die Vorgeschichten des Lukas- und Matthäus-Evan-
geliums*," p. 62.

Similarly the Legend of Martha and Mary would serve as an example for the message " One thing is necessary ", although the textual variants show that it was used rather in connection with the need for moderation. The Legends of the Triumphal Entry and of the Preparation of the Passover Supper would be related to Biblical prophecy, or to the Communion Service. The Legends of Mary, the shepherds, and Simeon would serve public worship at least by their prophetic words, although they exhibit quite different Christologies. But as for the rest, the Legends, by their nature, are interested in *secondary things and persons*. Here all sorts of people surrounding Jesus are put forward, the future significance of Jesus is shown during His childhood, and exemplary thoughts and deeds of religious men are brought out. But Legends leave it in the background that Jesus had waged war upon Jewish religiousness, that His appearance simply did not correspond to the wishes of pious Jews, and that He was attacked rather than admired.

The literary garb corresponds to this content. Legends put halos round men, and set in a transfiguring light the very things with which religious men deal. Hence everything belonging to the very fact of holy men may become significant in a Legend. Paradigms have to do with the message as such, and Tales with miracle. But Legends sometimes lack concentration, and their interests are manifold, because nothing proper to the fact of a man of God must be excluded. Hence in this case analysis cannot prove the type by examples as in our third and fourth chapters. Rather we must demonstrate by the narratives themselves and the interests which come to light in their statements whether and in what sense we are dealing with a Legend.

Chapter VI

ANALOGIES

In analysing the narrative material of the Gospels, we found three categories of narrative material—Paradigms, Tales, Legends; the first two types are essential for the synoptic content of narrative, the third type, however significant it may be as literature, was developed upon the periphery of the Gospel tradition. On the other hand, the Tale-like Legends and stories of miracles belong together in so far as both types are to be met again in different folk-traditions. The Paradigms, on the other hand, with their technical brevity, and with their concentration upon conceptions of a definite character which can be used in preaching, do not exemplify in any way a recognized type of literature as such.

The results thus gained can be assured and defined by asking how, in the narrower or broader environment of Jesus' life or in the construction of the Gospels, analogies to these narratives might be sought, i.e. the question is whether we can find current folk-stories originally isolated and of a similar character.

(i) Rabbinic Analogies.

Our question must be directed first of all to Jewish tradition as preserved in the *Rabbinic literature*. The relatively late editing of this literature is no objection to the comparison, for (1) the Rabbinic anecdotes appear in part to go back to a relatively early time, as is shown by the Tannaite introductory formula: " Our masters handed it down thus " ; and (2) the most important thing is to demonstrate not relation of dependence, but only of analogy.

Rabbinic literature, especially the Talmud, contains a large number of short stories with very varied contents. A large majority of them in their present text serve as examples of juristic discussions. Thus they give not hypothetical, but historical cases, or which claim to historicity. Even in the Mishna, the proper corpus of statutes, such cases appear now and again, though rarely. They stand amongst the legal regulations, but the first purpose of the author is not to record historical events, but rather to confirm decisions of the rabbis in regard to these events. The case is often introduced by the formula: " ma'aseh," " an event," " a proceeding," without its being possible to express a literary judgment of the narrative style. "Ma'aseh" is also to be found in the Gemara, the later part of the Talmudic corpus, not to introduce juristic cases, but human occurrences of various kinds. Hence " ma'aseh " would be originally a traditional introductory formula amongst others and finally, in the Middle Ages, was used to mark Jewish stories as such without differentiation of style.[1]

The nature of this Rabbinic narrative-material can only be determined if, first of all, we analyse its relationship to the Jewish tradition as a whole, which owes its framework and content to those narratives. The essential element in this tradition is the statute, the " Halakha ". The simplest connection of a statute with a story is made when a celebrated case of obedience to the law is recorded, especially if it be difficult or heroic. Even the Mishna contains isolated instances of such. In the Berakhoth ii, 5, incidentally on the saying that the bridegroom is exonerated from reading the Sh'ma on his marriage night, we have a narrative about Rabbi Gamaliel; he appears to have read the Sh'ma on his marriage night nevertheless, and to have replied to a question of his disciples that not for a moment would he be absent from the Kingdom of Heaven.

There is a great number of stories in the Talmud which have nothing to do with the preceding Halakha. But just

[1] Cf. Moses Gaster, *The Exempla of the Rabbis*, London and Leipzig, 1924.

because the bulk of the Talmudic material only comes into existence by such indirect connection with the Statutes, we are compelled to discuss it. The introduction of a story into the connection of the Halakha, although it does not properly belong there, is usually due to *association*. For example, if the matter dealt with is fasting in case of pestilence or the collapse of a building in a town, stories are told in which the presence of a saintly person gives protection from danger, the last being the " Gamzo " of R. Nahum, the teacher of Akiba. And once this name is mentioned, the legends of the name " Gamzo " (" this also ") are reproduced at the same time. According to them the saintly Rabbi said, " This also be for good " to everything he experienced, and, in fact, he enjoyed a wonderful fulfilment of this wish (Taanith 21a). Or else the question would be discussed whether a woman might marry again if her husband had disappeared in a lake and had never been seen again, either alive or dead. Then examples of surprising rescues would be told, and the opinion comes up that the rescue of a scholar would be known quickly enough to prevent his wife marrying again. Then in this connection wonderful rescues from shipwreck are told by Akiba and Meir (at bottom it is the same story in two very similar texts, and other parallels are also known). But we hear nothing more about the woman and her new marriage (Jebamoth 121a.)

The passage Sabbath 127a, b, shows how complicated such an associative connection may be. The corresponding Mishna contains the rule that on the Sabbath one might carry away four or five heaps of straw or corn if it be on account of " guests or to interruption of study ". At the mention of guests, the Gemara introduces somewhat about hospitality, as well as an enumeration of six good actions in which hospitality is mentioned first, and the favourable judgment of companion is mentioned last. Now there follow three stories on the subject : He who judges his companion favourably will be judged favourably. All three have the same conclusions.[1] We may assume, since this theme is also supported with two stories in the Aboth of Nathan viii, 5, 6 (fol. 19a Schechter) of which the second is similar to one of the Talmudic stories, that in Rabbinic Judaism stories were assembled according to certain leading ideas. In the Talmud these stories frequently came forward from quite other standpoints, but indeed in such a manner that the original point was not obscured, sometimes indeed so that the original connection of several stories is preserved although the Talmud did not require it. A striking example of this is offered by the astrological section, Sabbath 156a, b, about the influence of a birthday and birth-hour upon the fate of a person. The point in all three examples was to show that Israelites were not subject to the influence of stars, and that unfavourable oracles were not fulfilled in their case. But the first two of these three stories have yet a second point. It is said that a death by snake-bite did not happen as prophesied to a passer-by and to Akiba's daughter; and that the threatening snake itself met its death by accident. Both stories are confirmed in a similar way and in the same saying, viz. that this happened to them as a reward for doing well, and reference is made to Proverbs x, 2 : " Well-doing rescues from death." This passage of Scripture obviously furnished the standpoint which originally brought the two narratives into connection, and perhaps in a shorter text, without the oracle at the beginning. The bias against astrology was probably given only in the Talmud.

In this way we catch sight of pre-canonical connections amongst the Rabbanic stories. It is really self-apparent that not only material, but often also personal, connections existed which were preserved together in the *stories about a Rabbi*. Examples of this sort of thing can be given. In regard to the theme of praying for rain, Taanith 9b tells of weather prophecies. Rabbi Ulla (fourth century) tells that on one occasion

---

[1] The hero of the narrative says : " Just as you have judged me compassionately, so may God judge you compassionately."

in Babylon his prophecy of rain was not fulfilled. A story about this same Ulla then follows, how that once he upset his stomach in Babylon with dates. This has nothing to do with the matter of rain which is then handled further. But both stories begin in the same way with the words: " Ulla came to Babylon ", and obviously in these words we find the common element for which originally they were brought together. In the tractate Taanith a number of stories are recorded which deal with the successful or unsuccessful rain magic. In this connection a story about R. Chanina b. Dosa is told. Then there follow five further legends of this great miracle-working Rabbi, and then, after a few addenda, the series of stories about fasting and rain is continued (Taanith 24*b*, 25*a*).

The proof that many Rabbinic narratives stand to-day in a connection which does not correspond to their content or their point, leads now to another question in which or by which the special problem of the Talmudic narrative material first becomes quite clear. It appears we must reckon with the possibility that material *foreign in nature to the Talmud and its interests* has been introduced. That becomes especially credible (1) if we recall the bias of the Talmud towards Halakhic instruction, and, on the other hand, (2) if we observe how the material of many a Talmudic story escapes this bias in accordance with the law of its innermost nature.[1] We must content ourselves here by illustrating the problem with a few examples.

All kinds of ethical and juristic casuistry have the tendency to " construct " extraordinary cases in order to fix the leading pronouncement for such eventualities as are difficult to judge. It gladly seizes upon actual events of an extraordinary character, not in order to make the event with its special circumstances available for the future, but in order to hand

---

[1] The question has been raised most earnestly by Moses Gaster. He expressed the opinion that many narratives which were originally intended to be amusing changed their character when taken up into the Talmud : " They are told as an ' exemplum ', in order to teach a lesson, to convey a ' moralization '. They serve, so to say, as a basis for sermons " (op. cit., p. 6).

on the correct legal judgment. In the Tractate Baba Qamma
48*a* we read how a woman comes into another's house in
order to bake there, and how a goat of the owner ate some of
the dough and, in consequence, died. Raba ordered the woman
to pay the value of the animal. This is a story which might
well be true and belong to the time of Raba (the first half of
the fourth century). But it is not told because it is true, but
because Raba had to decide this case just the same whether
it was true or only possible. For the purpose of this Halakhic
decision no question would arise as to whether the event
were only hypothetical. Many other very complicated cases are
dealt with in the Mishna and the Gemara as only hypothetical,
e.g. the possibility that a man should have cut off another's
hand or broken his foot, or blinded his eye, or made him deaf
(Baba Qamma, 85*b*), or the many possibilities that someone
or something should be damaged by a goring bull, as when
an Israelite's bull had trampled down that of a Samaritan
(ibid., 38*b*), or when a bull had accidentally killed a slave or
a free man (ibid., 43*a*), or when it had rubbed itself against
a wall and this had fallen on someone (Mishna Baba Qamma
iv, 6). In this way all sorts of difficult cases are told and decided.
But all the while we should observe that these cases had not
grown up into stories, whereas the above-mentioned case of
the goat which died is put forward in narrative-form. From
this we may conclude that this case was handed down as
a happening, and thus probably was originally a happening.
But this makes it quite comprehensible that the Halakha
endeavoured always to increase its stock of cases which had
actually happened, and that it dealt with such stories also as
" cases " for an Halakhic decision, although originally they
were not told with this application. The question is whether
we can still prove this displacement of emphasis.

In the tractate Jebamoth (Mishna Jebamoth ii, 9) cases
are discussed in which the re-marriage of a woman is questioned
after news of the murder of her absent husband has been
received. In this connection the following case was put to

Rabbi Jehuda : " The case of a robber who was condemned
to death in the court of Cappadocia, and he said to them :
' Go and say to the wife of Simeon ben Kohen, I killed her
husband coming to Lud ' " (ibid., 25*b*). Thereupon the woman
was allowed to marry. Rabbi Jehuda set aside this case as
not decisive, etc. If we may assume that this narrative reproduces an event still told amongst the people, it appears to me
to be quite undoubted that in the first instance it was not
told with reference to the possible second marriage of the
woman. The real interest was the self-accusation of the
criminal at the point of death, for this was something which
could scare the hearers of a popular narrative. It was only
the scholars who were interested in the juristic question of the
case ; might the woman now marry again ?

The two stories of adultery from the Nedarim 91*b*, seem
to me good examples of marked obscuration and indeed of
contortion, and perhaps the problem can be made clearest
by this passage. Cases are mentioned in which apparently
there are evidences of adultery. We hear of a man who shut
himself in a house with a married woman, and when the
husband came he broke through the fence and fled. Raba,
the Amoraean, understood this case in the sense that adultery
had not actually taken place, for otherwise the man would
not have fled so openly. A second case follows in which the
strange man hid himself behind a curtain when the husband
returned. There lay some watercress of which a snake
was eating (apparently poisoning the cress). When later on
the husband was about to eat some of the cress the stranger
warned him " for a snake has eaten some of it ". In this case
also Raba decided negatively, since an actual adulterer would
simply have let the husband eat the cress and die. Now it
seems to me to be clear, at least in the second story, that the
Talmud does not give the narrative completely. It does not
tell how the man behind the curtain came face to face and
into conversation with the husband. It would be easy to
reconstruct the event in such a way that the stranger is sitting

at table with the married pair and betrays himself against
his will by giving that warning about the cress. The point of
the narrative as a whole seems clearly to be a self-accusation,
and not an exoneration as construed by the Talmudic jurist.
Thus in the Talmud we have not only an omission but
a distortion, for the original narrative was a very secular
story with a comedy point of an adulterer giving himself
away by a slip of the tongue at table. In the Talmud it becomes
a " case " in which, in spite of all suspicion, adultery cannot
be asserted nor its legal consequences allowed. The distortion
is not so clear in the first story, and under stress we may
accept the view asserted by Fiebig that the event is not given
as an anecdote, but just as a case laid before a juristic authority
such as Raba.   But the conduct of the accused person even
in such a view still remains uncertain, for he has awakened
the husband's suspicions by his clumsy flight. It seems to me
still the likeliest supposition that when the husband returned
the adulterer lost his head and betrayed himself in this way.
If so, we should have an anecdote here which was originally
secular and humorous, and was only twisted round in the
Talmud to be a case of insufficient proofs.

In any event the question about the origin of such Talmudic
passages comes forward here in full clarity : were they formed
from the beginning as cases, or were they first current as
anecdotes which were transformed into cases ? This question
can be applied to a great number of anecdotes contained in
Rabbinic literature. I will instance an example, striking on
account of its uniqueness. Following upon the Mishna statute
against conjuring the dead and soothsaying (M. Sanhedrin vii,
7), definitions of such arts are given. Sanhedrin 65*b* tells with
striking brevity that Raba had made a man and sent him to
Rabbi Zera. The latter recognised the origin of the image by
its dumbness, and said : " You originate from my companions,
return to your dust." If this narrative had been so brief and
pointless from the beginning as it stands here, it could have
been constructed as a case referring to almost any rumour.

The main point, therefore, is Rabbi Zera's answer, and not Raba's act. But if the narrative originally dealt with a miracle attributed to Raba, then naturally it would have been fuller on this point, and not confined to three words,[1] as in the original. But we are reminded by it that tradition ascribes to the Cabalistic miracle-workers of the Middle Ages the power to make artificial men. But if one takes the written name of God out of his mouth or from his forehead, the image immediately falls into dust. We should, therefore, look upon the tradition of Raba as the forerunner of such legends.

It is not easy to decide between the two possibilities. But since the barrenness of the narrative cannot be understood by its application to a clear juristic issue, I prefer to suppose that an old, vivid report has been artifically shortened and put into the Talmud. Our only point is to show in what way understanding of, and insight into, the process of tradition condition each other in these literary sources.

Every attempt to deal with the Formgeschichte of the Rabbinic narrative material is subject to the difficulty of deciding the categories at which we have just hinted. For decision about the category follows upon the determination of the leading interests, and this again must be taken from the Form of the story. If the Form is not preserved by the editors of the tradition, if it is broken up, if the original leading interest is replaced by another, then the original Form can only be regained by reconstruction, and the certainty about the process of the event is considerably lessened thereby. The examples just analysed show that we have to reckon with a three-fold manner of preserving the Rabbinic narrative material.

1. The narrative corresponds to the context in which it stands according to its original nature. That holds especially

---

[1] Such is the simplicity of the narrative which begins, without an introduction : רבא ברא גברא. Previously is the saying of the same Raba : " If religious people wished, they could create a universe."

of stories of an Halakhic kind, but also occasionally of Rabbinic legends concerning Rabbis (cf. p. 134 *supra*).

2. The narrative has no relation to the Halakhic context. It is recorded because another narrative is properly introduced in this connection, and itself is connected with this narrative either on literary grounds, since both belong to the same collection, or have the same beginning or conclusion; or by association, since they deal with the same persons or things, or are bound together by the same saying. In this way especially numerous legends have been preserved in the Talmud (cf. pp. 134 ff. *supra*).

3. The narrative was originally foreign to the context, but was fitted into it when an interest corresponding to the context was stamped on it to some extent obscuring or distorting the original character, often again abbreviating the report proper. In such a way old categories of popular narrative could find a place in the Rabbinic literature, and in this way secular material and even fairy stories have particularly been preserved (cf. pp. 138 ff. *supra*).

We do not need to say that the first-mentioned manner gives the greatest, and the last-mentioned the least, guarantee for the preservation of individual stories with the maximum original Form.

On the basis of this sketch it is now possible to inquire for possible analogies to New Testament narratives.

The *Halakhic stories* occupy a large space in the Talmud, and can scarcely be brought under *one* type by their Form. On the one hand, simple cases are dealt with which were brought to the Rabbis for decision and the answer consists frequently only of a saying. There is no narrative at all, for neither the questioner nor the effect of the answer upon the hearers is described. The point is simply to set down the decision of the Rabbinic authority. There are analogies to this among the sayings of Jesus which, in the same way, preserve for the Church the decision of the Master.

Other *cases* are told in the Talmud as stories; questions

are brought to the Rabbis, whose attitude to them characterizes them. Thus not only are stories of Hillel and Shammai collected in Sabbath 31a, but also theoretic and practical answers of the Rabbis are preserved in numerous other passages. Similarly in a few Paradigms, questions of a Halakhic or of an Haggadic kind are put to Jesus: fasting, rubbing ears of corn, but especially the tribute money and the Sadducean question are passages most strongly reminiscent of the corresponding Rabbinic stories. We must grant that the material difference is significant; for with the Rabbis the point is mostly the correct explanation or application of a legal prescription, whereas Jesus' answer goes far beyond an Halakhic instruction. It is also differentiated from the Halakha in so far as it gives nothing as an interpretation of a scriptural passage, but as the decision of " one who has authority ". The reference to David who ate the shewbread (Mark ii, 26) cannot be held as an Halakhic justification for breaking the Sabbath, and the Sadducees who, in the Halakhic sense, ask to whom the much-married woman would belong in the resurrection, receive not an Halakhic, but an Haggadic answer. It is true that in this case the passage Exodus iii, 6, is adduced as a proof for the resurrection, but only after Jesus had already decided the question at issue authoritatively: " they will be like the angels in heaven ".

But it is of the greatest significance in this connection that Matthew xii, 5, places, alongside the example of David who ate the shewbread, the Sabbath sacrificial ceremonial of the priests, according to Numbers xxviii, 9 f., and thus really adduces an Haggadic proof for Sabbath-breaking. Matthew, indeed, adds also, Hosea vi, 6, "I desire mercy and not sacrifice," a saying which in Matthew ix, 13, had already justified eating with the publicans. We can see how great was the need felt by the Christian circle of Matthew's gospel for the scriptural proof of the Halakha. At the same time we see in how small a degree the original formulation of the material was influenced by this means.

Another difference between these Paradigms and the Halakhic stories of Rabbinic literature now comes into view. By collecting Rabbinic decisions, Jewish tradition wished to attain to an effective legal statute, and for this purpose it hands on the Halakhic stories. Thus there arises from the examples of different generations a thesaurus of normative significance. The handing down of Paradigms, on the other hand, deals only with the decisions of one man. Their normative character depends upon the worth of his person and not upon the agreement of voices which have been preserved from different periods. So also the work of collecting the tradition is limited to a few decades, and not, as in the Talmud, extended to centuries. Moreover, the object of collecting Paradigms is not to create a new legality, but to illustrate preaching and to call to repentance.

The Rabbinic *miracle stories* offer a further possibility of comparison. If I see it rightly there are two interests which, above all, come into account in their formulation and handing down. On the one hand, it is sought to prove that the common course of the world is miraculously corrected by God and in this way He glorifies His special concern, the fulfilment of law. On the other hand, further miracles are told simply to glorify certain Rabbis or holy places. I shall not deal further here with these Place-legends as there is nothing corresponding to them in the New Testament.[1]

Those legends first mentioned, which prove the righteousness of God by the miraculous amelioration of world-history, and which might therefore be called *Theodicy-legends*, are to a large extent also personal Legends, since they give names to their heroes, who are mostly well-known persons from Rabbinic circles, and in such a manner as to increase

---

[1] I would mention as typical examples the narrative that the doors of the Nicanor-gate, while being brought from Alexandria, calmed a storm (*Joma*, 38*a*), the Legends of the secret place in which the ark was placed (*Joma* 54*a*), finally the narrative of the youths who before the first destruction of the Temple threw its keys into heaven (Taanith, 29*a*; cf. the exhortation to the priests to do the same, *Rev. of Baruch syr.* x, 18).

their fame. But the interest does not cling to the person so much as to his activity and to the value set upon this activity by God. When R. Gamaliel, after Eliezer b. Hyrkanos was banned, was himself overtaken by a storm while on board ship, he supposed it was a divine judgment and said, "Lord of the world, it is open and known to Thee that I did this neither for myself nor for the honour of my ancestral house but for Thy honour, in order that strife should not increase in Israel." Then the sea calmed (Baba Mezia 59*b*). The story says that Eliezer's banishment was confirmed by God. There is a material interest present in this case. The two narratives of the snake-bite (Sabbath 156*b*), which I mentioned earlier (cf. p. 136), reveal a similar interest behind the context in which they at present stand; in both cases the misfortune which would have taken place was not permitted by God, since the "heroes" of the legend were beneficent. So little depends upon these heroes, however, that the first of them is not even named. Erubin 63*a* speaks of a pupil of Eliezer's who decides a Halakha in the presence of his teacher. Eliezer thereupon says to his wife "this pupil will not live into the next year". And so it is. Here again, the emphasis is not on the miracle, for we know nothing detailed about the death. Nor is the point the excellence of Rabbi Eliezer, since what was intended would be applicable to any Rabbi. The basic idea is obviously that God by means of a miraculous punishment confirmed the prescription that a pupil was not to give a decision in the presence of his teacher. What small significance the nature of the miracle itself possessed is shown by a story from Berakhoth 5*b*, in which, as a conclusion in the meaning of the theodicy, two different miracles are given to choose from. Four hundred measures of wine belong to Rab Huna become sour. The question is : Which of his deeds had brought him this misfortune ? And those who argue the point convince him finally that his unsocial attitude towards his gardener was the fault, for he had deprived him of his share of the wine. Huna promised an improvement, and now the divine reward must cause the punishment to be reversed. The narrators know of two ways in which this could take place : some say the sour wine again became drinkable, others that vinegar so rose in price that Huna could sell his soured wine as vinegar at the full price of wine. The mode of the divine intervention is of little importance ; the main thing is that the righteousness of God withdraws the punishment.

A special type of miracle-narrative is thus seen in this theodicy-legend. The main point is not the miracle as such with its special circumstances and manner of completion, rather its point is to confirm law-abiding piety. God intervenes in order to recognize a good deed, not as otherwise known in the man, in order to show that a deed which was misunderstood was pious, and in order to show that the righting of a wrong was satisfactory. The miracle is not always told for its own sake, but for the benefit of the matter for which the Talmud stands, viz. *proclaiming a divine law* by which men must live.

These miracle-stories are therefore very much more significant for Judaism as a whole, than the tradition of miracle-working Rabbis and their prayer-technique which we have still to analyse, for these stories stand in close connection with the Judaism of the synagogue. Their " Sitz im Leben " or home is in the endeavour continually made in the synagogue to fix the relation between divine righteousness and human conduct. Its rise is therefore to some extent plain. The Jewish scholars in fact take every striking case of preserving life, or some other special benefit of fortune, as a cause for going over the question which, in the narratives of the harmless snake-bite (Sabbath 156*b*, cf. p. 136 and 143, *supra*), were expressly related to the persons who were saved : the question was " Then what hast thou done ? " i.e. in which sense have you deserved this miracle ? And thus a connection with an earlier virtue of the " hero " must be made with these very events. But also, as the story of the sour wine shows (cf. p. 145 *supra*), a divine recognition must be postulated from the standpoint of human action. Then it becomes unmistakable that many of these events are not miraculous in the present popular use of the term, but can be classified as in accordance with the law of cause and effect. In the ancient sense of course they are miracles, since an extraordinary divine causality appears in them. But in these more perspicuous proceedings we can see that the handing down of these passages was subject to the danger of exaggeration and of syncretistic influence to a smaller degree than other traditions. It is not interested in the greatness of the miracle, and not even, in the first place, in a comparison with other miracle-doers, but only in the connection between human conduct and divine confirmation.

A precaution becomes necessary if we designate as Legends these stories which serve theodicy. Their diction is not the same as is proper to the religious narrative—the Legend strictly so-called. Rather its style is influenced by the nature of synagogue-discussions, and does not show the honour with which elsewhere tellers of Legends regard the saintly person. But the intellectual coldness of the presentation is characteristic of most of the Rabbinic tradition. If, in spite of this, I speak of Theodicy-legends, it is in order to suggest that these stories mostly deal with definite saintly men mentioned by name, and, therefore, belong to the circle of personal Legends in the wider sense.

But it seems to me, however, that the difference between these theodicy miracles and the miracles narrated in the sense of genuine personal Legends, is of the highest significance for comparing with miracles in the New Testament. For we find also in Rabbinic Judaism narratives of miracles which in themselves have not the typical quality of miracle-stories, i.e. do not describe the technique and do not prove the reality of the miracle. The miraculous event is subject, rather, to another law : it is only to be understood from the central religious interest of the message which these miracle-stories serve ; in the Talmud it is the comparison between divine

righteousness and human conduct, in the gospel it is the
eschatological salvation whose coming can be traced in Jesus'
saving work. For naturally it is the Paradigms in the gospel
which, in so far as they record miracles, offer an analogy to
the Theodicy-legends we have depicted. The relation between
miracle and salvation which is assumed in these primitive
Christian texts is somewhat the same as the saying Luke x,
20, brings to expression : " Rejoice not because the spirits
obey you, but rejoice because your names are written in
heaven." The difference among the records of Jesus' miracles
which I have put forward in the previous chapters on the
basis of Formgeschichte proves to be materially appropriate,
and in a way is confirmed by the analogy of the Jewish
Legends.

Alongside the Theodicy-legends we find the miracle-
stories which glorify miracle-working Rabbis, and thus
are Personal Legends in the narrower sense. Amongst them
there are common miracles, proofs of great miraculous
power without special relation to law and law-abiding life.
These are miracles which almost approximate to the secular
sphere. This view probably holds good of the miracle in the
Sanhedrin 65*b*, of Raba's making an artificial man—if the
supposition is correct that this reference goes back to a record
originally more colourful and detailed (cf. pp. 140 f. *supra*).
Narratives of this kind are not too frequent in the Rabbinic
texts. But two characteristics seem to me to be significant
for the tradition of miracles in honour of certain Rabbis.

1. These miracle-working Rabbis were not of great ability
but of much prayer. It is characteristic that a specially great
collection of miracle-stories is to be found in the tractate
Taanith—which deals with fasting and prayer for rain
(Taanith iii, 1–9). God remains untouched in His majesty ;
the power of man cannot alter anything in the course of the
world as divinely ordered. Nevertheless a saintly person
can also bring an extraordinary request to the throne of God.
He is great then, not by his power, but by his place before

God : " I am in Thy sight like a member of Thy household," prays Rabbi Choni in a tradition already found in the Mishna (Taanith iii, 8 ; cf. also the Bab. Taanith 23*a*). But the same tradition shows also that Jewish faith believed the borders of the permissible were already passed in a very capricious, miraculous activity. Choni prays for rain, or rather compels it, since he swears not to leave the place (the circle drawn by the Rabbi) until God had sent rain. Rain then falls sparingly ; he requires more. Then the rain becomes too tempestuous, and only after a third prayer does beneficent rain fall. Then Simeon B. Shatach says to the Rabbi : " Were you not Choni, I would have put a ban upon you, but what can I do against you where you act wrongly towards God, and He nevertheless fulfils your wish, just as a child acts wrongly to his father and he nevertheless fulfils his wish ? " This manner of influencing the divine will is, therefore, regarded as not really permissible.

2. Miracles are not recorded of the great teachers of the law amongst the rabbis, but of others whose fame in the school is smaller. Characteristic of this is the story of the cure of the son of Rabbi Johanan b. Zakkai by the prayer of the miracle-working Rabbi Chanina b. Dosa. After his prayer had been successful, the great Johanan is driven to understand that his own prayer would not have been respected. When his wife asks in amazement : " Is then Chanina greater than thou ? " he answers, " No, but he is like a servant before the king ; I am like a prince before the king." Perhaps that means that it is not fitting for a prince to pray to the king with his head between his knees, as Chanina's attitude in prayer is described. Perhaps the suggestion is also that the relation of the lower person, the servant, to the king is more confined than that of the prince. In any case, from this tradition one sees that in regard to status there were conceptions which ascribed much more miraculous power to the lower than to the higher. And that was the intention when, after success in prayer, Chanina must confess " I am

neither a prophet nor the son of a prophet " (Jebamoth 121*b*
and Berakhoth 34*b*). Chanina's miraculous power is
well known, indeed it is recognized in heaven.[1] But the
greatness of a Rabbi consists not in power over demons or
sicknesses, but in the ability to explain them all and proclaim
the will of God.

The tradition about Chanina b. Dosa is of literary significance because the numerous miracle-stories which are recorded
about him [2] demonstrate two things, viz. the existence
of a collection of legends about a person, and the relatively
close connection of these stories with this person and his
special qualities.

After we have compared the theodicy-legends with the
Paradigms in the Gospels, the question at once arises as to
the relation between the miraculous Personal-legends and
the primitive Christian Tales. We see that certain traits
characteristic of the Tales occur also in the Jewish miracle
Legends. When Chanina b. Dosa heals R. Gamiel's son
at a distance (Berakhoth 34*b*), then, just as in John iv, 52,
the chronological agreement between the healing word and
the actual healing is demonstrated. When the same Rabbi
makes Rabbi Johanan's son well by means of prayer (Berakhoth
34*b*) the prayer technique is described. Thus Chanina puts
his head between his knees. Taanith 23*b* says that R. Jona
covered himself with a sack, went into a cave, and prayed
for mercy—and so he received rain.

Nevertheless the common quality of miracle-stories can
at times be demonstrated in the Talmudic Legends, although
significant differences are to be noted between the Gospel
Tales and the stories. The Tales narrate the miracles from
the standpoint of epiphany : by means of the miracle God's

---

[1] A female demon says that someone in heaven had cried out : " Beware of
Chanina and his knowledge of the law " (Pesachim, 112*b*, 113*a*). One sees here that
even the miraculous power was also conceived as combined with the ability of the
teacher. We often hear of a heavenly voice which proclaims that the world was
sustained for Chanina's sake (Taanith 24*b*, Berakoth 17*b*, Chullin 86*b*).

[2] Cf. Taanith 24*b*, Berakhoth 33*a*, 34*b*, Jebamoth 121*b*, Pesachim 112*b*, 113*a*,
Koheleth rabba I on 1[1].

power proves the authority of His emissary: the essential thing is that in what Jesus did is seen what came from God. The Talmudic narratives tell of human beings, about what the Rabbis effect by their prayers, about the power which they receive on account of their saintliness. Thus it is not remarkable that the motif of miraculous self-help, so seldom met in the Gospels, is frequent in the Talmud. On the other hand however, syncretistic influences do not appear to have played the part in the Rabbinic miracle-stories which we must occasionally assume in the early history of the New Testament Tales. This is connected to some extent with the general shyness of Rabbinic Judaism towards strange motifs. But again, the Jewish Legends were also protected from these secular motifs because they ascribe to the miracle-worker a sanctity on account of which God gives His answer in the miracle. They do not ascribe the miraculous power to the miracle-worker himself. Therefore it follows that there is not a real possibility in the Rabbinic narratives of a connection which would lead to strengthening the "human", i.e. the secular elements, and thereby to a foreign veneer upon the tradition.

(ii) Greek Analogies

In addition to anecdotes from Rabbinic literature, certain narratives of a popular character in Greek literature offer a comparison with the Gospel narratives. Here we are dealing with (1) traditions containing the sayings of famous men, especially of well known and popular philosophers, useful and edificatory for succeeding ages; (2) Tales incidentally introduced into longer historical or romantic narratives; (3) miracle records, epiphanies and aretalogies preserved in connection with some religious cultus.

There is no single name for the first of these categories. It is not sufficiently precise to call them "Apophthegmata" in the ancient sense, as the term is used both of the sayings

introduced without occasion, and of answers of a definite
character to a situation which is given briefly or at length.
According to Diogenes Laertius (iv, 7, par. 47), Bion left
behind many things worth remembering (ὑπομνήματα) or
"Apophthegmata" of a practical value. Then follow as
examples, among other things, sayings without any context :
"It is a great evil not to be able to bear evil" (par. 48). Others
have the introduction : "He used to say" (par. 49). Answers
given in specific situations are also cited : "Once when
asked who had the most worries, he answered, The man who
is most anxious for happiness (par. 48)". One of these examples
is expanded into a short narrative (par. 50). "On a voyage
with evil companions, he fell into the hands of robbers. The
former said : "We are lost if anyone recognizes us." But he
answered : "So am I if no one recognizes me." Similarly,
in the collection of "the finest Apophthegmata" which
Diogenes Laertius wove into his biography of Aristotle we find
both sayings without context and answers given in particular
situations (v, 1, par. 17–21). The various collections of
Apophthegmata in Plutarch (*Regum et Imperatorum ap. ; ap.
Laconica, Lacaenarum ap.*) contain, as a rule, circumstantial
replies, but also a few sentences apart from the occasion.

(a) Chriae

The large number of these differences makes it possible
to distinguish a character defined by marks of style, and thus
comprehensible as a category. It is the reproduction of
a short pointed saying of general significance, originating
in a definite person and arising out of a definite situation.
In the age of the Gospels, rhetoricians called such a small
matter a "Chria", as also did the Stoics in the first century
B.C.[1] The "Chria" is distinguished from the larger group

---

[1] Theon. *Progymnasmata* 5. χρεία ἐστὶ σύντομος ἀπόφασις ἢ πρᾶξις μετ'
εὐστοχίας ἀναφερομένη εἴς τι ὡρισμένον πρόσωπον ἢ ἀναλογοῦν προσώπῳ.
Citations in Diogenes Laertius imply that Hecaton of Rhodes, pupil of Panactus,
had published collections under the title "Chriae".

of " Apophthegmata " by its connection with a particular situation, even if this difference was sometimes misvalued by the collectors. It is differentiated from the Gnome by its connection with a person.[1]

The typical short forms of the " Chria " are those in which the saying is introduced either by a question, or by a personal remark, or by a very concise description of the circumstances in the genitive absolute : To the question how the educated differed from the uneducated, he (Aristippus) answered, " Like a tamed from an untamed horse."[2] He (Aristotle) said to the man who boasted that he came from a large city : " One should not be concerned about that, but whether one is worthy of a great motherland." [3] When someone marvelled at the sacred gifts in Samothrace, he (Diogenes) said, " It would be far greater if all those who had not been saved had given the like." [4]

In all three cases it is clear that the introduction to the saying only serves the purpose of giving the circumstances necessary for comprehension. In accordance with the style, the " hero " is only characterized by the actual saying, and the introduction does not portray his nature, but only the particular situation ; above all, the narrator does not give way to his pleasure in story-telling and describe an interesting situation. The more striking the saying, the greater the attention to concentration. This is supported by numerous examples from the biographies of philosophers by Diogenes Laertius, and similar short genuine " Chriae " are also to be found amongst the anecdotes of Socrates which Xenophon included in his *Memorabilia* (iii, 13). Moreover most of the fifty " striking and witty sayings " preserved by Lucian in his biography of Demonax (12–62) show the characteristics of the " Chria " and some of them are

---

[1] Theon. *Progymnasmata* 5. πᾶσα γὰρ γνώμη σύντομος εἰς πρόσωπον ἀναφερομένη χρείαν ποιεῖ.

[2] Diogenes Laertius ii, 8, 69.

[3] Ib. v, 1, 19.

[4] Ib. vi, 2, 59.

particularly remarkable for the terseness of their style.[1] On the
other hand the descriptions of the Sophists by Philosotratus
contain relatively few short and terse " Chriae " in among
their rich and varied materials.[2] The sayings reported are
often given in connection with a longer narrative, or interwoven into a biographical description. The work of the
author appears to have filled out, and even to have destroyed
the original form of the material in this case. Philostratus himself shows occasionally that he found such material in a collection
before his time. He calls them ἀπομνημονεύματα. He inserts
into the biography of Polemon i, 25[9], a special section of
witty sayings, and supplies it with a special introduction and
conclusion. The content of this section is six narratives,
of which five are genuine " Chriae ". The first narrative
is a literary editing of an anecdote filled out with descriptions
and exclamations, as a consequence of which its extent exceeds
that of the other five together. But there can be really no
doubt that he has a genuine " Chria " at the bottom. In
what way Philostratus embodied in his biographies an isolated
story handed down separately can be observed in his description of Herod Atticus ii, 1[9]. At the end of the preceding
section he had been dealing with the mourning of Herod for his
wife Regilla, on which account he had had his house draped
in black. It also tells how a wise man named Lucius had
endeavoured to deliver him from his excessive sorrow.
In ii, 1[9], we have, first of all, a comforting speech of this
Lucius, but it does not lead to any goal. Then follows the
anecdote according to which this Lucius sees Herod's slaves
preparing white radishes and he says : " Herod would not
do right to Regilla if he ate white radishes in a black house."
This witticism caused Herod to remove the signs of mourning.

---

[1] Thus Demonax answers the question what it looks like in Hades : " Wait and
I will write you from there " (43). Peregmius reproaches him for his scoff :
Δημῶναξ, οὐ κυνᾷς—he answers : περεγρῖνε, οὐκ ἀνθρωπίζεις (21).
[2] When a customs officer attacked Nicetas of Smyrna in court : " Cease yelping
at me," the latter answered : " Yes, by Zeus when you cease biting me." Philostratus,
Vita Sophist. i, 19[2].

Thus we have here a " Chria " of Lucius which has been inter-woven into Herod's biography. But now in loose connection there follows another " Chria " of Lucius which has nothing to do with Herod. Lucius sees how the emperor Marcus goes for teaching to the philosopher Sextus, and he cries, " By Zeus, the ' king ' of the Romans goes even in old age with his copybook to school, but my ' king ' Alexander died when he was only thirty-two." Then follows a conclu-sion in accordance with the style—and now Philostratus continues as if the connection had never been broken : " Thus the mourning for Regilla was ended, but the Athenians mitigated it for the daughter Panathenais . . ."

From these examples we can see clearly that Philostratus also had in front of him short stories which were originally isolated, and which contained striking and even witty sayings. These he edited in his own way. Another collection of witty sayings, under the title *Philogelos*, belonging to the fifth century A.D. shows how constant were the laws of style of this category.[1] This collection of 264 very short stories deals not with anecdotes of historical persons, but with types. The drunkard, the wit, the fool, and especially the pedant, the " scholastic ". But the style of these terse sayings is that of the " Chria ",[2] and it may very well be that many of these witticisms originally had a famous name.

The terse style of the " Chria " tolerates many extensions without spoiling the form. In place of a terse sentence we may find a longer one, or even a dialogue.[3] The description of the situation may require several sentences.[4] At the con-clusion the saying may be explained, or its effect described,[5]

---

[1] *Philogelos. Hieroclis et Philagrii facetiae*, ed. Alfred Eberhard, Berlin, 1869.

[2] Story No. 77 is about a σχολαστικός returning from the funeral of his son. He meets his teacher and says : " Pardon my son's absence from school, he is dead." This story was originally a witness not to the feeble intellect of the father, but to his phlegmatism; hence it was a " Chria " handed down in honour of the " hero ".

[3] It is diagnostic of the Socratic method that among the six " Chriae " given in Xenophon *Memor*. iii, 13, there are two in which only the to and fro of a debate eads to the deciding sentence (13³, 13⁶).

[4] Cf. Lucian, *Demonax* 16.

[5] Cf. Philostratus, *Vita Sophist*. ii, 4¹ ; xvi, 31².

but the concentration upon the saying itself always remains recognizable : the striking phrase, full of spirit and wit, or full of pride or folly in a ridiculous degree, is preserved for special honour or as a characteristic mark of the speaker. This differentiates the " Chria " from the witticisms of *Philogelos*, and this fettering to a person shows the home from which these stories arise : they were told in honour of a well-known man or to keep alive some joke or foible of his.

The quantity of the material[1] permits us to judge the relationship of the tradition of Jesus to the Greek " Chriae " and the Greek apophthegma in the narrow sense of the word. There is a similarity of *origin*, a wide difference of *content*, which influences the diction, and a certain but essential difference of *construction*. For the purposes of comparison in the Gospel tradition we may use the Paradigms (but naturally not the Tales) and in addition also, the sayings of Jesus which are set in a definite situation, and hence in essentials constituting the group which Bultmann calls Apophthegmata.[2]

The *origin* of both the Christian and the Greek tradition is unliterary. The circles interested in the hero, either as disciples or, amongst the Greeks, also as opponents, preserve expressions and events in order to maintain the mind and the manner of the hero as the normative standard (in the case of opponents as typical opposites not to be imitated). These short stories were handed down in isolation, at first in narrower and then in wider regions. Only gradually were they taken up into the broader connections in which they were preserved, either clearly defined or edited from a literary standpoint.

The unliterary character of the origin unites the two

---

[1] The collection made by von Wartensleben, *Begriff der Chreia*, 31 ff., contains over 500 examples even though it leaves the Sophists out of account. Naturally material is to be found in the *Vita Apollonii* of Philostratus, but here, however the problem of the source may be settled, we must reckon with more marked literary editing than in the *Vitæ Sophistarum*. For this reason anecdotes of Apollonius have not been adduced in our discussion.

[2] *Geschichte der Syn. Tradition.*

groups, but they are very widely differentiated by their *content*. In the Greek texts there is a large number of examples of witty repartee without material content, such as appropriate answers, startling paradoxes, sayings with a double meaning. This is what characterizes many of the " Chriae ". Of the fifty stories which Lucian gives in *Demonax* 12–62 I count only seven to which philosophical content can be ascribed. An essential side of Greek intellectual life comes forward here : the leaning to a clever play upon words, conceptions, and thoughts. The depth and breadth of Greek thought were expressed in other forms. These pointed anecdotes are dominated by the εὐτραπελία, the dexterity in jocular speech which Aristotle called educated insolence.[1] It rules to some extent in philosophical borders. It was not to no purpose that the Cynics made boldness the characteristic of philosophical advisers of mankind. And hence this brilliant art of giving a striking answer, even where it served no ethical or polemic purpose, but was concerned only with itself, was felt a valuable quality. But the New Testament, in the only passage which speaks of the εὐτραπελία (Eph. v, 4), counts it amongst the vices.

This shows the essential difference between the two groups. The originators of the tradition of Jesus were ἰδιῶται τῷ λογῷ; elegant speech was altogether foreign to them and especially when its effectiveness is an end in itself. The causes of this difference in essence are very manifold. The originators and mediators of this tradition, even if they were educated, nevertheless had no share in that world of culture out of which the witty sentences of the " Chriae " arose. In addition the Semitic character of the words actually spoken hindered elegant imitation in Greek. And finally the content of this tradition excluded altogether every presentation founded upon wit, punning, or an elegant and brilliant manner of speech. For the word and work of the Master

---

[1] Aristotle, *Rhetoric.*, ii, 12, πεπαιδευένη ὕβρις. According to the *Nicomachian Ethics*, ii, 7[13], it is the correct mean between buffoonery and lumpishness.

were determined by reference to the end of the world.   In
this landscape of the world, in this circumstance of an urgent
time, in this period of the approaching divine judgment,
that kind of word was forbidden which was only brilliant
or only intended to arrest the hearer.   Jesus Himself replied
occasionally, mostly outside the Paradigms, in "striking"
words, but His call to repentance or exhortation to preach
is connected with a simple brushing aside of objections.
Before "Let the dead bury their dead" stands "Follow
thou me" (Matthew viii, 22).   Even Jesus speaks occasionally
in paradox, but the puzzling character was intended to cause
repentance.   When He requires anointing and washing of one
who was fasting, as if he were going to a feast (Matthew vi, 17),
the apparent foolishness of the requirements is itself meant
to produce a right attitude.

     The method of speaking is determined by the content.
In spite of their brevity the Christian texts have a certain
warmth and fullness which grip one.   Without speaking of
Jesus as the "Lord" in the course of the narrative they
deal with His figure as that of the Lord, His word as normative,
and His act as decisive.   A certain coolness and terseness is
proper to the Greek stories ;   the wit is biting and the scorn
is effective :   the opponent is mercilessly vanquished indeed,
to the satisfaction of the hearers.   Along with this difference
of inner character there goes also a certain difference of the
outer construction.   It is true that the Paradigm concentrates
upon the word and act of Jesus, but the situation is really
described, whereas the "Chriae", as a rule, only give the
most essential presuppositions for the saying.   Thus, the
build of the Paradigm, in spite of all its brevity, is nevertheless
more attractive and satisfying than the composition of the
"Chriae".   The severity of the style of the Paradigm is seen
rather in the unconditional relation of all the motives to the
central matter.   But in the "Chriae" it is seen in the sparseness
of the data.   As compared with the Greek, the Christian

texts deal with a large number of topics : the faith of a man
seeking health (Mark ii, 4 f.), the spite of the opponents
(iii, 2), the reluctance of Jesus (x, 14), the zeal of the rich man
(x, 17). The character of this construction is, of course,
conditioned also by the Semitic spirit of the language which
is also noticeable to some extent in the diction of the Gospel
narratives. Its inclination to parataxis, to a parallelism of
sentences, is quite obviously opposed to the overburdening
of the sequence of the sentences such as many more-detailed
Chria-like constructions show (cf. p. 155 *supra*). But
parataxis is not the only thing to which the fuller mode of
description in the Paradigms is due. Thus at the end of the
story of the children (Mk. x, 13–16), which is a very short
Paradigm, the attitude of Jesus to the children is described
with not less than three verbs, but they are not placed loosely
alongside one another, rather the first and the last are subordin-
ated as participles to the middle one.[1]

The difference of construction is conditioned by the
content in so far as very often in the Gospels the action and the
saying are related to one another. The saying prepares either
for an action or serves as its explanation. The concentration
of the " Chriae " simply upon the saying is thereby impossible
in the Paradigms.

In this place, however, we must mention that there are
source-passages in the Gospels in which the saying alone is
prominent, and which are therefore outwardly much nearer
to the " Chriae ". I am referring to those sayings of Jesus
which are furnished with data as to the circumstances. We
may claim for the precanonical tradition at least four passages
in Mark and Matthew in which the saying of Jesus needs
data as to the situation. Jesus utters the saying about refusing
signs as an answer to the Pharisees who require a sign (Mark
viii, 11 f.). The words " foxes have their holes " and " let
the dead bury their dead " are replies to the words of would-be

---

[1] Mark x, 16, καὶ ἐγκαλισάμενος αὐτὰ κατευλόγει τιθεὶς τὰς χεῖρας ἐπ' αὐτά.

disciples (Matthew viii, 19–22).[1] In Mark ix, 38–40 Jesus answers in the same way the mention of an exorcism in His name, and in Matthew xviii, 21 f. the question about the duty of forgiveness. A great difference exists, however, between these well-defined sayings and Chriae, a difference which is due to the variety of content. Nevertheless in construction and in the method of concentrating upon the word of the hero there exists a strong relationship. This is explained by the nature of the case. The sayings cannot be reproduced without indicating in what situation they were spoken—and this holds good both of the Greek and of the Christian writings. The meaning of the communication is, in both cases, found exclusively in the saying itself.

The analogy of the " Chriae " may help to explain a development within the tradition of Jesus' sayings. In view of the wide occurrence of Chrie-like material it must have been easy for Christians, when they had become authors to a certain extent, to dress the sayings of Jesus in the form of " Chriae ", when they would become more striking and impressive. Traits handed down popularly received a literary dress and ambiguous sayings were explained.

An example of this development is perhaps to be seen in the transformation which the passage about the greatest command (Mark xii, 28–34) received in Matthew's Gospel. The concluding dialogue between Jesus and the scribes has dropped out, and the whole of Matthew xxii, 35–40 consists only of question and answer. The fragment from Fayoum [2] published by Bickell seems to me to show a Chria-like transformation still more clearly. Obviously it is not a Gospel fragment, but, if its beginning be filled out in the

---

[1] A third instance occurs in Luke ix, 61 f., where the would-be disciple wishes first to say farewell at home. Jesus answers : " No man, having put his hand to the plough, and looking back, is fit for the kingdom of God." This saying is of so general a character that its introduction and fixing into this context must be held as the work of the evangelist.

[2] *Ztschr. f. Kath. Theol.* 1885, 498–504.

manner customary to-day,[1] it comes from a collection of the sayings of Jesus which were supplied with chronological data. The dialogue of Jesus reported in Mark xiv, 27, 29–31, is here abbreviated in so far as Peter's reply is given only in the genitive absolute, and thus in the genuine Chria manner, and is condensed in the extreme.[2] Everything is directed to the prophecy of the denial.

We must now deal with the evangelist Luke. Both in form and material he constantly reached out towards literature as such. In Acts he is independent; in the Gospel he keeps within the boundaries of a tradition which has already been developed. Naturally he has given many words of Jesus a literary turn where possible. Thus he has supplied six parables with data of a situation in the way that the Chriae would have given them in sentences (Luke x, 29; xii, 13; xiv, 15; xv, 1; xviii, 9; and xix, 11). In the same way he has put words of Jesus within the framework of brief data as to the occasion (xi, 1; xxii, 24); and also the third example (ix, 61 f.), added by Luke to the two sayings about followers in the source, is surely the Chria-like formulation of a current saying otherwise without occasion (cf. p. 160, note 1). And so he transformed the stories into smaller pictures. He shortened the situation so that the whole has the effect of a Chria, as is seen in his strikingly compressed formulation of cleansing the Temple (xix, 45). Or else he shortened the introduction until it was a mere opening bar (cf. p. 155 and note 2); in this way the whole of the compressed description of Jesus' Baptism (iii, 21–2) leads up to the heavenly voice. Or else, finally, he made a single striking sentence out of several sayings of Jesus, as is the case in the saying about His true relatives (viii, 21).

---

[1] I am here assuming Wesseley's reconstruction (*Patrologia Orientalis*, iv, 173–7) according to which the introduction runs: ἐν δὲ τῷ ἐ]ξάγειν ὡς ἐ[ι]πε[ν] ὅτι ἄ[παντες ἐν ταύτῃ] τῇ νυκτὶ σκανδαλισ[θήσεσθε κατὰ] τὸ γραφέν κ.τ.λ. The union with the time-datum appears to come from a logia-collection.

[2] [κατὰ] τὸ γραφέν is already an abbreviation of the Markan finite verb, and only properly: [εἰπόντος το]ῦ πέτ· καὶ εἰ πάντες ο[ὐκ ἐγώ].

But, above all, in a large number of cases—I count eight—
Luke gives words of Jesus in such a construction that they
appear as answers to short questions or as assertions from
the opposite standpoint.   Then the whole of the little picture
has the appearance of a Chria ; xi, 27 f. offers the best example :
a woman in the crowd cries, " Blessed is the womb that
bare thee and the breasts which thou didst suck " ; Jesus
answers, " Blessed are they that hear the word of God and
keep it." Whereas we receive the impression here and in
xiii, 1, xix, 39 that the situation may have been handed down
to the evangelist and that only the pregnant style is due to
him ; in other cases the correspondence between situation
and saying is by no means convincing.   We see that Luke
artificially created constructions of that character.   The
saying about the faith which can remove a tree is introduced
in Luke xvii, 5 by the quite unconditioned request, " give
us faith," which is certainly formulated by Luke.[1] The same
holds good of the question " Lord, will only a few be saved ? "
(xiii, 23), which was meant to introduce the saying about
the narrow door which was handed down also in the Sermon
on the Mount.   In xvi, 14 a saying against the Pharisees
is joined up with a very colourless notice of their scoffing at
Him.   In the case of the well known word about the Kingdom
of God " among you " which carries its significance within
itself, it is very questionable whether its introduction by
a quite colourless Pharisaian question (xvii, 20) meets the
sense of the saying.[2] We may raise a similar question about
the saying xiii, 31–3, for it is very doubtful whether Jesus'
word was directed against the " fox " Herod.   Probably

---

[1] This can be seen particularly clearly in the first words : καὶ εἶπαν οἱ ἀπόστολοι
τῷ κυρίῳ—speaker and hearers are characterized in the Lucan manner.

[2] But this very introduction corresponds verbatim to the plan of the Chria :
ἐπερωτηθεὶς δὲ ὑπὸ τῶν Φαρισαίων πότε ἔρχεται ἡ βασιλεία τοῦ θεοῦ, ἀπεκρίθη
αὐτοῖς καὶ εἶπεν.
What is meant is the signs of the Kingdom which alone could be objects of
apocalyptic " observation " (παρατήρησις). The only question remaining is
whether these signs are already " among you " or " within you ". The latter would
refer to eschatological repentance, the former, which seems to me more probable,
to the eschatological movement.

here also the introduction is the work of the evangelist,
who is always interested in the great ones of the earth.[1]

A good example of a certain tendency to construct Chria-
like narrative forms is offered by the story of the man working
on the Sabbath (Luke vi, 4 D) which is artificially introduced
into the context. If we isolate it we find the pure Chria
form.[2] " When he saw a man working on the Sabbath, he
said to him, " Man if you know what you are doing you are
blessed, but if you do not know, you are accursed and a trans-
gressor of the law." The first words are not narrative, but
give the situation with a participle. Hence we do not learn
what sort of work it was which broke the Sabbath. In a
Paradigm the introduction would have been (say) " On the
same Sabbath he saw a fisherman minding his nets, and said
to him . . ." Thus this record of the Sabbath-worker is by
no means a Paradigm, as I held in the first edition of this
book, although a Paradigm might be its original basis ;
and the extra-canonical tradition might have approximated
the section to the current Greek form by depicting the
circumstances as briefly as possible.

Moreover this example shows that the general tendency
of Chria-like formulation hangs together with the tendency
of the form universally current. This manner of abbreviating
the circumstances and giving the concluding saying as
strikingly as possible is, therefore, apart from a few exceptions,
not that of the original tradition, but is indicative of the
secular style into which the gospel tradition was entering.
The relative originality of the primitive Christian Paradigm
in Greek literature comes out here once more. It is not a

---

[1] Goguel, *Vie de Jésus*, 333 f., deduces the trustworthiness of this tradition
directly from the introduction in which the Pharisees strangely appear as giving
warning advice. But if this framework is due to the literary tendency of the
evangelist to handle tradition in a Chria manner—as the analogies make it seem
probable—then the strange introduction of the Pharisees would be explicable
otherwise: Luke lets them come forward without historical dubiety, as in xvi, 14 ;
xvii, 20 ; as the usual opposite numbers of Jesus.

[2] This introduction causes a tautology : τῇ αὐτῇ ἡμέρᾳ is a superfluous time-
datum alongside θεασάμενός τινα ἐργαζόμενον τῷ σαββάτῳ.

literary originality for which we must praise the author's craft of those who handed down the tradition, but pre-literary. The objective, i.e. use in preaching, conditions the Form and this is neither so complicated in a literary way as is the Chria, nor depicted so vividly as is the Tale.

(b) Tales

The Tale, the second of the analogies from Greek literary history to be mentioned here does not need any detailed analysis for our purposes. For this " narration of an interesting single event," often inserted in larger works of narrative content from the time of Herodotus to Apuleius, cannot be more closely defined by the regularly returning peculiarities of its diction. What is to be generally characteristic of its nature, namely narrative fulness, has already been dealt with in connection with the early Christian Tales. That which can otherwise be established as typical in the Christian Tales, refers mostly to the topic of the healing miracle, and can thus only be compared with the Greek records of healings which we are about to discuss. But the Greek Tales contain such varied material that things in common can only be established with difficulty. Moreover the editing quite obviously applied to the Tale, when incorporated into larger works,[1] makes it difficult to recognize the Form in which it was current in isolation.

For our purposes it is sufficient to establish the following. In ancient times there were finished detailed descriptive stories in the Greek language which described interesting single occurrences. They were of popular origin, at first

---

[1] This can be particularly well observed in Josephus. He narrates Archelaus' dream of the ears of corn and Glaphyra's dream of her dead husband (*Wars*, ii, 7³, ⁴; *Ant.*, xvii, 13³, ⁴), in such a manner that on each occasion that it is possible to detect how the editorial work in the " *Antiquities* " has been carried further; digressions and " philosophical " remarks have entered. From this we may conclude that also other *philosophica*, e.g. the instructive warning in the story of Manahem's prophecy to Herod, *Ant.*, xv, 10⁵, come from the author.

current in isolation, then taken up in works of a literary character in an historical or biographical connection ; but thereby they have frequently undergone some literary editing. In this Form they have come down to us. In the same fashion Jewish material has come into Greek literature. This is proved by Josephus (cf. p. 164, footnote 1) ; the Gospel story of the young man at Nain (Luke, vii, 11–17) also offers an example of this, if the above-mentioned assumption (p. 71) of its use by Luke is correct. Again in the case of the *pericope adulteriæ* (cf p. 75) one may imagine a like development. A certain breadth of the narrative is betrayed in this story by virtue if its paradigmatic content, but this nevertheless in the mixed form of Legend. As its commencement shows,[1] in its present form it is adjusted for a connection. This rouses the suspicion that the text has been otherwise worked up. And the wealth of variants confirms this suspicion, for the difference between the texts rests not solely upon popular variation, but perhaps upon editing.[2] Then here also we would have before us an edited Tale.

This narrative is also distinguished from the New Testament Tales by its lack of miracle content. But the Tale need not always contain a miracle, even when the extraordinary, and thereby the wonderful, is preferably clothed in the broader narrative fashion. Since the Gospel Tales, all and every one of them, relate miracles, we must here also still take into consideration as analogy the conventional method of relating miracles.

In the Greek language miracle tales have not only come down to us as edited Tales, but also in the official records of the cultus. The most famous are the healing reports of Asclepius in Epidauros ; but there must also be taken into

---

[1] John, vii, 53 καὶ ἐπόρευθεν ἕκαστος εἰς τὸν οἶκον αὐτοῦ.

[2] The addition in John viii, 8, in the text of U is a literary editor's work, intended to give a practical application to Jesus' writing in the sand, an act really indicating pre-occupation and repulse of the interrogators : (ἔγραφεν εἰς τὴν γῆν) ἑνὸς ἑκάστου αὐτῶν τὰς ἁμαρτίας.

account other inscriptions from sancturies, as well as aretologies so far as they are pre-literary.[1]

The therapeutic records of Epidauros are also edited,[2] though not by writers, but officials. As can be seen from the style and the content of the individual records they had quite different material at their disposal—and in order to understand how such wonder-tales arose it is not unimportant to picture the possibilities which came into consideration for these editors.

In Epidauros, as also for the establishment in Lebena [3], it is frequently a question of working up the data to be found on votive-tables and consecrated gifts in the sanctuary. That the content of these texts has not been faithfully preserved, but has been revised in honour of the god and thereby the miracle has in certain circumstances been exaggerated is evidenced from the Epid. Text No. 1.[4] The ancient inscription on the consecrated gift in the text of the Stele said simply that Kleo for five years had a growth in her body and whilst asleep in the temple was delivered therefrom. The text preserved on the Stele relates in addition that Kleo gave birth to a son who cleansed himself at the fountain and ran about with his mother. The legendary motif is recognized in the fact that the child was from birth spiritually and bodily developed.[5] Its incorporation is occasioned here by the explanation of the tumour as pregnancy: the child carried about in the womb for five years must have the qualities of a five-year-old. In another case, No. 10, the report of the

---

[1] e.g. *P. Oxy*, xi, 1382, ed. Weinreich. Still other inscriptions from the second and third centuries A.D. come from Epidauros and must be taken into account here as parallels. Cf. *I.G.*, iv², 126, 127. As also the inscriptions from Lebena, *Reconditi della R. Academia dei Lincei*, 1901, pp. 300 ff.

[2] The latest edition is Herzog's *Die Wunderheilungen von Epidauros. Philologus Suppl.*, xxii, iii, 1931.

[3] Herzog, loc. cit., pp. 51 ff.

[4] The number refers to the enumeration of the miracles upon the four Stele according to Herzog.

[5] In the Protoevangelium of James, chap. xix, the motif is applied to the new-born Jesus. Cf. my monograph, *Jungfrauensohn und Krippenkind. Heidelb. Sitz. Ber.*, 1931–2, No. 4, p. 51.

cure shows the union of a consecrated gift with the motif of a fairy tale.

There was a beaker (cup) preserved in the sanctuary which, on being broken, was restored whole by the god. Certainly our text does not cite the inscription, but casually mentions the dedication. The why and where of the miracle is, however, fully and charmingly related in a short story, how the boy who broke the beaker sought in vain to match the pieces together again, and how by the word of a chance stranger he was directed to the helpful god—" for even Asclepius of Epidauros could not mend the beaker." In this case also probably the content of a shorter votive inscription is bound up with a current Tale.

In a series of cases it is clear that the miracle is not necessarily bound up with the Epidaurian cultus. That a sick woman borne upon a stretcher was cured by an unknown wanderer who just by virtue of his powerful presence is recognized as a god (the Greek has " parousia ") could have been otherwise told. Then the editors would have added that the sick woman came from Epidauros and according to the direction of the god must pay according to Epidauros. That such editorial work is present is evidenced from the artificial insertion of the technical value of the incubation-dream in the description of the meeting : " It seemed as if at Cornos there appeared to her and her companions an impressive-looking man." This fiction of a dream is immediately relinquished in the course of the relation of the story. The story of a treasure which finally, after a puzzling oracle, is found where at a given time the shadow of a stone lion falls (No. 46), is proved by the parallels as a legend which was originally independent of Epidauros. Again the story No. 47 is only connected with Epidauros through the mention of the name of the god. Herzog [1] has amplified it by conjectures as follows : that the fisherman (Fischtraeger) who did not permit the god to have part in the result of his trade (calling), as he had promised, is

[1] Loc. cit., pp. 26 ff.

then himself attacked by the fishes. It is quite possible that here we have an emphasis upon the ancient *ius talionis* : in the manner in which we have sinned, so are we punished. For that very reason we have to recognize in the story a Legend, vividly related, which was only afterwards connected with the Epidaurian god.

These examples are only intended to show that the miracle story takes a considerable place among the healing narratives received by us. As in the cases just dealt with, stories are recorded which were not originally bound up with the cult of Epidauros. Or, the healing stories already to hand have been elaborated and adorned by including Tale motifs. This was the case in the first miracle we analysed. No. 2 is to be judged after the same fashion : a woman, after receiving the conception prayed for in the sanctuary, is then, however, supposed to have been with child for three years because she had forgotten to pray to the god for the birth. Only after renewed incubation does she finally give birth to a girl. Here we have obviously an account of guaranteed conception, with the known motif of a desire which was voluntary but badly understood.

But these examples indicate that the records of Epidauros do not rest solely upon the art of the Tale. There are a large number of stories on these stele which tell of actual therapy. These cures and surgical operations are represented as dream-processes in which the god takes part. But there can be no doubt that actual occurrences are reported here, even if sometimes in an exaggerating and crude fashion : e.g. therapeutic measures which were used by the priests in the sanctuary during the time of incubation.

And now it is characteristic of the tradition connected with the place that these healing stories are related for the most part according to a fixed stylistic scheme, whereas the style of those Tale-like records is for the most part in the form of a lively story, but, as is conceivable, lacks uniformity. The following is the stylistic scheme of the therapeutic

Tales : first the illness is described ; then there follows, in expressions varying very little, the description of the incubation and the appearance of the god [1] ; after the operation or the cure the success is demonstrated, and this again in a phraseology which is frequently used.[2] In the more detailed accounts this scheme is filled out. At the commencement the illness of the patient or even his unbelief is described. The middle part of the record may be taken up with the special difficulties of the operation. The conclusion confirms occasionally not only the success, but the actuality of the operation, inasmuch as it allows the person healed to take note of what has occurred when he awakes.[3] These variations only witness to the fact that the underlying form is fixed.

The rise of this, the simplest form, is not conceivable without some historical foundation. As a matter of fact, healing in Epidauros took place not only by consultation, [4] but also by the aid of surgical operation or therapeutic measures. What actually occurred has often been exaggerated into the fabulous in the reports—it is not to be regarded as medical so much as divine assistance—and, as already shown, this has been exaggerated by the interpolation of material proper to Tales.[5] But the basis of this type of healing report—in contradistinction from the type first discussed—is the handing down of something which mirrors what actually happened. For

---

[1] The most usual formulæ are : ἐγκαθεύδων (ἐγκαθεύδουσα) ἐνύπνιον (or ὄψιν) εἶδε· ἐδόκει.   Or, again, frequently ἐνεκάθευδε (or καθύπνωσε) καὶ (or ὡς δ'ἐνεκάθευδε) ἐνύπνιον (or ὄψιν) εἶδε (ὁρῆι)· ἐδόκει.   Finally we find also ἐγκαθεύδοντι (or ἐγκοιμαζομένῳ and also ἐγκοιτασθέντος δ'αὐτοῦ) ὄψις ἐφάνη or similarly.

[2] The commonest endings are : ἁμέρας δὲ γενομένας (or γενηθείσας) ὑγιὴς ἐξῆλθε (or ἐξῆρπε) and καὶ ἐκ τούτου ὑγιὴς ἐγένετο (or ἐξῆλθε) ; again, we find also ὑγιὴς (ἀσκηθὴς) ἀπῆλθε or ἐξῆλθε.

[3] On awakening the patient either holds in his hand the foreign body which has been removed by the operation (Nos. 12, 13, 14, 30), or he finds blood on the floor (No. 27) or some broken piece on his clothing (No. 41).

[4] A good example is given in I.G., iv², 126, where Apellas feels the first improvement in nine days, but remains in the temple until he is free from all inconvenience. The conclusion runs : χάριν εἰδῶς καὶ ὑγιὴς γενόμενος ἀπηλλάγην.

[5] The record No. 13 is very instructive for such extensions. It is here narrated, in the brief schematic style, how leeches were removed by operation from a man's breast. It says : "He had swallowed them because he was deceived by his stepmother ; he had drunk a mixture into which they had been put."

the rest we should give the same favourable judgment to the not very numerous accounts which report cures without incubation, but within the sacred area of the sanctuary, on the ground of supernatural therapeutic or related psychical influences.[1]

From this analysis of the Epidaurian healing records we get traditional material which enables us to perceive a certain analogy to the Gospel tradition. In the Epidaurian texts we have an older tradition of numerous healing processes, of course often in conjunction with the inscriptions concerning dedicatory gifts, but always in the uniform formulation preferred by the official editors. At the same time, there is incorporated into this collection a group of healing stories containing matter which is known to come from miracle Tales and which has been brought into connection with the Epidaurian Asclepius. Here again an historical cause is not to be excluded, but it is often overgrown by already existing motifs of popular Tales, and many a Tale may have been attributed to the god of Epidauros which has no historical basis. The entire collection serves a uniform purpose : the pilgrims who read them in Epidauros are to be strengthened in their faith in the healing power of the god, and to be confirmed in their hope of healing. The original records of cures, found in reports of cases cured through holy (consecrated) gifts and tablets, certainly arose from the desire to thank the god and to exhalt his name ; the Tales (found on the stele) were originally dictated by pleasure in miracles. But in our texts all these records and materials are taken up and shaped in style in order to serve the work of the sanctuary by fortifying those seeking to be cured.

Thus we are here dealing with a tradition of varied origin composed of single accounts which have been edited for the purposes of a cultus. On the one hand the records mirror

---

[1] A dumb boy regains his speech when the temple servant asks for the expression of thanks for healing (τὰ ἴατρα) ; a dumb girl when she is frightened by a snake (5, 44). A lame man, whose stick had been stolen, was able to pursue the thief; a blind man, who had lost his flask of ointment, suddenly saw it (16, 55).

processes from the work of the cultus, and that in a style
which has been laid down. On the other hand the records
have come into being by the inflowing of Tale-like materials,
of entire Tales or single traits, i.e. under the influence of
traditional material of alien origin. The foreign quality of
certain of the records does not mean that the fundamental
soundness of the others is to be questioned. The two groups
originally were executed differently. In the one case the
" Sitz im Leben " is to honour the god who heals ; in the
other, the satisfaction of a curiosity which may perhaps have
been merely a " pious " search for miracles, or perhaps only
a need for entertainment. These groups were brought together and edited about the fourth century B.C. for the purpose
of the cult of Asclepius. Their final orientation is thus closely
related to their execution, which in the one group has to
be regarded as the original.

Within a certain compass we have an analogy here to the
building of the Gospel tradition. In the Gospels also it is
possible to distinguish between the basic tradition of the
Paradigms and the less basic tradition of the Tales, which
contain either alien materials or at least strange motifs, i.e.
originating in the sphere of Tales. Here again the editors
have brought together varying matter and put it under a
single viewpoint. And here again this final orientation is
related to that which had to be accepted for the Paradigms
as original " Sitz im Leben ".

In how far the analogy between the Epidauros reports
and the Gospel stories is only a limited one, need not be
established here. Naturally the building up of the tradition
attached to the person of a wandering leader of a band of
disciples, a leader who laboured in public by word and deed,
would obey other laws than the tradition bound up with a
sanctuary in which apparently the god, but in actual fact his
servants, undertakes cures in secret upon the patient either
asleep or in a state of trance. It can be understood that the
stronger cultistic and local connection is more pronounced in

the stylization of the Epidauros-Texts : the " firm " phrases of the therapeutic records are much more stereotyped than the corresponding sentences of the Paradigms. The relationship of the tale-like narratives here and there, however, rests far more upon the trait of the miracle-tale than upon the peculiarities of these very two traditions. But all these limitations are at bottom understandable. The Epidauros-Texts were not examined here in order artificially to connect things far removed from each other, but rather to illuminate the one traditional process from the other.

(iii) Patristic Apothegms

Alongside the Jewish and the Greek writings yet another group of traditions is worthy of consideration, viz. that belonging to the early Church, written in Greek, but apparently by men of the Coptic language. The immediate objection, that early Christian texts ought not to be used in reference to the use of the primitive Christian tradition because the later traditions might be dependent upon the earlier, carries little weight, for biblical influence can only occasionally be detected in the texts in question.

The subject-matter is the Apophthegmata Patrum, the fifteen hundred to two thousand fragments of tradition of the sayings and experiences of the anchorites in the desert round about Scete, preserved for us in several collections arranged according to different standpoints.[1]   Wilhelm Bousset, whose last labours were given to this tradition, not only brought out the literary inter-relationships of the surviving collections, but also reconstructed their early history. The " fathers "

---

[1] The greatest service in illuminating this tradition, as well as the first beginning of a comparison with the gospel tradition has been rendered by Wilhelm Bousset *Apophthegmata*, Tübingen, 1923. The Greek text of the *Apophth. Patrum* (reprint of Migne, *Patrologia græca*, 65, 71–440), ed. Cotelerius, and the Latin text of the *Verba Seniorum*, or *De Vitis Patrum*, v, vi (Migne, *Patr. latina*, 73, 851–1066) are the oldest and most important collections.

who are the originators of the logia and the heroes of the anecdotes, belong to a relatively brief period : the latter half of the fourth and the first half of the fifth Christian centuries. The earliest of the surviving great collections, the Greek apophthegmata, Migne *græc*. 65, p. 71 ff., appears to have arisen between A.D. 460 and 500.[1] Its forerunners were small collections. The Abbot Poimenus (died c. A.D. 450). and his school appear to have taken a large share in building this first tradition.

In none of the other analogies examined here is the process of tradition marked out with such brevity or so readily grasped, and it is this very process which offers the most essential similarities to the history of the tradition of the gospel-material. The collecting of the logia and anecdotes took place during a period of about one hundred years, and was completed apart from literature proper. Even the large collections are throughout pre-literary ; there are no biographies but only materials consisting of independent passages. Finally the entire tradition of the logia crossed the boundaries of a language, for those Fathers, strange to Hellenistic culture, spoke Coptic, whereas the collections are Greek. These three peculiarities of the process of the tradition place it alongside the process of tradition which created the Gospels, for in the latter, as in the former case, independent fragments were collected soon after their rise, fixated in an unliterary manner, and indeed, in another language.

Of course, we must take notice of essential differences. Like that of the Rabbis, the Patres-tradition had to do with a multitude of " heroes " ; tradition dealing with a single man, a fact which gives the Gospels their stamp, is not present. Moreover, the " Sitz im Leben ", the practical reference of the tradition, scarcely offers any comparison. The Apophthegmata serve in the first place the problem of maintaining the devotions of the great anchorites, and then they are meant to put forth

---

[1] Bousset, *Apophth.*, pp. 66–8.

teachings to which the monks should conform.[1] Obviously
then the purpose of the great collections lies in this direction ;
they are books intended to be read aloud, books whose
reading would bring the ideal of the hermit-life before the
hearers.   Nothing is said about preaching, especially of
missionary preaching, but at best the glorification of the
monastic life and the promotion of its following.

If we now turn our attention from the process of handing
down to the content of the tradition, once more numerous
parallels appear to the material set down in the Gospels. Here
also the tradition consists of logia and anecdotes ; but again
many of the anecdotes have no other purpose than a logion
although they nevertheless give the occasion in detail. The
real tradition of logia is independent of context, very often
without any occasion, often also told as an answer to a question
or a request, and hence a certain fixedness of the introductory
phrases is unmistakable.[2] The anecdotes also are introduced
and, sometimes, continued according to pattern.[3] There are
short, longer, and very long stories, but individual types are
hard to differentiate. Many of the longer narratives seem to
rest upon the connecting up of several anecdotes. Thus
Bisarion is depicted in a fortnight's prayer with his hands
stretched towards heaven, then his journey with the Abbot
Dulas is described, during which he miraculously provides
a drink of water for the thirsty Dulas. They come upon a
completely silent hermit and, on their return journey, mean-

---

[1] The difference of interests is well illustrated by the different arrangement of
the great collections, for the Greek *Apophth. Patr.* give the passages each time
according to their " heroes " and the arrangement of these " heroes ", even of the
Scetic fathers, is alphabetical. The collection of the Latin *Verba Seniorum* is entirely
dependent upon the Greek, but mostly follows an arrangement according to subject :
de quiete, de compunctione, etc.

[2] The logia containing no question are introduced by εἶπεν (ἔλεγεν) ὁ ἀββᾶς
or εἶπε (ἔλεγεν) πάλιν. If there is a question, it is ἠρώτησεν, ἐρωτῶντός ποτε
or ἠρωτήθη . . . καὶ ἀποκριθεὶς εἶπεν.

[3] The intransitive of παραβάλλειν in the meaning of " come to someone " often
serves as for the introduction ; though often one finds " It used to be said about
Abbot so and so " (ἔλεγον or διηγήσατο περί). Often a visitor says εἶπε μοι
ῥῆμα ; the effect of the word or work of the hermit is often given by κατενύγη
ἔβαλε μετάνοιαν αὐτῷ.

while having visited Abbot John, they find him dead in his cave, and when they bury him they discover that it is a woman (*Apophth.*, Bisarion 4). But even what is recorded in shorter passages is manifold. Clever or significant answers are very frequent, as well as proofs of self-humiliation or of refusing all reward ; in this way the special quality of the hermits of Scete becomes quite obvious. On the other hand, there are stories which apply to the monks of Scete what has plainly been recorded elsewhere. Thus Bisarion makes Dulas drink fresh water out of the sea (*Apophth.*, Bisarion 1)—a miracle that was already told of Serapis.[1] A dead man was asked by Makarius about the place where he had deposited treasure (*Apophth.*, Makarius 7)—the same thing occurs also in the Rabbinic tradition.[2] Various cures are narrated, including even raising from the dead.[3] But there is also the motif, so foreign to the Gospel-material, of miraculous self-help, for when Ammonas has lost his way and prays about it a hand is stretched out from heaven showing the road.[4]

Thus we have here as in the texts from Epidauros indigenous and foreign materials side by side in the same tradition. It is indubitable that these traditions are very close in time and place to the matters of which they tell and hence that perhaps in conventional form, but in all essentials faithfully, they have preserved much of both the words and the deeds. Nevertheless passages are to be found in between which are either current stories, as already shown, or else contain current motifs [5] ; or, on the other hand, show by their nature that they have nothing to do with historical happenings.

---

[1] Aelius Aristides, *In Serapim*, 29. [2] Bab. Berakhoth, 18*b*.
[3] *Apophth.* Gelasius, 3, Sesoes 18. In the second case the miracle takes place without the knowledge of the miracle-worker, for he thinks the dead man is alive and says to him ἀνάστα, ἔξελθε ἔξω.
[4] *Apophth.* Ammonas, 7. According to the Bab. Taanith, 29*a*, a hand is stretched forth out of heaven and takes the key of the Temple before its first destruction.
[5] *Apophth.* Bisarion, 2, tells how the Abbot led by prayer crosses a river and in doing so sinks into the water only as far as his ankles. Much better than the story of the sinking Peter who had not to cross the water, an analogy is offered by the well-known Buddhist narrative of the lay-brother who, impelled by joyful thoughts of the Buddha, walks over the river Aciravati (Introduction to Jataka, 190, German

What often appears enigmatic to-day to an observer of the synoptic tradition, viz. *the existence side by side of an indigenous tradition with its proper character, and foreign materials, or materials deranged by foreign motifs*, finds something corresponding to it in the Apophthegmata. We had to demonstrate something similar in the case of the Epidaurian texts. But here the part played by the official editor in shaping the text was not small whereas in the apothegms the editor seems to have been concerned with the various groupings of the material, but not to have systematically worked over the records themselves, for the Greek clothing in the language of the texts seems older than the collections of apophthegmata. Moreover in yet another reference is this monkish tradition nearer to that of the synoptics than are the Epidaurian records, for the apothegms of the Fathers, unlike the former, narrate not only striking and miraculous happenings, but also they contain—and this for the greater part—sayings and simple, non-miraculous events. Of course, there also comes to light here the difference between the monkish stories and the Paradigms of the Gospels for whereas all the latter are adapted for the sermon the former are intended simply to conserve the memory of their " hero ", and hence their style is necessarily different—less urgent, less conscious of purpose. There is a similarity between the apothegms and the rabbinic texts in another reference in so far as the former also occasionally name the bearers of the tradition.[1]

Similar things are to be found at bottom in every popular process of tradition. It is the merit of Karl Ludwig Schmidt [2]

translation in Aufhauser, *Buddha und Jesus*, Kl. Texte, 157, p. 12), cf. *supra*, p. 116. Admittedly the motif of fear is lacking during the miracle in Bisarion's case, and that this is characteristic for both the story of Peter and that of the Indian. But both Bisarion and the Indian lay-brother were questioned after the miracle by another—Bisarion by his disciple and the Indian by the master himself—and both assert they had walked as if on firm ground, although Bisarion only felt this στερεόν when the water reached to his ankles.

[1] There is quite a chain, e.g. in Poimen, 144. Abbot Joseph reports that Abbot Isaac said : "I once sat beside Abbot Poimen and saw how he entered into ecstasy," etc.

[2] Die Stellung der Evangelien in der allgemeinen Literaturgeschichten, *Eucharisterion für Gunkel*, ii, 50 ff.

to have applied to Gospel research this viewpoint which is in essence self-apparent, and he has at least indicated the similarity by a number of examples from various times and countries. Beside the *Apophthegmata Patrum* he mentions the *Littérature orale de la Haute Bretagne* (Paul Sebillot), the German *Volksbuch vom Doktor Faust*, the popular Christian saints' lives, the Franciscus-tradition, Goethe's record of the feast of St. Rochus at Bingen and the legends of the great Maggid of the Chassidim. Here in fact we find a multitude of standpoints from which we can study the law and modelling of such traditions, and this would hold good even if perhaps not all the mentioned complexes of tradition have truly unliterary formulations as their foundation. But in this sphere we are not likely to reach more than a general comparison of the history of tradition, for the differences of content and the remoteness of periods and cultures are too great and as a consequence the formulation is subjected to laws which have been variously drawn up. Hence it may suffice to hint at this broad, indeed boundless, region.

Chapter VII

THE PASSION STORY

In the earliest period there was no connected narrative of the life, or at least of the work of Jesus, i.e. a narrative comparable to a literary biography or the legendary life of a saint. The stories contained in the synoptic Gospels, whose essential categories I have attempted to describe, were at first handed down in isolation as independent stories. Folk tradition as contained in the Gospels could pass on Paradigms, Tales, and Legends, but not a comprehensive description of Jesus' work.

We have already mentioned an exception in the Passion story (cf. pp. 22 f. *supra*). Its relative self-sufficiency strikes everyone who reads the old description of the Passion which has come down to us. It contains only one narrative passage which can be immediately separated out—the story of the anointing of Jesus in Bethany (Mark xiv, 3–9)—which stands out from the framework of the Passion story as an isolated narrative. It was probably first introduced artificially into the story because the action of the woman was given a reference to the burial of Jesus and thereby a second point was put alongside the first. But in any case it breaks up a closed connection, and for this reason cannot be claimed, as we shall show, for the earliest form of the Passion story. But a case where a self-sufficient narrative stands out in this way from the Passion story could not be repeated. The record of the Passion of Jesus runs, as it seems at first glance, in a closed sequence from the Sanhedrin's plan for the death of Jesus to the empty grave.

In no respect is that remarkable. For what we know of the Christian message make us expect a description of the whole Passion in the course of a sermon, at least in outline. Every formulation of the message as preached mentions the facts of the Passion and the Easter story. They contained the decisive soteriological event, whose understanding gave a basis for Christian faith from the divine, not the human, standpoint. The man who understood this shocking event, the execution of Jesus, on the basis of the Easter faith, as a victory, was a Christian. But he who understood the Passion in this way saw in the resurrection of Jesus the first act of the final resurrection of the dead. Thus the Passion story was also the beginning of the eschatological process. We can understand that the interests of preachers as of believers was given in greater degree to the Passion than to any other event in the life of Jesus.

It is understandable and also obvious. The Passion story is narrated by all four evangelists with a striking agreement never attained elsewhere. Even John, who deals freely enough with the facts reported by tradition, binds himself to this tradition in the highest degree when describing the Passion. There is so much that he illuminates and clears up, but he, like the others, records the Last Supper, the arrest on the Mount of Olives, the trials before the High Priests and the Procurator, the denial of Peter, the crucifixion, and the discovery of the empty grave. He follows the *via dolorosa* like all the evangelists before him. Since for him, not the death and the resurrection, but the " going to the Father ", was the decisive event in salvation, a correct reproduction of the Passion story was really not to be expected. But since he nevertheless makes the report, and does so in relative agreement with the others, obviously the firmness and domination of the tradition determines him. The force of the events is so great that little room remains for an independent interpretation of the happenings.

Thus the Passion story is the only piece of Gospel tradition which in early times gave events in their larger connection. We may suppose that even this description contained passages which were at first current isolated in the Church. There was e.g. a tradition of the Last Supper which was comprehensible apart from connection with any other narrative passages, and which had an independent introduction. We know this bit of tradition from 1 Cor. xi, 23 ff.: " The Lord Jesus, in the night when he was betrayed, took bread, and when he had given thanks, He said . . ." Similarly a few other parts of the Passion story, e.g. the denial of Peter, may have once existed separately. But they occur in our Passion story no longer as separate passages like that of the Anointing ; they have already been woven in. And that is exactly what differentiates the Passion story from the Gospel tradition as a whole, i.e. its early composition as a connected narrative. It was introduced by a passage which, through and through founded upon the context, never had a separate existence, for it does not bear the marks of a story fettered to a certain situation, but shows itself as a summary binding together of events presupposed for the understanding of the Passion story and deducible from the later course of the happenings. If we exclude the story of the Anointing because it was only artificially put into this context (cf. pp. 178 ff. *supra*), Mark xiv, 1 f., 10 f., reads :—" Now after two days was the feast of the Passover, and the unleavened bread ; and the chief priests sought how they might take him with subtlety and kill him : for they said, Not during the feast lest haply there shall be a tumult of the people. And Judas Iscariot, he that was one of the twelve, went away unto the chief priests, that he might deliver him unto them. And they, when they heard it, were glad, and promised to give him money. And he sought how he might conveniently deliver him unto them."

We do not learn how and when that happened for both situation and dialogue are lacking. The only thing recorded was what could be deduced from what happened later from the purpose of the Sanhedrin and the readiness of Judas to betray.

This introduction leads to the entire Passion, and would

be in place only at the beginning of a connected description. But this description must be earlier than Mark's gospel since it contradicts his chronology. It sets for the decisive motive of the secret arrest of Jesus the nearness of the feast, which would only make sense if Jesus had come into the power of His opponents before the feast. Hence, according to this record, the arrest took place before the Passover evening. But in Mark's opinion Jesus and also the Jews celebrated the Passover that evening. Thus Mark cannot have been the author of this introduction and, therefore, also not the originator of the connected narrative. The composition of the Passion story is earlier than Mark.

Thus the earliest Passion story must have had another conclusion than that now found in Mark, for the reference to the appearance of the Risen Lord in Mark xiv, 28, seems strange. The Gospel does not tell of such an appearance, but only refers to it again in Mark xvi, 7, " You will see him there as he told you." To a certain extent the Easter happenings in Galilee are thereby put outside the book. They are known, but the story of Jesus ends with the record of the empty grave if Mark ends with xvi, 8. But, as seen from xiv, 28, it was not this ending that the author was preparing for.[1] Thus the very content of the record gives evidence of an older account.

We cannot determine its exact range. We can only say at once what certainly was not contained in this record— by its contradictions to the tendencies of the points which marked the older account. The Anointing is one of the matters which was not original to the Passion story, since it interrupts the flow of the introduction xiv, 1, 2, 10, 11. So also the story of the empty grave must have been lacking, because xiv, 28, requires a different ending. Moreover the introduction to

---

[1] If our judgment of the Fayoum Fragments is correct as put forward on pp. 160 f. *supra*, this is therefore to be regarded as a Chria-like abbreviated reproduction of a bit of tradition, and it appears in no way surprising that Mark xiv, 28, does not correspond with the Fragment, for Mark xiv, 28, is only in place in a connected description.

the Last Supper, xiv, 12–16, was not present in our account which made the Passion take place before the Feast. On the other hand, the story of the Last Supper is to be differentiated from this Legend (cf. p. 121 *supra*) by the fact that it makes no mention of the meal as being a Passover. Thus we have every reason to regard one form or another of the story of the Last Supper as old and as a part of the earliest Passion story. We might delete from the early account such other scenes or parts of scenes as possess artificial links in the narrative. That is the case with the scene in Gethsemane, for the second and third prayers of Jesus are only referred to. The threefoldness had to be mentioned, but nothing was known of three prayers. In the same way the trial of Jesus before the Sanhedrin has become obscured in the present text by the passage from the accusation of profaning the Temple to the proof of the Messianic claim " but even so their witness did not agree " (Mark xiv, 59). In both these cases the early record contained only *one* utterance of Jesus, His prayer in Gethsemane much like Mark xiv, 34 f, and His word *re* the Temple. But perhaps the scenes were altogether lacking, in which case the notice in Mark xv, 1, would be the only mention of the Sanhedrin.

Finally, in this connection, we must take notice of the fact that *eyewitnesses* of the Passion story appear to be mentioned. We observe that in Mark xiv, 51, and xv, 21, two quite insignificant persons are introduced into the narrative, the unnamed young man who flees leaving his garment in the hands of the bailiffs, and Simon of Cyrene who carries the cross of Jesus and who is described as the " father of Alexander and Rufus ". In both cases the persons are characterized by features of minor significance The unnamed young man plays a part which is comic rather than dignified, and the report does not very well fit in with the style of the Passion story. Simon of Cyrene, however, is of importance in the Passion as one who helped to carry the cross. We are not told in what temper he took his part, but we are told the names of his sons! But what at first seems strange is explicable if we suppose that the readers knew both the unnamed young man and the sons of Simon. In this case these remarks would draw the readers' attention to the actual eyewitness of the events. Elsewhere Mark introduces no such references. They seem alien because elsewhere Mark's record lacks every personal moment. The evangelist put forward the story of salvation, not individual happenings. It follows that these two references are older than the Gospel. The two parallel writers, Matthew and Luke, support this view since they say nothing of the unnamed young man nor of the sons of Simon. Hence we must ascribe these references, and also the events which they were intended to prove, to the older record. In fact it would not be far-fetched to look for such links between the events and the church, links made in the old record whose readers still stood close to the generation of the eyewitnesses. There are very important data which were based upon the testimony of those present at the time, viz. the arrest of Jesus and His execution. And this interest would give significance to what was secondary at least to those who still remembered the persons mentioned.

Nevertheless we may still doubt whether the denial of Peter is told according to the report of an eye-witness. No express reference of this sort is given in the text, although the denial may have been found in the earliest record. For it is highly probable that an appearance of the Risen Lord to Peter in Galilee, which we must assume as the end of the early record, stood in relation to the denial of the Master by the disciple, such as that Peter was taken back after his fall and received a special forgiveness for a special guilt. It so, then the earliest record (Mark xiv, 29–31) would belong to Mark xiv, 28. But if the denial was prophesied it had to be narrated.

If in some such way the probability is established of a pre-Marcan record of the Passion story, and if its content is at least to some extent made clear, we may inquire into the meaning and purpose of such a connected narrative. If a Christian undertook to tell the Passion of Jesus as a whole, and if he undertook it at a time when only isolated stories of the life of Jesus were told, there could have been only one object for such an undertaking, viz. to describe that meaning of the events which was founded on the Easter faith. What happened in Jerusalem at that time must have been so offensive and ignominious that a record of these things could only seem a document of shame and disgrace.   Only if one were convinced not only that Christ lived with the Father, but also that the disgrace of the arrest and the torture of the crucifixion had taken place in accordance with God's will—only then could the record be made with any meaning. That here God's will had been done, all who knew the Risen Lord guessed and, indeed, knew.   It was proved for them by the Old Testament. Indeed, the earliest surviving message, that of Paul in I Cor. xv, 3 ff., speaks of Jesus' death " for our sins according to the scriptures ", and of the resurrection " on the third day, according to the scriptures ".   It is often emphasized in the primitive Christian witnesses that " this stands written of Him ", but definite quotations from the Old Testament are not adduced in this connection (cf. Luke xviii, 31 ; Mark xiv, 21, 49 ; Luke xxiv, 26 f., 44 ff.). Perhaps an old custom is continued here.   It is probable that scriptural proof was at first only a postulate, a postulate rooted in the Easter faith.   But this faith guaranteed the assurance that the very Passion of Jesus was in accordance with God's will, and God's will was to be found in the scriptures. Thus the witness of the scriptures may have been spoken of before it could really be adduced.   Then in certain Old Testament passages, e.g. Psalms xxii, xxxi, lxix; Isaiah liii, the Passion of Jesus was found depicted in advance. These passages were read again and again as the evangel of the Passion. From this there grew, of a certainty still before the use of Mark's gospel, a conception of the *via dolorosa* and of the hour of suffering. Connected records must accord with these conceptions, and thus these motives which had been at home in the Old Testament came into the text of the Passion. This took place, without citing the Old Testament words, simply in the form of narrative. This was enough for an informed man, for he would feel the agreement between record and scripture, and would see God's will announced in the latter and worked out in the former. We may assume that even the earliest record told events from the Passion which only had significance because they were known to be announced by scripture. Then everything shameful and dishonouring done to Jesus—arrest, mishandling, dividing of garments, contemptuous treatment, was legitimatized in the Passion story, for it happened according to God's will.

Hence these Old Testament relations with the Passion story did not arise from exegetical zeal, but from an understanding of the story of salvation. The Passion had its home, not in teaching and uplifting the individual, but in carrying the message to the church, i.e. in the sermon. The point was to show that a paradoxical event, without human sense, represented the beginning of the Last Day, and was thus a part of the fulfilment of salvation. The Christ had to suffer such things (Luke xxiv, 26).

If we would understand the meaning of the basis in the Old Testament, we must put aside the modern error—that the earliest narrator evaluated things much as our present-day consciousness does, and meant to describe stirring and heroic events, or to illumine a historical happening. The earliest Passion story was neither stirring nor heroic. It contained no word speaking of the human greatness of Jesus in suffering, none intended to appeal to the human feelings of the reader. We can express this view with complete confidence because Mark's Passion story itself shows the same character. If we read, say, the story of the arrest or the trial before Pilate without reading any construction into the text, we shall be astonished at the bareness of the description and the absence of any traits that show the feelings of those who took part and that work upon the feelings of the readers.

Nor is the attention of the narrator directed to the historical process. The very section which, because it fixes the date of the death, we might with all probability ascribe to the earliest record—I mean the description of the plot and of the arrest (Mark xiv, 1 f., 10 f.)—is indicative of this point. For not the least attempt is made here to bring the events into historical connection, or to indicate, at least, the motives of the Sanhedrin and the traitor. Matthew was the first to tell of a gathering of the opponents and a dialogue between the chief priests and Judas. What is in Mark, and what we derive from the earliest record, is a short notice of the events which could be deduced from the further course of the Passion—and nothing else. It was known that the Sanhedrin had got Jesus into their power before the feast by a *tour de force* and that the arresting party had made use of Judas, a disciple of Jesus in the undertaking. Thus they must have decided upon the former and agreed upon the latter; and there is nothing else in those four verses (Mark xiv, 1 f., 10 f.). They describe no situation and depict no process, but only offer what could be deduced.

Hence the first concern of the earliest record is not to confirm the story, but to make clear what in the Passion took place by God's will. This purpose was served by finding in the Old Testament the motivation which of course penetrated the early narrative and was an essential element in Mark's. But we must differentiate here between quite different applications of the Old Testament. Reference may be made to scripture without adducing any particular citation (Mark xiv, 21, 49). Or we may have an express citation (cf. Mark xiv, 27, " I will smite the shepherd "), or a complete citation without the introductory formula of citation, e.g. the last utterance of Jesus (Mark xv, 34). Further, we must mention the passages where the application of significant words from Old Testament passages gives the man who is aware of the facts the right connection even though "scripture" has not been mentioned at all. Thus the dividing of Jesus' garments is told after Psalm xxii, 18; the offering of the vinegar to the dying Jesus follows Psalm lxix, 21. When the crucified Jesus is derided, the passers-by wag their heads—the narrative obviously linking up with Psalm xxii, 7—and when He is mis-handled after the trial, the spitting and beating with rods probably links up with Isaiah l, 6. Further we hear of the robbers in order to fulfil Isaiah liii, 12, "he was reckoned among the evil-doers". And must the scoffs of the robbers (Mark xv, 32) be referred back to the Passion Psalm which speaks of the scoffs of those "who scoff at thee" (Psalm lxix, 9)? If we read the Psalms which have supplied most material for the Passion story, i.e. Psalms xxii, xxxi, lxix, we are struck in all three by the mention of the cry (xxii, 24; xxxi, 22; lxix, 3). Just as it is obvious that Jesus' dying has been modelled on these passages, so the clauses of the surrounding description may have been important for the scene in Gethsemane. Finally, we may ask also whether the description of the traitor as one present at the supper ("who eats with me", Mark xiv, 18) may be in some way related to Psalm xli, 9 ("who eats my bread").

Whereas those first four Old Testament references—parting the garments, drink, scoffing, mishandling—may be clearly recognized by the wording, the last-mentioned cannot be demonstrated with certainty. But the possibility of a connection with the Old Testament cannot be denied at once, if one remembers that proof passages about suffering were from the beginning read in connection with the Passion story. The best proof of this is the fact that in the other Gospels the Old Testament colouring increases in a significant way,[1]

---

[1] Matth. xxvii, 3 f., makes a record about a meeting and a decision out of an introductory notice about the purpose of the Sanhedrin τότε συνήχθησαν οἱ ἀρχιερεῖς καὶ οἱ πρεσβύτεροι . . . καὶ συνεβουλεύσαντο . . . This obviously comes from Ps. xxxi, 13: ἐν τῷ συναχθῆναι ἅμα ἐπ᾽ ἐμὲ τοῦ λαβεῖν τὴν ψυχήν μου ἐβουλεύσαντο. The scoff of the passers-by already described by Mark according to Ps. xxii, is recorded by Luke xxiii, 35 with the words: εἱστήκει ὁ λαὸς θεωρῶν. ἐξεμυκτήριζον δὲ οἱ ἄρχοντες which are doubtless modelled on Ps. xxii, 7: πάντες οἱ θεωροῦντές με ἐξεμυκτήρισάν ἐμε.

and, indeed, without express quotation. In the Passion story it was not meditative quotations that were needed, such as Matthew introduced in depicting the life of Jesus, but a description of the story of salvation. The Old Testament passages on suffering were read as normative sources for the Passion story.

At this stage of our considerations we can no longer put off the question whether these descriptions coloured by the Old Testament must not be declared unhistorical *in toto*. Doubtless in a few places the Passion has been enriched from the Old Testament, i.e. the biblical passages have begotten history. This view holds good, e.g. when Matthew says the price of the betrayal was thirty pieces of silver. The information was not given in, but read out of, the scripture. It comes from the same passage (Zechariah xi, 12 f.) which had provided material for the Judas-legend (Matthew xxvii, 9). But it would be wrong to apply this conclusion to all the data which are described as fulfilments of the Old Testament. Some of them with great probability are to be regarded as authentic on general historical grounds. The soldiers, indeed, had a right to the garments of the criminal, as can be proved from the Digests (cf. *Digesta* xlviii, 20[6]). The scorning is probable in itself, and the mishandling is at least credible. But all this is narrated, whether it was known, deduced, or sought for, simply because God's will was seen in it as revealed in scripture. Certainly much more could have been told of the process of the crucifixion, either on the basis of tradition from Simon of Cyrene, or on that of acquaintance with the usual procedure of an execution. But in spite of this, if the record was not made more ornate it was because it was limited to facts understood to be soteriological because they were in the Old Testament.

In this connection we must regard it as significant that none of the Synoptics tells of nailing the hands, although the classic Passion-Psalm (xxii, 16) speaks of piercing the hands and the feet. Since only the Easter narratives of Luke and

John hint at it (Luke xxiv, 39; John xx, 25, 27) we may still ask whether the silence of the crucifixion records, in spite of the possibility of an Old Testament basis, does not suggest that the earliest narrators conceived the event otherwise and assumed that the body was made fast by binding. That, again, would show that at first one was very shy about inventing details of the Passion story which, however supported by biblical citation, would be contrary to what one believed one knew of the happenings. Hence we cannot always, nor at once, reach a verdict about the historicity of a motif by showing it had an Old Testament basis.

If these fundamental observations of Old Testament motivation hold good both of the Marcan record as well as of the demonstrably earlier records, we must raise the question of the meaning of the Marcan Passion story. A considerable part of the material was, as we have shown, ready to hand. To show in what sense he shaped the tradition we must analyse the passages in which any case of difference between Mark and the earliest record would have to be proved. As far as I see, three sections come into account for this purpose.

1. Mark has prefixed to the Last Supper the introductory Legend (xiv, 12–16) whereby the supper was changed into a Passover (cf. p. 182 *supra*). But this change has no such literary cause as would be due to the writer's intention. Rather it was conditioned by the cultus. Here is expressed the interest of churches which celebrate the Supper as a continuation of the Jewish Passover. This need not be only in Palestine or Syria. It is conceivable that elsewhere the ritual which was used by Christian Churches, derives from the Jewish Diaspora, and thus the special element was gained in this way. By accepting this Legend, Mark admitted this understanding of the Supper and, of course, at the same time brought into being the incongruity between the legendary introduction and the record (xiv, 22–5). Luke, however, put aside this incongruity.

2. Mark replaced the narrative of an appearance of the

Risen Lord to Peter by the Legend of the empty grave, for
this seems to me to be the conclusion of Mark's gospel.
I am assuming that the earliest Passion story contained one
or more appearances of the Risen Lord to Peter and the
disciples.   Such a narrative may be deduced from the old
record in Mark xiv, 28.   From I Cor. xv, 5, we know that it
existed at an earlier date.   We perceive a trace of its existence
in the reference in Luke xxiv. 34.   We can derive some conception of it from John xxi and the Gospel of Peter.   I assume
further that Mark xvi, 8, is the conclusion of Mark and, therefore, that the text as contained in the old MSS., Codices
Vaticanus and Sinaiticus, as well as the Sinaitic Syriac, is
complete.   In this case the concluding words would have, not
a psychological, but a literary significance : " The women
said nothing to anyone, for they were afraid," means that
the narrative of the empty grave was still unknown in wide
areas.   We grant that by this conclusion Mark did not create
the story of the empty grave.   This is a Legend with a life of
its own whose purpose was to demonstrate the resurrection
by the fact of the empty grave.   The fact that the women
are mentioned at the beginning, superfluously after xv, 47,
seems to prove that it was originally independent of this
connection.   There is a genuine legendary note in the story :
concern about the stone ; miraculous help in the fact that it
is already rolled away ; a divine interpretation of the whole
given by the angels ; and the flight of the fearful women.
Thus this conclusion belongs to the old Legend.[1]   But the
command in xvi, 7, does not belong to it, for here the
evangelist appears to have joined the Legend of the grave
with the traditions already at hand in the church.

Obviously various traditions of the appearances of Jesus
were current in the Church, either due to the Easter faith,

---

[1] The assurance that at first (before the death of the miracle-worker) a specially
secret miracle was not spoken of is found also after raisings of the dead in
Apophth. Patr., Sisoes 18, Gelasius 3. Here the silence seems to be desired on personal
grounds, but there is always the purpose of explaining why such a miracle did not
become generally known.

or even bringing it into being. Not only did the disciples receive appearances, and not only in Galilee did this phenomenon take place. James, the brother of the risen Lord, also became a witness of the resurrection as Christians knew in Paul's time (I Cor. xv, 5). Beside the Legend of the grave, the story of Emmaus is the only Easter Legend in the New Testament which has been preserved in an almost pure form,[1] and since it deals with two adherents of Jesus the variation of the scenes of the action is found in the early tradition. Thus the appearance to Peter was not the only event normative for the Easter faith, the faith that Jesus lived with the Father and would come again was reported in a similar way in the legend of the Emmaus road. A central Easter phenomenon, therefore, had to give expression to the fact which, according to Jewish pre-suppositions was to be accepted without question, that the body of Jesus had not remained in the grave. Even Paul did not found his Easter preaching upon this fact, because the message handed down to him said nothing of it. But it is comprehensible, still upon the basis of the same Jewish pre-suppositions, that a legend of the empty grave would be developed if there were narratives of appearances of the risen Lord even on Jewish soil. And only at this stage is it really comprehensible that this narrative—central because dealing with the empty grave itself and because handing on the assumption of other appearances—ran the course of the older traditions. Thus Mark accepted this Legend of the grave in place of the appearance to Peter. Its conclusion really depicted the effect of the angelic message upon weak human beings and, at the same time, explained why nothing had hitherto been known about the empty grave. This conclusion now became the conclusion of the Gospel. But at the same time Mark points to the appearances: he makes the angels repeat the promise of xiv, 28, and add: " there you will see

[1] It is quite understandable that this Legend also when taken up into a Gospel should be conjoined with the rest of the traditional material. This was done by the verses Luke xxiv, 21*b* (or 22) to 24. The old Legend of Emmaus was naturally intended to record not only a first appearance, but also a first message.

him." [1] This reference leads beyond the scope of the Gospel to the whole sphere of the primitive Christian experience of the risen Lord.

Hence the grave-legend is no invention of Mark's and thus it is no part of our consideration to bring out the meaning of Mark's Passion story. Here, as often, Mark is one who hands down, not one who moulds.

3. The third section in which we may have the right to suppose the evangelist intervened is the scene before the Sanhedrin, for here the phrase " but even so their witness did not agree " (xiv, 59) shows at least an incongruity. An accusation is brought forward and supported but it is not effective, because a second reason must be mentioned. Thus we have in front of us not a unified narrative, but an interfusion of motives. It is hard to say what was in the earliest report (cf. pp. 182 f. *supra*), but easy to say what motive the evangelist Mark wished to bring out. It is the motive which is decisive in his narrative : the confession of Jesus as the Messiah. We must not put the historical question in advance whether the trial took place at all, or whether and in what sense Jesus at that moment described Himself as the Son of Man who was to ascend and come again immediately. Christians could scarcely have possessed real information about such a discussion. The traditional news, perhaps passed on by Alexander and Rufus (Mark xv, 21) that Jesus was condemned as a royal pretender, was the historical point of departure. But what Mark means to describe in xiv, 61–3, is that a supernatural majesty flamed in the midst of all the shame of Jesus, and while the criminal was dying His heavenly future was

---

[1] That the verse, Mark xvi, 7, has been interpolated can be deduced from the context for xvi, 8, follows on xvi, 6. That the women " fled from the sepulchre ; for they trembled and were amazed " is not the consequence of comforting words promising an explanation as in xvi, 7, but of a puzzling event as narrated in xvi, 6. Moreover, it is impossible for the old Legend to have ended with the disobedience of the women to the heavenly command without letting such disobedience be punished. The matter would be different if the heavenly command in xvi, 7, had never been given, for then xvi, 8, would deal not with opposition but only with human fear.

announced to the world. This is the first high point of Mark's Passion story, and quite clearly it is made known as such by means of everything which, as part of the hostility of the world, stood in the sharpest contrast to this announcement : viz. the sentence of the Sanhedrin which the narrator could at once assume ; the mishandling which was deduced from Isaiah l, 6 ; and Peter's threefold denial which probably was already found in the material handed down from the earlier report (cf. pp. 183 f. *supra*).

The death scene constitutes the second high-point. First we must speak here of the last word of Jesus. The narrator regarded it as of special significance, as can be seen from the misconception of the hearers who, out of Elohi or Eli, " my God," make a naming of the prophet Elijah. We are reminded of the well-known misunderstandings of the Fourth Gospel, which always serve to increase the quality and the meaning of the preceding utterance, for its right understanding is closed to mankind. But then we must completely exclude the possibility discussed ever anew, that in the last cry " My God, my God, why hast thou forsaken me ? " a final doubt, indeed collapse, of Jesus is expressed. In this view one assumes a chronicler who, concerned only with history, faithfully hands on to the next age also what is painful and, to Christendom, intolerable. There never was such a chronicler, for the whole Passion story was written for the edification and not the bewilderment of Christians. A narrator who brings out the last utterance of Jesus in this way—by means of misunderstanding— did not understand this utterance as one of self-renunciation. Similarly, the very literary character of the Passion story excludes such an interpretation. For that utterance of Jesus is the beginning of Psalm xxii, a Psalm which opened up to Christians the true understanding of the Passion in a quite essential way, and whose words were quoted, a few verses before the cry, to express the scoffing of the passers-by (Mark xv, 29 ; Psalm xxii, 7). One who repeated this cry of a Jew praying in deepest stress did not express an utterly unholy striving against God. A Bible word on the lips of a dying man means a religious reverence for the Bible, and, in any case, union with God. Either it was known from actual hearers that Jesus used this word from the Psalm as a prayer before His death, or else it was desired to carry out the fulfilment of the Psalm up to the last moment, and hence it was put on the lips of Jesus. But in no case did this cry express a doubting sense of abandonment, for to quote from the Bible is always a proof of faith.

But that even among the earliest Christians offence was taken at this last utterance of Jesus was a sign that the symbolical meaning of Biblical quotation was no longer understood. Luke replaced the last cry by a milder word from the other Psalm of suffering, xxxi, 5; the Gospel of Peter corrected it into " My power, my power, why hast thou abandoned me ? "; the MS. D read the Marcan text as " Why hast thou put me to shame ? " But these are misunderstandings arising from an attitude which no longer sets value upon a biblical word as such.

Drinking the vinegar follows upon the last cry of Jesus, once more a " fulfilment " corresponding in this case to Psalm lxix, 21,[1] and then the last cry is mentioned. One who read the Psalms of suffering found that all three psalms mentioned that last cry (cf. p. 187 *supra*). But the phenomenon accompanying the death of Jesus, the rending of the Temple veil, can no more be interpreted according to Matthew than the scoffing when Jesus was mishandled (cf. p. 193 *supra*). In Matthew the veil of the Temple signified one cosmic event among others, the earthquake, the opening of the graves, and the rising of the dead—and it is to be understood

---

[1] Nor must we fall into the mistake here of interpreting like Matthew and put the phrase ἄφετε ἴδωμεν εἰ ἔρχεται Ἠλίας into the mouth of the scoffers (like Syr.^sin) in order to give it the meaning of refusing the vinegar. " Let be, we would see whether Elias will come." For ἄφετε is comparable with our " wait " and is added to the first person of the imperative (cf. Moulton, *Prolegomena*, p. 175 f.) The one who is acting wishes to lengthen the life of the criminal by means of the vinegar even though according to Ps. lxix, 21, this drink is a torment and not a refreshment.

accordingly. In Mark the veil is recorded as a single " sign " and would have to be interpreted from its own self were not another event narrated alongside it which, rightly understood, was also intended as a " sign ", and from which also the meaning of the Temple phenomenon is to be derived. I refer to the confession of the centurion. He recognizes in Jesus the Son of God (not, shall we say a son of the gods) —and that is a miracle since it lies outside historical and human " possibility ". No one saw that better than Luke, who ascribes to the centurion only the knowledge which was in fact accessible to human power, for he says " this was truly a righteous man ". Here only the psychological miracle is intended, known in numerous martyrologies, viz. the executioner convinced by the martyr. Mark is dealing with a greater miracle, the conversion of an unbeliever by the dying Saviour. It is not the word or the virtue of a man which is operative, but the saving power of Christ's death as a whole.[1] Thus the record of this conversion is not an edifying legend with which the death of Jesus was adorned, but the last proof of the supernatural sending of Jesus to earth, and thus a " sign ". The first Gentile was converted and in his word the Gentiles give their answer to the death of Jesus.

But then the rending of the Temple veil is a parallel, for this is the answer of Judaism. While the Jews only scoff at the dying Jesus, the ancient holy place of the Jews bears witness that something decisive has happened. Thereby the material may have been afforded to the evangelist by the Jewish tradition [2] that forty years before the destruction of the Temple its doors were miraculously opened, really to suggest perhaps the impending departure of the Numen.[3]

---

[1] οὕτως therefore does not refer to a single event as D. interprets οὕτως αὐτὸν κράξοντα, but to everything which happened there (cf. Luke τὸ γενόμενον).

[2] *Pal. Joma* 43c *Bab Joma* 39b, Jos. *Wars* vi, 53; cf. also Tacitus *History*, vi, 3.

[3] If Mark is a witness of this tradition his Gospel can scarcely be dated before A.D. 70, for the tradition of the ominous signs in the Temple could surely have spread abroad only after it had been proved by the catastrophe. So also the Legend of the graves seems to me to indicate a time when no demonstration on the spot was any longer possible, for otherwise something of the sort would have been hinted at.

In this way Mark gave light and shade to the death of Jesus, in that Judaism and Paganism acknowledge the significance of the hour.

Thus in the two high points, the trial and the crucifixion, Mark clearly and obviously gave expression to the soteriological understanding of the Passion, and he concluded this record of God-willed happenings with the message of the angel " He is risen ".

Since we are here dealing with the meaning which the narrator derived from the Passion story, we must examine the Passion record of the other Gospels, although the total quality of these books is not now in debate.

As in other cases, Matthew deleted details and in this way rationalized the Legend of finding the Upper Room (Matthew xxvi, 17–19). He made many things clearer or developed them more highly, and thereby, on occasions, departed from the meaning of the Marcan text,[1] and then the clearer text-form of Matthew often tempts the interpreter to understand Mark's record according to Matthew's model. Finally Matthew increased the Passion material by introducing details copied from the Old Testament, e.g. the thirty pieces of silver, the gall in the drink, the detailed formulation of the scoffs of the passers-by (Matthew xxvi, 15 ; xxvii, 34, 43). He increased the material also by taking up Legends or legendary extensions of the narrative, such as the description of the traitor and his death, Pilate washing his hands, and the sentries at the grave and their expressions (xxvi, 25 ; xxvii, 3–10, 24, 25, 62–6 ; xxviii, 11–15). Such traditions were obviously present in the church already.   Even if

---

[1] Simple clarifications are : xxvi, 3, 57, the naming of Caiaphas ; xxvi, 27, " all ye drink of it " in direct speech ; xxvi, 49. χαῖρε in Judas' greeting ; and so on. Changes of sense as compared with Mark are : xxvi, 68, the scoffing cry προφήτευσον understood as that Jesus blindfolded was to guess his tormentors (since this same meaning is found in Luke xxii, 64, it does not originate in the evangelist but was current in the church); xxvii, 29, the κάλαμος is in the first place a sign of majesty and only then becomes a means of torture ; xxvii, 49, the cry ἄφες ἴδωμεν was meant to prevent giving vinegar to drink ; xxvii, 54, the exclamation of the centurion is referred to the earthquake.

Matthew could not take up all of them, yet he indicated the place where these traditions belonged. We have already shown (cf. p. 117 *supra*) that the short notice about Pilate's wife (xxvii, 19) is to be understood in this way. But Matthew xxvii, 51–3, only touched upon the miracle after the death of Jesus, whence the cloudiness in the dating, viz. already on Good Friday the dead are awakened in their miraculously opened graves, but they only come into the Holy City and appear to many after the Resurrection of Jesus. In the same way the Easter record of xxviii, 2–4, is content with hints : an angel rolls away the stone from Jesus' grave and sits upon it, but it is not said that Jesus proceeds from the grave.

But all these are changes which at bottom show nothing more than that tradition lived a wider life as is seen in its growth or diminution. We cannot derive a special and new understanding of Matthew's Passion story from these features. But it does seem to me that another group of variations bears witness to such an understanding, I mean a *Christological understanding*. It is very clear in one small detail, when it is said of Joseph of Arimathæa in Matthew xxvii, 57, that " he also was a disciple of Jesus ", whereas Mark xv, 43, says that he also awaited the Kingdom of God, that the text from Matthew corresponds to the Christian connection with the person of its Master. The same understanding is appropriate if the disciples do not simply " take offence " but " take offence in me " on the betrayal night (Matthew xxvi, 31, 33, 38, 40). There is also Christological significance in the fact that Matthew xxvii, 17, 20–2, puts Barabbas and Jesus very emphatically in antithesis.

But Matthew's Passion story, and only his, is distinguished by moments of the highest Christological significance which show Jesus even in suffering as the plenipotentiary Son of God who is master of His own fate. " My time is near " is the wording of the message to the owner of the room (xxvi, 18 f.) ; with the words " Friend, do that for which thou hast come " (xxvi, 50), Jesus Himself gives the signal

for His arrest.   He makes the disciple with the sword hold his
hand by reminding him that He Himself is in authority over
all the hosts of angels, but that the scriptures must be fulfilled
(xxvi, 52–4).   The saying against the Temple in the trial
scene, given by Mark as the prophecy of a new temple " which
is not made with hands ", is in Matthew an expression of Jesus'
authority to dispose : " I *can* break down the temple of God
and re-build it in three days " (xxvi, 61).   Nothing more is
said about the incongruity of the witness (Mark xiv, 59).
The chief priests do not put the question about the Messiah,
as in Mark, as a preliminary to a further point, but in order
to draw the consequences from such a claim of Jesus.[1]
And Jesus answers the solemn adjuration not with a prophecy
about the Son of man (Matthew xiv, 62) but with the
announcement : " From henceforth you shall see the Son of
man sitting at the right hand of power " (Matthew xxvi, 64) ;
the Lord of the Church will *now* sit at the right hand of God
and work in the world.   Finally, his presentation cannot
end with the mere announcement of Galilean appearances.
The Risen Lord must reveal Himself as the One to whom all
power is given, who wins all people for Himself, and who
is with His own until the end of the world (xxviii, 16–20).
In this way Matthew's Passion story becomes a Christological
revelation.

It scarcely needs to be said that Matthew, remaining
altogether within the framework of tradition, presented the
Passion from a standpoint of which the fourth evangelist,
with a freer formulation of tradition, afterwards gave a
dominating expression.

John presented in his own way the initiative taken by Jesus
at His arrest.   His status as a King at the trial, and the victory
that lies in going to the Father.   That is his individual achieve-
ment, but we can see from Matthew that the presupposition

---

[1] Mark xiv, 61, πάλιν ὁ ἀρχιερεὺς ἐπηρώτα αὐτόν—Matthew xxvi, 63, κα
ἀποκριθεὶς ὁ ἀρχιερεὺς εἶπεν αὐτῷ, although ἀποκριθείς is lacking in many
Egyptian MSS.).

of this presentation was already at hand in the Church. The
Christological illumination of the whole is, of course, in
Matthew, the work of this one author (whereas many another
variation in the same Gospel derives from the Church and
is only set down by Matthew); but the editing undoubtedly
corresponds to the Christology of the Church, which not
only recognized God's will in the Passion, but could also
worship the glory of Jesus Christ.

The execution of the Passion story is quite different in
Luke. To be clear as to the meaning of his conception is
a particularly urgent duty of the exegete. Luke works more
independently than the other two synoptists, and thus we
must expect that he would bring his understanding of the
material to quite clear expression. But a knowledge of his
conception as a whole is the presupposition for the exegesis
of certain questions of detail.

Of course, Luke, like Matthew, is a witness to the further
development of the Passion and Easter stories in the Church.
The messengers who prepare the room are named in Luke xxii,
8; the influence of the Old Testament is broader; in
Luke xxiii, 35, the scoffing follows Psalm xxii, 7 (cf. p. 187,
note 1, *supra*); and the scene before Herod, quite unessential
to the process of the trial, is interpolated because the friend-
ship between Pilate and Herod (Luke xxiii, 12) was read into
Psalm ii, 1 f. Above all, in the Easter story (Luke xxiv, 6),
interest turns from the Galilaean to the Judaean appearances.
Thereby room is given not only for the constitution of the
Church in Jerusalem (Luke xxiv, 49), but especially for the
Easter legend of Emmaus which, as in no other Easter story,
presents the solution of the riddle of the Cross. It also deals
with an event outside the circle of the disciples which therefore was not taken up elsewhere in the canonical text.

We owe these changes rather to the growth of tradition in
the Church than to the special style of Luke. Everything
which serves the purpose of *historization* holds good as the
work of the evangelist in the Passion story as elsewhere,

i.e. the presentation of a graphic and comprehensible historical connection, with which Luke concerned himself also in describing Jesus' work. By this effort Luke overcame the incongruities of the dating with the general notice Luke xxii, 1 and 7), which speak of the "approach" and the "presence" of the Passover. Moreover, in xxii, 15–18, he has clearly interwoven the Last Supper into a Passover meal, and we must show later in what way this has affected the history of the Eucharistic text. Further Luke paid some attention to the technical proceedings at the betrayal and at the trial: the arrest takes place "far from the multitude" (xxii, 6), and thus a traitor was necessary who knew Jesus' customary lodging for the night (xxi, 37; xxii, 39); the Sanhedrin can only assemble in the morning (xxii, 66) and the mishandling of Jesus during the night is not the fault of the rulers, but the servants (xxii, 63–5); a genuine accusation is formulated before Pilate (xxiii, 2); the darkness at the hour of Jesus' death is "explained" as an eclipse, and the rending of the Temple veil as a sign which precedes the death (xxiii, 45).

Finally, Luke remained true to his custom in this place also by bringing sayings, handed down to him without introduction, into a connection which appears to be due to their sound. In this manner Luke invented the speeches at table during the last Supper; the word to Simon (xxii, 31 f.) is the clearest example. True, it speaks of the danger of Satanic temptation for him and for all. By implication, however, it promises not backsliding but that his "faithfulness" shall continue, and finally, indeed, perhaps a *vaticinium ex eventu* that he shall have a leading place among the disciples. In Luke this word serves as an introduction to the prophecy of the denial. We do not know whether it belongs to the Passion at all. In tradition, it in no case belongs to the prophecy of the denial as the change of name from Simon to Peter (xxii, 31–4) clearly shows. An eschatological saying referring to the impending struggles and advising the purchase of a sword is interwoven into a dialogue, and prepares for the blow of the sword at the arrest (xxii, 35–8). Similarly the sayings about service and waiting at table have been introduced into this description of the meal (xxii, 24–30), but the parallels show that it had nothing to do with it originally.

But even yet the characteristic quality of the Lucan Passion has not yet been described, for it is still not clear from what standpoint the evangelist understood Jesus' Passion and explained it to his readers. This standpoint can be detected : for Luke, the suffering Saviour is the Man of God who is attacked by evil powers and who, with His patience and forgiveness is a model of innocent suffering. Luke regards these events in the place where he consequently puts them not as the completion of salvation, but as the story of a saintly man closely united with God. The literary consequence of this view is that Luke presents the Passion as a martyrdom. There were Jewish martyrdoms, as is proved by the literary record of them in the Martyrdom of Isaiah, and in II and IV Maccabees. Since these were read among the Christians the evangelist could expect that if he presented Jesus as a martyr he would be understood by Christian readers.

The presentation of Judas' betrayal (xxii, 3) is significant. Satan, who at one time, " until an opportune moment " (iv, 13), had left Jesus alone now uses the person of Judas to make a decisive attack. It corresponds with this that Jesus at His arrest does not speak of the hour which God has sent nor, as in Matthew xxvi, 18, of " my time "; rather He says : " this is *your* hour and the power of darkness " (Luke xxii, 53). Gethsemane in Luke no longer means that the Son bows in secret to the counsels of the Father and with only His most trusted disciples near. This special secrecy about the event is not retained nor is the threefold prayer. Now, in the foreground, there stands the appearance of the angel in answer to Jesus' prayer, together with a description of the wrestling in prayer (xxii, 43 f.).[1] Both these are typical experiences

---

[1] Indeed, the textual tradition of xxii, 43 f., is divided in such a way (A.B. f. Syr^sin, ital. omit the verses) that we cannot at once deny the possible correctness of the view that the verses are an interpolation. But what remains after their deletion is quite

of a martyr. In consequence of Jesus' warning against such pretence the Judas-kiss is never given at the arrest, but the sword blow is here dealt with in detail, although in Mark it is a subsidiary matter. It is introduced by a saying about the two swords which was later so much debated (xxii, 48). This saying combines the eschatological proverb about buying swords with the Passion, and says nothing more than that two weapons are at hand. The blow with the sword is emphasized by the cry of the disciples : " Shall we smite with the sword ? " (xxii, 49). But the use of the sword is not denied in such a way as would place the whole matter in the scheme of salvation, like Matthew xxvi, 52 : " He who uses the sword shall be destroyed by the sword." Jesus' denial here is an isolated matter, and it is in accordance with the framework of the Legend that Jesus heals the wounded ear (Luke xxii, 51). In the same way the soteriological presentation expressly omitted angelic help (Matthew xxvi, 53) ; but the legendary form makes use of a strengthening angel. So also the trial in the High Priest's palace is not the main thing, but rather the unique event of the denial most impressively concluded by the glance of the Lord upon the fallen disciple (xxii, 61). The trial scene itself is stripped of its solemnity, as also of the promise of the Parousia. It serves only juristically to confirm the claim to be the Messiah, which claim is necessary for the accusation before Pilate (xxiii, 2).

Everything that follows, however, is interwoven with proofs very characteristic of the category of a martyrdom, viz. that the martyr was able by his attitude to convert opponents and the unprejudiced ; Pilate asserts three times that he found no guilt in Jesus (xxiii, 4, 14, 22) ; the women, who as onlookers take no part, are informed by Jesus that all this affects themselves and that their own fate is to be

trite for it has then neither the soteriological air of the scene as in Mark or Matthew, nor the legendary air of the full Lucan text. The evangelist Luke could not have written in this way.

deplored [1]; the martyr prays for the executioners,[2] and promises to the penitent thief who confessed Him that he would share His own blessed martyr lot.[3] He dies with an expression of reliance upon God on His lips,[4] and in this way convinces the centurion by His patience. The change over to something which is unique is here particularly clear. It is not paganism which now speaks, as in Mark, and confesses the Son of God; rather a single person speaks who expresses something very much less, viz. the conviction of Jesus' innocence which is all that can be reached at this moment by human criteria: "this was a righteous man." But the multitude which in the soteriological presentation (Matthew xxvii, 25) defiantly takes the responsibility upon itself and thus brings the curse upon the Jewish people, here strikes its breast and goes home, frightened by the martyr's blameless suffering.

All this rests upon a unified conception and therefore cannot be traced back to a source but to the only "author" among the Synoptics. It is, however, clear that Luke in this presentation departs from the line which the other Gospels follow and, because of the "literary" needs of the "historian", endeavours to give a human and psychological presentation. Many mediæval Legends followed him in this respect. But the Church's understanding of the Passion-story remained at first soteriologically orientated. That holds good also of the early non-canonical writings as far as we know

---

[1] A traditional logion is certainly made use of in xxiii, 27–31, for at least the conclusion—about the green wood and the dry—points to an entirely different situation.

[2] As in xxii, 43 f., here also there is the difficulty—that part of the tradition (B D*, W. Θ Syrˢ sa bo) omits the prayer for the enemies, but probably the omission is to be explained in both cases by the influence of the parallels. In quite another wording, in Acts vii, 60, the prayer is indicative of a martyr; such a far-reaching interpolation of such a content would, however, be unexampled in the Gospel-text.

[3] This special reward of the martyr is the subject matter of the promise in Luke xxiii, 43—and not a doctrine of immortality foreign to Judaism. Cf. Sifre to Deut. xxxii, 4, § 307, where the philosopher who is told of the fate of the martyr Chananja b. Teradjon and his family says: "To-morrow I shall have my part with them in the future world." Cf. G. F. Moore, *Judaism*, ii, 391.

[4] A citation from another Psalm of suffering, Ps. xxxi, 5, has taken the place in Luke xxiii, 46, of the one from Ps. xxii, 1, as in the old tradition (cf. p. 194 *supra*).

them. In the Gospel of Peter, in the Passion story which the fourth evangelist employs,[1] also in the conceptions of the Passion story to which Justin bears witness—everywhere the Passion is presented as a fulfilment of the Old Testament, the accomplishment of the Divine will, and as the completion of salvation. Thus, in spite of all extensions and intermingling of other kinds of interests which may be demonstrated in them, these later records have preserved the original concerns of the ancient narrative.

Our present examination has hitherto not dealt fundamentally with the question which stands in the foreground of the usual view of the Passion story, viz. the problem of its *historicity*. This question can, in fact, only be dealt with when the meaning of the record has been made clear. Only when we have seen from what standpoint the narrator intended to speak, can we ask what it meant to report on the basis of tradition.

We have already shown that the Passion story itself points to eyewitnesses of the Crucifixion (Mark xiv, 51 ; xv, 21), viz. the unnamed youth at the arrest, Simon of Cyrene for the Crucifixion (cf. p. 182 *supra*). Nevertheless both happenings are represented as fulfilling the Old Testament. At the Crucifixion, that becomes clear in the smallest details which are narrated with Old Testament references which can still be traced. Its historicity is, of course, not to be contested throughout on this account, but neither can it be proved (cf. p. 188 *supra*). At the arrest the Old Testament reference is only expressed in the concluding word of Jesus " but the Scripture must be fulfilled " (Mark xiv, 49). For the rest, we have here a short, cool record in which, for example, the attempted opposition with the sword is only

---

[1] That John uses a record not identical with one of the synoptic records is best seen in these non-synoptic motifs of which the evangelist makes no use in the meaning of his theology, viz. the date of the death, the prophecy of the traitor, the denial of Peter, the condemnation on the Sabbath, the lots about the garment, omission of the crucifragium, which appear to me to offer the most important mark of such a tradition.

reported, not set aside nor made good again by a miracle. Hence this record may be traced back to those eyewitnesses and thereby the historicity of the *betrayal* and the traitor is assured. A disciple of Jesus was required in order to reach without sensation the place in which Jesus was accustomed to lodge by night. Luke worked out this connection particularly, but only by means of small incidental remarks. Thus he probably is following not a special source, but his own reflections. As a matter of fact the old introduction to the Passion (Mark xiv, 2, 10 f.) had already presented the situation in such a manner that the necessity of a secret arrest by the help of a confidential person from Jesus' circle was in sight. If the surprise were to take place quickly and without remark a traitor was necessary also in order to show Jesus in the darkness of night to the bailiffs to whom the Galilæan "prophet" was perhaps quite unknown by sight. Hence the greeting "Rabbi" and the kiss. Since both stand together, perhaps the kiss should not be regarded as a special wickedness, but simply as the customary greeting of the teacher by a disciple.[1] In any case only the co-operation of the disciple made the arrest successful.

Whereas the probability and the historical importance of a tradition of eyewitnesses shine through here, in other sections of the Passion story the question of a tradition is loaded with difficulties. This holds good above all in the institution of the *Last Supper*. As Paul bears witness in 1 Cor. xi, 23–5, there was widespread in the Church an independent tradition complete with an independent introduction about the words of institution. Since at the distribution of the bread and wine these words ordered repetition, we may suppose that this form of the words was pronounced in celebrating the Eucharist. Granted that that does not seem to have been customary in the Corinthian Church up to the

---

[1] As a rule kisses are recorded by the Rabbis, we must admit, as signs of the recognition of the pupil by the teacher—as especially in the famous scene in Chagiga 14*b*. Further examples in Strack-Billerbeck i, 995.

time of Paul's letter, it probably was so amongst the Greek-speaking Christians of Syria (Antioch, Damascus) to whom Paul had adhered when he became a Christian.[1]

It is obvious that the form of the word of institution also in Mark is determined by the tradition wihch was bound up with the rite. The text of Mark xiv, 22–5, avoids not only the historization which would bring the Passover character of the meal to expression according to xiv, 12–16, but also every soteriological interpretation which would prove a special understanding of the happenings within the borders of the Passion story. The section has an introduction also, which makes it appear as relatively independent.[2] Thus we may characterize its content just as in the text cited by Paul as an ætiological tradition of the rite. Similarly the sentence which stands in the middle " and they all drank of it " (the cup) in Mark xiv, 23, is not simply narrative, but indicates, as a parallel to " and he gave it to them ", what was the essential thing in the proceeding, viz. that all drink of one cup, just as they have all received from one loaf.

The true texts, Paul and Mark, are not far removed from each other in content ; they can both be conceived as derived from the same Aramaic original form. When the Pauline text adds " for you " to " this is my body ", we have an explanation which expresses the idea that this body was sacrificed for them. Mark, again, has a similar word about the blood : " poured out for many ". Both interpretations, therefore, contain the idea of sacrifice. In both cases we may ask whether the words were not first introduced into the Greek tradition, for each writer has them in a different place. The rite deals with a communion—you are one in eating and drinking of

---

[1] Thereby for the sake of this correspondence I understand παρέλαβον—παρέδωκα, like 1 Cor. xv, 3, as an indication of this tradition from the circle of the Lord (ἀπὸ τοῦ κυρίου), and thus without reference to a revelation (so Lietzmann, *Messe und Herrenmahl* 255).

[2] Mark xiv, 22, καὶ ἐσθιόντων αὐτῶν does not fit correctly into Mark's context which had already said (xiv, 18) καὶ ἀνακειμένων αὐτῶν καὶ ἐσθιόντων. Hence the words are probably an old introduction of the material handed down in the cultus.

the same loaf and cup—and the utterance, at least that in connection with the bread, adds the reference to Jesus— you are *My* body, hence one in Me. But then those interpretations concerning the sacrifice seem to obscure the sense, for the disciples are the body of Jesus, but not His sacrificed body. But the man who caused the addition in Mark xiv, 24, seems to me to have encumbered the whole formulation of the word used in dispensing the cup, and I would regard this as later than the Pauline form. A Jewish Christian Church with its dread of blood would scarcely have made Jesus say " this is my blood " (in the cup), but rather " this cup means a new covenant which is instituted by my blood, i.e. by my death ".[1] This conception stands formally as far as possible from the word used in dispensing the bread and appears to me, therefore, to deserve preference. It is naturally orientated on Jeremiah xxxi, 31, whereas the Marcan conception gives the antithesis to Exodus xxiv, 8, " this is the blood of the covenant poured out by me," in opposition to the blood of the covenant which Moses sprinkled upon the people.

The chief difference between the Pauline and Marcan recensions lies in the verse Mark xiv, 25, where Jesus promises that He will not drink wine again until the day when He will drink it new in the kingdom of God. The usual critical theory clearly finds here a completely different conception which is not compatible with the preceding words of institution. Rather it originates in a lost record which, it is believed, can in any case be reconstructed out of Luke. But the question is nevertheless whether Mark xiv, 25, cannot be understood in connection with the preceding words of institution, as seems to me, in fact, to be the case. If the action of the Last Supper without any explanation obviously represents the founding of a fellowship, and the word about the bread just as obviously traces this fellowship to a union with Christ

---

[1] Cf. also Macgregor, *Eucharistic Origins*, pp. 64 ff., who emphasizes this idea, although as a critique of the authenticity of the words as such.

—not only *a* body, but *My* body—then xiv, 25, offers the
explanation of the founding and of the word. The founding
of this table-fellowship in the invisible union with the Person
of Jesus is necessary, because the visible union which had
hitherto existed is ceasing. Jesus will only preside again over
this table-fellowship when He can do it in the Kingdom of
God. This connection between Mark xiv, 22–4, and xiv,
25, comes out, as it seems to me, without the least forcing
of the text, but it is missing, indeed, if we see in the explanatory
words essentially a prophecy of death, and in the prophecy
essentially a joyful outlook. Neither can be justified for the
breaking of the bread and the dispensing of the cup are
Communion rites, and this significance dominates also the
accompanying words. And in the prophecy the " not again "
of the departure comes just as much to expression as the
" drinking it new " in the promise of the kingdom of God.[1]

My construction of Mark xiv, 25, seems to me to be confirmed also by the observation that Paul expresses the same
thought, for he himself adds to the words of institution the
explanation that the Church, by this eating and drinking,
celebrates or proclaims the death of the Lord " until He
comes ". Obviously, therefore, Paul knows of an eschatological terminus *ad quem* in connection with the Eucharist : when
the fellowship of the Parousia commences this memorial
table-fellowship ends. Perhaps he had in mind a parallel to
Mark xiv, 25, which spoke of the coming of Christ instead
of the coming of the kingdom of God. Perhaps the eschatological conception in the Eucharistic rite known to him was
expressed in some other manner. In any case, we can see from
his words that the content of Mark xiv, 25, belongs to the
words of institution.

With all these observations we reach a certain probability
in regard to the Eucharistic tradition which lies at the basis

---

[1] If Mark xiv, 25, were only a promise the wording would be οὐ μὴ πίωμεν.
In limiting the refusal to Jesus the thought is contained that the disciples will drink
again. The reunion is self-explanatory with the outlook upon the kingdom of God.
Matthew xxvi, 29, brings this out expressly in μεθ' ὑμῶν.

of the traditional passages in Mark xiv as well as in 1 Cor. xi : the utterance accompanying the bread without the interpretation handed down by Paul, the word accompanying the cup in the Pauline form without the Marcan interpretation together with the eschatological saying (Mark xiv, 25) as its basis. But we do not reach final certainty about Jesus' words, because we must reckon with the fact that, from the beginning, the development of the tradition took place amongst what were really the interests of the cultus. Hence, especially, the question cannot be answered whether Jesus spoke anything about the new " covenant " when dispensing the cup.

At present many scholars believe that by the help of the Lucan text they can get further, i.e. to a second tradition. Thereby the short text offered by D and a few old Latin MSS. (Latin Luke xxii, 19b and 20) is given special value. The usual wording of Luke xxii, 15–20, is rejected, because it is regarded as a text expanded from 1 Cor. xi. Both views seem to me to be erroneous. A text offered by such a stately tradition as Luke xxii, 15–20, in the wording of the Egyptian MSS. cannot be so lightly thrust on one side. Moreover, the form of the words of institution (xxii, 19 f.) cannot be understood in any way as an interpolation, but as an evolutionary product of the type which is demonstrated in Mark xiv and 1 Cor. xi. This growth retains and strengthens in a comprehensible manner the elements of value for the cultus : the command to repeat (only in the case of the bread), and the two interpretations applied to the bread and the cup.[1]

---

[1] Amongst the narrative clauses the clause introducing the dispensing of the cup, Luke xxii, 20, offers a wording much as in Paul (ὡσαύτως and μετὰ τὸ δειπνῆσαι. The introduction to dispensing the bread is related to both Mark (λαβὼν ἄρτον . . . καὶ ἔδωκεν αὐτοῖς) and Paul (εὐχαρισήσας ἔκλασεν). The word about the bread has the same form as in Mark, but the explication is not the one found in Paul (τὸ ὑπὲρ ὑμῶν) but an extended form (τὸ ὑπὲρ ὑμῶν διδόμενον). The word about the cup is almost entirely in the Pauline form (although without the command to repeat), but is enriched with an explication (τὸ ὑπὲρ ὑμῶν ἐκχυννόμενον) that at least reminds one of Mark (τὸ ἐκχυννόμενον ὑπὲρ πολλῶν). The words appear formally to belong to ποτήριον, but, following the analogy of the explication of the word about the bread, must be joined to αἷμα. The explication of the word about the cup obviously comes from a text in which αἷμα stood in the nominative. The language of the formulas in Rev. (i, 8, etc.) show that such apparent offences against grammar were tolerable exactly in cult-texts.

The Lucan text of the words of institution, therefore, does not appear to rest in any way upon a literary assimilation to the two variants of Mark xiv and 1 Cor. xi. Rather it is to be understood as a third variant, which in the development of the explanatory words has proceeded further than the other two.

But now the tradition of the words of institution in Luke follows upon the description of a Passover meal, xxii, 15–18, in which Jesus utters an eschatological saying in regard to the Passover lamb as well as the Passover cup, of much the same text as Mark xiv, 25. The origin of this complicated text is no enigma. There is an incongruity in Mark when the Legend of finding the room announces a Passover meal and yet Mark xiv, 22–5, does not describe a Passover meal. Hence Luke placed importance upon describing a Passover meal. With this object he applies a prophecy of suffering (xxii, 15) and a command to divide the cup (xxii, 17). But in both places he adds a corresponding variation of the eschatological pronouncement of Mark xiv, 25. Luke now joins the words of institution to this record, presumably in the form offered to him by his tradition of the cultus. Hence the whole Lucan record presents an attempt to give the words of institution the force of history by putting them in the framework of a Passover meal. This framework and what belongs to it, as well as the dividing of the eschatological words into two sayings, is naturally the work of an evangelist who was pondering such an historization. In this way he made a text containing four actions :

Passover Meal : I. Passover Lamb, xxii, 15, 16.
II. Passover Cup, xxii, 17, 18.
The Lord's Supper : III. The Bread, xxii, 19.
IV. The Communion Cup, xxii, 20.

As it seems to me we can only evaluate the much-discussed and mostly highly-valued form of the text in the MS. D, if we compare it with the other corrections of the text as seen in the textual history. It is then apparent that all these corrections pursue the object of lessening the number of the four actions either by changing the grouping or by deletion. And even the D text means an attempt in this direction,[1] and is, therefore, to be given equal worth with the other corrections. It does not come into account for the reconstruction of an old tradition. We must content ourselves, therefore, with the record of the cultus gained from Mark xiv, and 1 Cor. xi, for it was in this form that the Churches of Syria and Palestine preserved the memory of the Last Supper.

The question of the historicity of the scene in Gethsemane is of quite another form. If we consider this section in the context of the Marcan Passion we must first of all free ourselves from the prejudice which has also obscured the understanding of Jesus' last cry on the cross (cf. p. 194 *supra*)— as if a conscientious chronicler had narrated in this case that even Jesus, in the stress of that moment, had shown a trace of human weakness. The scene as it stands to-day in Mark does not bear witness to a disillusionment—for then it would not have been accepted into the Gospel at all—but to a certain understanding of a revelation. Like the entire Marcan Passion it is orientated not psychologically but soteriologically. Its high point is the antithesis between Jesus' agonized resignation to the will of God (xiv, 36) and the unsuspecting sleep of the disciples who know nothing of " the hour ". That no historical tradition comes to expression here—and indeed, against every Christology—is seen in the fact that every kind of eyewitness is excluded from the essential part of the scene, since the witnesses are asleep. The essential content is

---

[1] Syr[sin] gives the arrangement xxii, 15, 16, 19, 17 (with καὶ μετὰ τὸ δειπνῆσαι from 20), 20 (words of institution in a varied form without " explication "), 18 ; i.e. i is united with iii, and ii with iv, so that only two actions are recorded. Syr[cur], b, e, read : xxii, 15, 16, 19, 17, 18 ; i.e. iii follows upon i, and ii is put in the position of iv. Really only two actions are recorded as i serves for introduction. Marcion (cf. Harnack, *Marcion*, p. 214 f.) certainly deletes 16, probably also 17, 18. Thereby i has become wholly introductory and so united with iii and iv. Syr[vg] deletes 17, 18, whereby the first of the two cups is omitted. The order is i, iii, iv. D. deletes 19*b*, 20 ; whereby the second cup is missing. The order is i, ii, iv.

presented as a mystery to which only the three intimate disciples were admitted, just as in the case of the only Marcan instance of raising the dead, and in that of the Transfiguration. But this comparison shows also the uniqueness of the scene, for the three intimate disciples do not now experience, as formerly, the revelation of Divine glory in Jesus ; indeed, toward the end of the scene the separation of the three disciples from the others is left altogether out of consideration. Hence it is artificial. And the real proceeding, Jesus' going to and fro between the place of prayer and the disciples, is also seen to be invented ; for the second act of prayer (xiv, 39) is not completed with words of prayer, and the third (xiv, 41) is in any case only referred to. We can see in the scene of the denial in what way those three actions were narrated in an edificatory style. Thus I cannot regard the scene either as an historical tradition nor as a Legend current originally in isolation. Luke himself filled it out with a " legendary " content, but waived the threefoldness of the act of prayer (cf. p. 201 *supra*).

Now, however, we are in a position to ask out of what elements the scene was constructed. We may gather from Hebrews v, 7, that independently of the Gethsemane tradition the view existed in the Churches that Jesus in His time of suffering had prayed to God for deliverance with strong crying and tears. This conception probably rested upon the Psalms of suffering which were read as a record of the Passion, and all three of which (Psalm xxii, 24 ; xxxi, 22 ; lxix, 3), speak of cries and in addition to that of extreme stress and of prayer for deliverance (xxii, 20 ; xxxi, 9, 10, 22 ; lxix, 1 f.). A presentation of the Passion must take account of this, and perhaps the oldest record used by Mark did so (cf. p. 187 *supra*), perhaps with a lament of Jesus and with the content of His prayer, and thus, to some extent, with a description of the same content as Mark xiv, 34 f. Mark built this material up into a process. A traditional word of Jesus gave him cause for this, when it exhorted watchfulness and prayer in the last days, i.e. Mark xiv, 38, originally of equal importance to Mark xiii, 35, Luke xii, 37, but differentiated from these parallels by the use made of the conceptions of flesh and spirit. Mark understood this exhortation as a warning about natural sleep and, on this account, he put together the scene of the sleeping disciples. He also put the prayer of Jesus (xiv, 36) into direct speech with an application of the metaphor of the cup of suffering which was probably already common, and with the emphasis upon what was for him the main thing, Jesus' submission to the will of God. The whole grew, if only by suggestion, into an occurrence by extending the prayer into three acts of prayer, and by separating off the three disciples in the way already found in the Gospel tradition (Mark v, 37; ix, 2). In this way the material gathered out of the Old Testament became a revelation of Jesus' obedience in opposition to the inert and dull disciples.

Again, an eyewitness' description of the proceedings when Jesus was interrogated before the High Priest and before Pilate is impossible. In the scene before Pilate (xv, 1-5) Mark clearly indicates that he only knows that the question about being a king had played a part. This was known in the Church, since the reason for the execution was published in the usual manner (Mark xv, 26). But, as we have shown, (cf. pp. 192 f. *supra*) Mark made the trial before the High Priest into the main point of the whole Passion story. We see from xiv, 59, that in doing so he was not writing simply according to his own criteria. Perhaps occasioned by the old record (cf. p. 182 *supra*) Mark brings in a threat of Jesus against the Temple, but does not wish it to be decisive, and so explains that the witness was not sufficiently confirmed. Naturally this does not do away with the genuineness of the utterance, for obviously it deals with a saying which was current in tradition without an occasion, and which was taken up into the Passion story like " watch and pray ", or Luke xxii, 25 ff., 31 f., 36. Hence there was obviously no old tradition, duly confirmed, about the trial before the High Priest.

This point is not unimportant, since lately the question has been raised [1] whether the Roman method of executing Jesus shows that there never was a process before the High Priest. The result of that process must have been stoning. Carrying such a thing out was not forbidden the Jews at that time, as John xviii, 31, and the usual opinion would hold, but was permitted in spite of the Roman rule. We cannot deal with the question here, whose discussion is not yet ended, but we must maintain that the only tradition preserved in the trial scene, the word against the Temple, is not bound up with this situation.

On the other hand, an old tradition appears to be present in the narrative of Peter's denial. It cannot be decided along with the verdict in regard to the trial scene, since, in any case, according to Mark xiv, 1 f., Jesus' arrest was carried out by the Jews, and thus the prisoner had first to be brought into the High Priest's palace. The meaning of the Marcan story is clear: even xiv, 29–31, Peter's declension is put forward as a special example of a general backsliding of the disciples in accordance with scripture, i.e. the will of God. But the scene itself (xiv, 66–72) along with the preceding mishandling of Jesus, constitutes the opposite number to the self-revelation during the trial, although the opposite number is much more ample than the main scene ! As a story the denial is full, and it is logically narrated ; a girl recognized the disciple by the light of the fire ; he denies, and leaves her ; she follows him into the forecourt and draws the attention of the people there to him ; he denies again but by his speech they recognize him as a Galilæan ; and then comes the third act of denial. The cock-crow at this moment is dramatically effective. Indeed, the whole composition must be held quite artistic. It has its own importance, for no element points to a soteriological content such as is suggested

---

[1] Lietzmann, " Der Process Jesu," *Sitzungsber. d. Preuss. Akad.*, 1931, phil.-hist. Kl., 313–322. Also Büchsel, *ZNTW.*, 1931, 202 ff. ; Lietzmann, *ZNTW.*, 1932, 78 ff. ; Burkitt, *JTS.*, 1931, 64 ff.

in xiv, 29–31. We may, therefore, assume that the narrative is not conceived as a soteriological presentation of the Passion, nor even as an element of the oldest report. It was narrated in the Church from the standpoint that it shared in the fate of Peter.

But, it may be asked whether this was only of human and psychological interest, and whether we are here dealing purely with a Personal Legend intended to surround a secondary person in the sacred story with the glamour of miraculous protection by God, or with saintly heroism (cf. p. 105 *supra*), since the narrative lacks this glamour. A legend might tell of a saintly person's fall, but then it would have to tell of his reconversion. The words " then he began to weep " depict the repentance, but not the acceptance of the sinner. The interest of the Church in this event seems to have another basis, and also Mark xiv, 28 (as well as Luke xxii, 32, in the evangelist's intention) points to another context. Peter was the first witness of the resurrection, and only the appearance of the Risen Lord restored him to the right of a disciple, or at least the author of John xxi, 15–19, seems to be of this opinion. The Church's interest in Peter's fall could be explained if the event were felt in some way to be the pre-supposition of the Easter appearances. The oldest record of the Passion story may have borne this construction since it puts the promise of the appearances (Mk. xiv, 28) alongside the prophecy of the denial (Mk. xiv, 29–31) (cf. pp. 181 f. *supra*).

Then the question could be answered as to how this event ever came to be narrated among the Christians, for then no doubt could exist against the assumption that Peter himself had reported it, though not in connection with a description of the Passion so much as in connection with his Easter experience. But the possibility cannot be excluded that the unnamed disciple of John xviii, 15 f., comes into account as the guarantor of the story. Here we must set out from three pre-suppositions which, in spite of all critical doubts, seem to me highly probable. Firstly, we must grant that John's denial scene was not adapted by the author to his special purposes in any theological manner. Hence it belonged to the tradition which lay in front of the author (cf. p. 204, note 1, *supra*). Secondly, we must get rid of the suspicion that the other disciple is introduced here tendentiously in order to excel Peter.[1] Finally we must regard the figure of the unnamed disciple as quite historical, and identify the disciple " known unto the High Priest " (John xviii, 15), with that John who, according to Polycrates, had carried the frontlet of a priest.[2] If these presuppositions are correct, the unnamed disciple also may have added to the Church's knowledge of Peter's conduct.

Moreover, even in the best case of building such a tradition, we must insist also that the description of the denial in the Gospels rests upon a Tale-like formulation. This holds in regard to the individualization of the three acts, but especially of the cock-crow. Perhaps originally at the bottom there was a proverbial use of the cock-crow, or even the second cock-crow, as an indication of time (Mark xiii, 35), and this was then developed dramatically.

Thus historical and critical considerations may enable us to

---

[1] In order to substantiate such a suspicion we may refer to John xxi, 21–3, and, even if in another sense, to John xx, 3–10. But matters stand otherwise with the denial. The other disciple is no opposite number to Peter, for he does not confess, although Peter denies. Again the reputation of Peter is not diminished by the co-operation of the other, for nothing concerns reputation here. The other disciple forthwith disappears and is only mentioned to explain Peter's entry in the courtyard. Thus he plays neither a legendary nor a soteriological rôle, but one that can only be understood historically.

[2] According to xx, 2, the " other disciple " is the Beloved Disciple. The surprise about his death, assumed in xxi, 23, shows that he is a historical figure. Hence not all the mentions of the Beloved Disciple can yet pass as early tradition, but probably if any passage, then this one, John xviii, 15, may, on account of its wholly untheological character (see the preceding footnote), lay claim to rest upon tradition. But then it becomes of the highest significance that Polycrates of Ephesus in his letter to Victor of Rome (Euseb. *H.E.*, iii, 31, 3) says of the Beloved Disciple John (whom he does not call apostle and whom he ranges after Philip): ὃς ἐγενήθη ἱερεὺς τὸ πέταλον πεφορεκώς. This may be exaggeration, but, nevertheless, it remains probable that the Beloved Disciple (who only appears in Jerusalem) belonged to a priestly family, and so in fact ἦν γνωστὸς τῷ ἀρχιερεῖ as John xviii, 15, says.

produce events in the Passion story, which might always claim some probability, both in the positive and in the negative sense. But such judgments can only be pronounced after the meaning of the Marcan presentation has been made clear, and this without regard to the question of historicity. Only then do the Form-constructing forces come to light, which effected the formulation of pieces of tradition. Thereby, in spite of superficial unity in the character of the Passion story, widely varied interests come into question. But nowhere else must we be more aware of subjectivism than in examining the Passion story.

Chapter VIII

SYNTHESIS

The only long connected passage of a narrative kind given in the old tradition was the Passion story. We saw in Chapter V that the connected passages in the Gospels of the childhood in Luke and Matthew were the work of the evangelists. The tradition of Jesus' words consisted of individual stories and sayings. If one wished to give the Church a connected presentation one must undertake to bring them together and provide connecting links.

As far as we can see the first who undertook this work was the composer of the Gospel of St. Mark. We may guess that he was in any case the first who wrote in Greek, because the material of his book is even now relatively little worked over. But this supposition naturally is not fully certain. From the character of the material we can conclude only that Mark did not take over some similar account, but rather that he acted independently in making his synthesis. The Passion story is an exception, but those passages are not exceptions which have been claimed for the so-called Ur-Markus as I have already attempted to show (cf. pp. 41 f. *supra*). The reasons which we can adduce for the existence of such a primitive synthesis prove only the existence of primitive stories, viz. the Paradigms. In the main body of his book which deals with the work of Jesus, Mark brought together in his own way passages from the tradition preserved in the Churches, i.e. what were essentially Paradigms, Tales, Sayings, and a few other fragments of tradition, such as the description of the Baptist and his death, the Baptism and the Transfiguration of Jesus, etc. He crowned and concluded the whole with the Passion story and the narrative of the Empty Grave.

But before we can examine the work of the evangelist as a collector and editor, we must consider the question as to what extent the originally single pieces were already joined together as complexes such as Mark employs. That narratives were united even in the old tradition, is seen most clearly in the interweaving of the story of Jairus with the healing of the woman with the issue. The union is so close here, that we cannot regard it as originating in the evangelist as editor. Mark's manner of combining is seen in the verses, Mark vi 45 f., with which he joins the narrative of walking on the sea, with that of feeding the 5,000. Probably the whole cycle, Mark iv, 35–v, 43, arose before Mark. Here it is topography which holds at least the first stories together, for the healing of the demoniac had to take place in Gentile country, and hence there must be a sea-crossing. Elsewhere also similarity of content may have brought certain passages together before Mark's time. We may even imagine that the cases of dispute had been brought together. But at least the group Mark ii, 1–iii, 6, as it stands to-day in the Gospel, has been constructed by the evangelist. This is proved by the pragmatic concluding sentence iii, 6, which refers to the Passion story and hence comes from Mark, but which is clearly conceived as the concluding member of this group. Thus not much can be said with certainty about the older narrative cycles.

Much more important for the moulding of the material were the tendencies of the collections and groupings of Jesus' sayings. In the following Chapter we shall deal with the rise and preservation of the general tradition of Sayings. Already in Chapter VI, when speaking of the *Chriae*, we have dealt with the formulation of individual sayings by indicating its cause. Now the question is, how, by setting them in a framework, or casting them into a dialogue, sayings were joined together into a kind of conversation scene. Whether this was due to Mark, or was earlier, is hard to say, but it is easy to see that the passages compounded of questions are not original. This holds especially of the disputes over being in league with the devil (Mark iii, 23–30), handwashing (vii, 5–23), and divorce (x, 2–12).

There can be no doubt that, in all three cases, originally isolated sayings have been brought together by the action of a cause. In Mark iii, 23–6, we are dealing first of all with the metaphor of the Kingdom, and the house divided against itself is perhaps an original reference to the reproach that Jesus cast out demons by Beelzebul. Upon this there follows the metaphor of binding the strong man, which probably was current in isolation. If its relation to Jesus' healing work is original, it would represent Jesus as the victor over demonic powers, but would not meet directly the reproach of being in league with the devil. The saying about blaspheming the Spirit (iii, 28–30), the original isolation of which is clear from iii, 30, makes the conclusion. The real cause, standing at the end of the saying, is still preserved, " because they said He had an unclean spirit." The whole composition is held together by the accusation, " He has Beelzebul and he casts out demons by the prince of demons." It is very possible that the passage already lay before the evangelist in this form. He must then have biographically evaluated the occasion, which was handed down without the circumstances, and made the scribes come from Jerusalem (iii, 22). He puts their attitude alongside that of Jesus' relatives, whom he mentions here (iii, 21) in order to prepare for their appearance in iii, 31.[1]

In the dispute about washing hands (Mark vii, 5–23), two little independent details stand out at once, still betraying their independence by special introductions. The first detail is the accusation of breaking the fourth commandment by the practice of Corban (vii, 9–13), which has nothing at all to do with the question of hand-washing. The second detail is the saying about true cleanliness (vii, 15), which relates to eating and not to washing.

This saying now receives two explanations (vii, 14–19,

---

[1] There can be no question of an original speech.

20–3) which do not suit its radical character, and which show themselves moreover to be Church doctrine, because they are given here esoterically in the circle of the disciples. This whole double exegesis can only be understood from the interest of the Churches in the food question. Standing before the words just examined is Mark vii, 6–8 (which makes use of Isaiah xxix, 13), " Thus you break the commandment of God and hold the tradition of men." The theme of what follows is given thereby. The thought, which recurs again in a new form in vii, 9, well suits the Corban saying vii, 10–13, but is by no means an answer to the opponents' question about hand-washing which, in great detail, introduces the whole section (Mark vii, 1–5). This question, with which the words of Jesus do not deal at all, has probably been placed in front of the whole composition only by the evangelist, but the connecting of the words of Jesus (at least in vii, 6–15) may be older and have commenced with the prophet's word, vii, 6–8.

In the divorce section an element of tradition forbidding divorce and re-marriage is also clear, and is found also in the parallels. It is appended as esoteric teaching (Mark x, 10–12) to the main saying (Mark x, 9) : " What God has joined let no man put asunder." This is given as a deduction from the creation story (x, 6–8). The differentiation from the Jewish law of divorce precedes (x, 2–5). We may doubt whether it originally belonged to the central passage (x, 6–9), because the little dialogue appears to be artificial. But even should an individual element of tradition be present, we might assume that Mark already found at least the connected passage, x, 2–9 ; according to x, 1, he wishes to open the journey to Judæa with a piece of Jesus' " teaching ".

Here, as in the two other cases, it is impossible to give a certain demonstration about the scope of the original details of the tradition. There is therefore little point in adding a few more to the number of hypotheses about these three sections. In our connection I was only obliged to make clear

two things important for the history of Form. Firstly, it
is striking how widely these "conversations" differ from
the dialogues of the Paradigms. There everything has point
either in silencing or convincing the other man, or in justifying
Jesus' attitude. Paradigms are intended to present events
out of which it will be seen how Jesus, by word or act,
proclaims the approach of the Kingdom of God. In the
"conversations" analysed here, the pointedness of the
dialogue is entirely lacking. The point is in the individual
saying, or group of sayings. But these are united by elements
of dialogue into highly artificial wholes. We cannot find any
category of "disputes". Moreover, in these compositions
eschatological furnishings are lacking throughout; the
thought is nowhere expressed that the passing of the old
order is conditioned by the approach of the Kingdom of God.
Thus also the "conversations" of this character do not lead
to any goal; they do not describe events in the sense of
Paradigms. Each time Mark endeavours in the introductions
to arrange them biographically; and we must deal with the
sense which these sections receive in his sketch. But no such
sense resides in the combinations themselves. Their Form
is due to another standpoint; by placing together materially
related words of Jesus the intention was to convey to
Christendom a "teaching" of Jesus on important questions
of church life. Thus it is not to be wondered at that once
and again actual problems of the church crop up, whether
they do or do not suit the biographical occasion which the
evangelist has given the whole. Hence in the Beelzebul
disputes the blasphemy of the Spirit is dealt with; in the
section about washing hands we hear about foods; in the
matter of divorce about re-marriage. These interests have
naturally influenced in many ways the tradition of Jesus'
word, till often the original Form cannot be reconstructed
even where we have parallel passages.

A second principle for the history of Form follows from
all this. The one who assembled these sayings and groups

of sayings cannot usually be Mark, whose interests, otherwise directed, can be recognized in the biographical motives at the beginning of each section. Even when he adds something, the assumption is probably justified that words of Jesus on similar or related themes had been assembled as teaching for the Church before Mark's time.

Alongside the narrative pieces there were complexes of some such kind, which Mark used when he began to transform the tradition into a narrative of Jesus' work. For his aim was to narrate, as is proved by the predominance of narrative pieces of tradition and by the "historizing" of complexes of sayings already proved. We have now to ask how the evangelists make a book out of the traditions.

In the analysis of the Tales I have already drawn attention to the *pragmatism* of St. Mark's Gospel. It is expressed in remarks of the simplest character which are intended to prepare, at the right time, for what is to come. This is seen especially in the conflict with the Jews, iii, 6; xi, 18; but also in isolated instances, as in iii, 9; vi, 31. The passages where Jesus enjoins that His miracles should be kept secret as in v, 43a; vii, 36; viii, 26; probably also vii, 26, serve also the purpose of uniting isolated passages. In my analysis I have already examined these passages to some extent.

They are intended (i) to show that Jesus did not wish Himself to be honoured as a miracle-worker, and (ii) to make it plain how, in spite of so many proofs of His supernatural power, He was not recognized as the Messiah. Thus the theory of the Messianic Secret constitutes a fundamental idea beneath the presentation as a whole.[1] It is the general category under which both Paradigms and Tales may be brought. The fact that it does not come forward more

[1] The working out of this conception is due to Wrede: *Das Messiasgeheimniss in der Evangelien.* I should like substantially to reduce the number of witnesses brought forward by Wrede for this theory. Thus, e.g. the secrecy of the success of the miracle does not belong here. Cf. *supra,* pp. 93 f.

frequently and that it has not led to greater changes in the single stories shows with what relative faithfulness Mark has reproduced tradition.

Although it is in contradiction to entire historical probability, this theory of the Secret is to be found also in a few of the passages (i, 34; iii, 12) in which Mark endeavours from his own materials to give a condensed representation of the work of Jesus. In these collective notes (i, 32–4; iii, 10–12; vi, 54–6) the vividness and the pointedness which characterize Paradigms and Tales are lacking. They are generalizations, where what is instanced in detail in single stories is now said of a number of cases without any detail. They are intended to signify nothing more than that Jesus continued to work further in the manner already described. In actual fact the collector, whose material consisted only of isolated examples, possesses hardly any other means of expanding these individual instances into a representation of the whole. No objective pictures of the life of Jesus were in existence. We can quite recognize this even in the colourless collective notices, and nothing else is to be expected owing to the nature of the conditions under which the tradition was formed. The little which Mark ever knew over and above the fixed tradition of the life of Jesus, e.g. geographical matter or names of Apostles, he included in the narrative almost without any addition. In this way arose the *incidental remarks and references* like iii, 7 f.; iii, 13–19. Also probably the framework of the instructions for the sending out of the twelve (vi, 7 f., 12 f., 30) belongs here. Obviously only this saying had been handed down, but Mark deduced from it the proceeding of the sending out, and invented a framework of remarks which rather mentioned than narrated the proceeding without any closer details. We cannot determine how closely the evangelist came to historical reality. But that he was concerned with a description of would-be history and not with a collection of sayings is shown by the fact that he gives in indirect speech the first of the two sayings which he reports, that about

sending out the messengers.[1] Here as elsewhere a certain
colourlessness strikes one in the enclosing remarks. Questions
which the situation puts forward are unanswered. Whence
comes the increase of numbers described in Mark iii, 7?
Whither does Jesus send out the disciples (Mark vi, 7), and
with what gospel? In iii, 13, does He call them to Himself,
and how is such a " calling " possible? Especially in this
passage iii, 13, are we struck at once by the lack of vividness
in the description; but this very lack shows once more the
conservatism of Mark who only collected such notices and
lightly touched them up yet without making Legends from
them.

The most significant of all the means used by the evangelist
for creating a lively connection among the fragments of
tradition has not yet been mentioned. This has to do with
the *interpretation of tradition*. The evangelist, in making his
collection, strives to do this by setting a number of traditional
events in a particular setting. He shows how and why they
must have taken place in accordance with the Divine Plan
of Salvation. We have already observed in dealing with
Paradigms that isolated, illustrative, or explanatory sentences
were placed even in the mouth of Jesus (cf. pp. 63 ff.
supra)—not even the words of the Lord were to be passed
on without interpretation !—thus it must not seem strange
to us if even these explanatory passages are given as words
of Jesus. But we are not concerned at the moment with
individual words within the borders of the narratives so
much as with relatively independent minor matters which
have little or only a quite loose connection with the fragments
of tradition, and which are easily seen to be the work of
the collecting evangelist. Among these passages are to be
placed above all the prophecies of sufferings in Mark viii,
31; ix, 30–2; x, 32–4. These three passages stand almost

[1] Mark vi, 8, says καὶ παρήγγειλεν αὐτοῖς, ἵνα μηδὲν αἴρωσιν . . . The
second verb μὴ ἐνδύσησθε stands indeed in the second person and thus
prepares for passing over to what follows. The second saying is then (vi, 10) introduced with a special insertion καὶ ἔλεγεν αὐτοῖς.

without connection in the narrative, and are intended also
really to bring forward not an isolated event, but one which
was frequently repeated. "And they departed thence, and
passed through Galilee; and he would not that any man
should know it." "For he taught his disciples, and said . . . ."
Introductory passages such as these show that the words about
the sufferings were introduced without any special reason and
also had no connection with the traditional material. That
they were introduced by the collecting evangelist is seen
from their regular distribution in chapters viii–x. The aim
of thus introducing them is the same as when prophecies
dealing with similar things are taken up into the story of the
Passion, as in announcing the betrayal, the denial, and
especially the general "offences" (Mark xiv, 27) (cf.
Chapter VII). In all these cases the point is not to prove that
Jesus was not taken by surprise by the events of the Passion,
but rather to show how and why the passion and death of
Jesus were willed by God. This teaching, substantiated in
this "offence" passage by a scriptural quotation, is expressed
in the prophecies of suffering by the term "Son of Man".[1]

The Son of Man, i.e. the Messianic "man" coming from
Heaven, "had" to suffer, otherwise he would not be the
"man from Heaven", nor would he be raised to God, nor
be now worshipped by the Church, nor accepted in the near
future as the "man" from Heaven coming with the clouds
of Heaven. What Mark reproduced therefore in these words
is in brief the preaching of the Church about the Son of Man.
Thus he explains first of all what he intends to depict, and
so binds up the life and sufferings of Jesus with the faith and
hopes of Christians. And in this sense we can probably understand Mark ix, 11–13, a passage in which the sufferings of the
Son of Man in accordance with the Scriptures are described
and confirmed. And this is done in such a way that it would

---

[1] For the doctrine of the Son of Man, cf. Bousset, *Kyrios Christos*, ed. ii, pp. 14 ff.
For the understanding of the words of announcement, cf. my remarks in the
Abhandlungen Zür Semit. Religionskunde für Baudissin, p. 138, note 1.

seem that the promised Elias Redivivus as the forerunner of the Messiah has already appeared in the person of the Baptist, and has suffered " as it was written of him ". Those are sections whose content is theology and whose origin is reflection, but not the theology or reflection peculiar to the evangelist so much as the theological view which had been spread far and wide in the Churches by preaching. In so far as Mark introduced such words into the traditional material, he formed out of the fragments handed down a picture of the Son of Man as the Church believed Him to have been.

Quite evidently the *editing of the parables* by Mark has to do with our understanding of tradition. The technique of the evangelist can be seen clearly enough in the parable-chapter Mark iv. Sitting in a boat, Jesus relates the parable of the sower to the multitude standing on the shore. This situation is evidently a creation of the evangelist, as there can be no question of a Paradigm or Tale or of any narrative complete in itself. Such could not have had an isolated existence nor could it have been passed on. Rather the evangelist himself prepared the scene by a little pragmatic remark (Mark iii, 9): Jesus causes a boat to be held ready in order if necessary to avoid the crush. The evangelist used this situation also afterwards as a connecting link, in so far as he depicts Jesus remaining in the same vessel and then (iv, 36) undertaking the journey across to the other shore (cf. pp. 74 f. *supra*). The composition of the parabolic preaching has been often observed and examined. The first parable is related within the borders of the seascape, but Jesus gives the interpretation (iv, 10–25) only when He is alone with the disciples. Then two more parables follow, apparently without change of scene, and yet we learn from the conclusion of the section that these two parables were spoken publicly and indeed (iv, 36) in the boat. The part which contains the interpretation appears therefore as a parenthesis. But perhaps it would be more correct to hold that Mark had created the whole situation in order to fix the tradition and afterwards to continue the narrative. Meantime, however, on account of the interpretation, he appears to have completely forgotten the situation. The interpretation and the words which Mark adds to it therefore constitute another independent section (iv, 10–25). Certain isolated sayings in the chapter, such as iv, 21, 22, 25, of course come out of the tradition, for they also receive testimony elsewhere. But the whole section is a composition by the evangelist, as is shown by the splitting of the connection of the parables. Mark's object in this section is to express the view that the divine element in the parables is visible not to secular, but only to opened eyes. By this means he justifies the detailed, half-allegorical explanation of the single parable of the sower. At the same time he assists his readers to gain a right understanding of the work of Jesus. He means to suggest that if the multitude had not understood the creator of these parables in His meaning and did not honour Him as the Messiah, yet that contingency was contemplated by Jesus. For the value of the Gospel was concealed in the garment of the parabolic form, and it was only granted to eyes favoured by grace to recognize the secret of the Kingdom of God— to open eyes such as had been given to the disciples and now to Christian readers.

In the last analysis the conversation in Mark viii, 14–21, which unites the two stories of feeding the multitude, must be understood from the same standpoint, i.e. that of the attempt to replace the tradition into its historical context. It is the work of the collector because it presupposes the other two stories. The evangelist made the saying about signs follow upon the Feeding the Five Thousand, since obviously that saying had been handed down to him with the occasion that belongs to it (Mark viii, 11 f. of p. 159 *supra*). Joining on to this, and continuing the polemic against the Pharisees, is the first word which Jesus speaks at the beginning of the journey across the sea, giving warning about the " leaven of the Pharisees and of Herod "—a traditional saying, since there is no reason in this connection for naming Herod. Luke is aware of the saying, and in xii, 1, uses it against Pharisaic hypocrisy. It has a deeper sense in Mark. When the disciples misunderstand, and think of the forgotten bread, Mark makes Jesus answer with a reference to the two feedings : " Do you not understand what was meant by that ? " The disciples, i.e. the readers, ought to know after the repeated experience of miraculous feeding that Jesus continually gives them true bread. To a certain extent the Johannine thought of the bread of life is apparent. Johannine is also the manner in which the deeper sense of the saying about leaven is touched upon by means of a misunderstanding. The composition as a whole is the work of the evangelist, who gives traditional material—here the narrative of the feeding and the saying about leaven—to his readers in a soteriological sense.

Only after we have seen how Mark combines and interprets his material, what interests he brings to it, and what picture of Jesus he tries to gain from it,—only then it appears to me to be in place for us to ask *with what object and from what standpoint Mark undertook this synthesis of tradition at all*. This question should not receive the facile answer that Mark in any case only worked up the narrative material of the preachers into a book. He by no means confines himself to the Paradigms. He included also Tales. He must have had definite ideas in bringing together such various elements. What those were, we can naturally only gather not from tradition but from those peculiarities of Mark's book which we ascribed on good ground to its composer.

As one such peculiarity we have already recognized his theory of the Messianic secret. To the evangelist the life of Jesus as a whole is only comprehensible on the assumption that Jesus intentionally kept His real status secret. He was the Son of God, but He did not reveal to the people who He was. This is the reason why He could be so much misunderstood and even sent to the Cross. A second characteristic of Mark's book, which its composer stamped upon it, is the conception of the parables as mysteries. It is true that like the miracles they signify an epiphany of the Divine in the world. But this is only for the chosen to whom it is granted to see the mystery of the Kingdom of God. To the majority of the Jews the parables were unsolved riddles, as is proved by their attitude towards the preaching of Jesus. Moreover, we can recognize the work of the editor-evangelist in the grouping of the material, at least in those places where a perfectly definite object is recognizable in the arrangement. The confession of Peter makes a turning point. After the disciples were convinced of the status of the Master, there commence the prophecies of suffering which certainly originate from the evangelist (cf. p. 226 *supra*). The divine confirmation of the Messiahship follows in the form of the transfiguration. It is easy to understand the meaning of this grouping : Jesus is the Messiah, but in the eyes of the world, until the Resurrection, He is despised, suffering, and mortal. His divine glory is patent only to the narrowest circle of the elect. From these characteristics we recognize the aim of the Gospel. It is to represent Jesus as the Messiah, but without placing His work in a supernatural sphere which had no room for tradition—although this was done in the Fourth Gospel. It is also to emphasize those characteristics in the tradition which disclose Jesus as Messiah, but at the same time to show why He was not recognized as Messiah by the people and why He was opposed, despised, and finally sent to the Cross. In this way the gospel of Mark was written as *a book of secret epiphanies*. Both the Paradigms and the Tales can be brought under this heading.

This view is confirmed if we glance once more at the commencement of the Gospel. Mark begins with the incident of the appearance of John the Baptist, which also constitutes the beginning of the preaching of salvation in the kerygma of Acts x, 37, and xiii, 24. But Mark is not concerned with the preaching of repentance by the Baptist, and it finds no place in his book. The Baptist is regarded only as a prophet of Jesus, i.e. as one of those who in consequence of divine illumination know of the status of Jesus.

Thus everything which the evangelist has to say about John the Baptist orientates in the Old Testament words with which the Gospel begins. But this is at the same time the best way of passing over to the record about Jesus, and thus it comes about that in Mark Jesus' appearance upon the scene of the events completely lacks both preparation and introduction: we hear nothing of His home nor of His upbringing. Even the question so often discussed in the Church about the motive which made Jesus approach the Baptist's movement remains unanswered. No other introduction is necessary for Jesus than what was given to the evangelist by tradition; the tradition of the coming and the Messianic preaching of the Baptist. We see in what degree this Gospel is still unliterary, for an author would have given a biographical introduction, just as Luke tried to do in his own way (iii, 1 ff.). But at the same time it becomes clear that this presentation is dominated by a soteriological motive. In bringing the appearance of the Baptist to expression it was intended to depict his significance for the Christian Church. The story of Jesus' baptism now follows. It is perhaps no longer, as originally,[1] the story of a divine adoption, but is intended as an epiphany of Jesus, although not an epiphany to a world which was not yet capable of receiving it. The heavenly announcement is not meant even for the Baptist, because, according to Mark's view, he scarcely had need of it.

---

[1] The most certain sign of this is recognized to be the other form of the voice from heaven in Luke (according to D. and other MS.): "Thou art my Son, this day have I begotten thee." Contrary to my earlier view (*Die urchristliche Uberlieferung v. J. dem Taufer*, p. 63), I now regard this form as old, but as precanonical and unjustifiably introduced into D. from the unregulated tradition. But also the canonical test can be understood as a formula of adoption. Mark, however, by no means understands that Jesus only became at this point what he had not hitherto been. He tells the incident with the feeling that now the heavenly status of Jesus is for a moment visible, i.e. for him it is the description of an epiphany, but as usual without witnesses or, if the Baptist were aware of it, at least known only to a very small circle.

It is meant for Jesus Himself, and, we may venture to add, for those initiated into the secret of the status of Jesus, i.e. the readers of the Gospel.   Thereupon follows the period in the wilderness where Jesus is tempted of the devil, surrounded by wild animals, and ministered to by angels.   It is a typical picture of one sent by God, who is preparing himself for carrying out his mission.   But even this picture remains hidden from the eyes of the world and is only visible to those of believers.   Secret epiphany, that is the characteristic of Mark's first section.   From this standpoint Mark gathered and edited tradition.

We can understand that a writer who had this aim did not confine himself to the Paradigms reproduced in the course of preaching.   He included also Tales which told also of epiphanies, sometimes even of epiphanies to a trusted circle.   The Tales harmonized well with Mark's aim, although for us Mark's proper theory of a secret seems very artificial when applied to such deeds as the raising of the little girl (cf. pp. 72 f. *supra*).   But in addition to Paradigms and Tales, Mark included in his book a third feature, viz. the words of Jesus.   The question about the rise of this Word-tradition can be answered only in a wider connection.

CHAPTER IX

EXHORTATIONS

The Paradigms contain words of Jesus of a general character. But primitive Christendom preserved many more such sayings. Mark preserved a few collections of sayings, Matthew and Luke far more. We are concerned principally with those passages in which these latter agree almost literally with each other apart from Mark, and out of whose relationship the "Two-source theory" has proved with great and proper certainty the existence of a common source, Q.

These researches have brought the whole matter to a high degree of probability, at least within certain limits.[1] But this welcome result of the criticism of the sources must nor blind us to the fact that in other directions the source Q remains an unsolved problem.

It does not seem to me that the question about the language in which this source is written requires any detailed examination. The text used by Matthew and Luke was Greek,[2] otherwise there would have been no such agreement. All the genuine sayings of Jesus were translated at the same

---

[1] Adolf Harnack, *Sprüche und Reden Jesu*, 1907. Engl. trans. *The Sayings of Jesus*, Williams and Norgate.

[2] The testimony of Papias in Euseb. *H.E.*, iii, 39[16], reads : Ματθαῖος μὲν οὖν Ἑβραΐδι διαλέκτῳ τὰ λόγια συνετάξατο, ἡρμήνευσεν δ' αὐτὰ ὡς ἦν δυνατὸς ἕκαστος. This testimony cannot be referred to the source Q. Papias undoubtedly means our Matthew, and, exactly as in his notice about Mark (op. cit., iii, 19[15]), wishes to justify some defect of the work we know not what. The justification is probably to be found in the notice that Matthew wrote in Aramaic and that the translations were done by various people. The implication is that it was in this way that we finally received our Gospel according to Matthew, but nothing is said as to how. Even if Papias were here only reproducing an old report, this would, nevertheless, not refer to the source Q. For here a book is intended which was current in the church under the name of Matthew, and the intention was to exonerate the Apostle from certain defects of this book. Therefore what Papias refers to is the Gospel of Matthew as current in the churches. Moreover, the notices of Papias are formulated already from the standpoint of literary Christians to whom the Apostles were authors.

time. But it seems possible to conceive this process in such a way that even in bilingual Churches it was handed on in Greek, and that these Greek sayings were brought together in a Greek-speaking region. This is much more probable than the other case, that the Aramaic words were first assembled and then translated as a connected writing. For in this case we shall have to assume even for the earliest Christian generation a certain literary activity—and that is out of the question.

So also we know nothing certain about the extent of the source Q, for we can only deduce Q in the places where the two parallels, Matthew and Luke, give the text in a somewhat similar fashion. We are not able to say how much of material special to each writer comes from Q. The very arrangement of the sections of Q is by no means determined by a certain agreement in the sequence in Matthew and Luke.[1]

But the greatest doubts arises when we consider the literary category of Q, for we have not the slightest idea whether and in what way this writing, deduced piecemeal, can have constituted a book. And, in especial, we cannot be certain about the historic or biographical framework which the individual speeches probably had. We see the approximate nature of such a framework in the section about the messengers of John (Matthew xi, 2 ff.), which Luke has edited like a historian (vii, 18 ff.). We find no such framework to John's preaching of repentance, nor to the temptation of Jesus, because the introductions (Matthew iv, 1 f., and Luke iv, 1 ff.) obviously depend upon Mark. These introductions do not appear to have been very extensive. In these, as in other questions, we must be careful not to speak with too great self-confidence of Q as a definitely ascertained entity.

---

[1] B. H. Streeter, in "The Four Gospels", pp. 273 ff. *The Reconstruction of Q*, judges the question much more optimistically. At the end of the chapter, p. 291, he gives a list of the passages claimed for Q, and immediately speaks of these passages as " a document the purpose and character of which are perfectly intelligible ". But that is precisely the question because of the very fact that there is no guarantee of the completeness of the list. The same scepticism applies to other writers.

As long as we leave this fact out of sight we run the danger of reckoning with as much certainty upon the source which we do not know as upon Mark which we can see in front of us. We tend to forget that we are dealing with a hypothetical entity. If, however, we remain conscious of the limits of our knowledge, then certain over-refined, as well as oversceptical, influences concerning the worth or lack of worth of the source fade away automatically, because they depend on the assumption that Q can be defined with certainty as to its extent and nature ; and this assumption is false.

By such a systematic self-limitation, we abandon the possibility of reconstructing the source in its fullness. For even in the case of sections which can be reconstructed, we must earnestly ask the question whether they all really belonged to the same " writing ". This may appear doubtful and has, in fact, been doubted.[1] The present position of research into the source Q warrants our speaking rather of a stratum than of a document. We clearly recognize the effort of the churches to gather together words of Jesus in the manner of Q, but we do not know whether the result of these efforts was one or more books or indeed any books at all. Thus from the point of view of literary criticism, the sections of the source which can be reconstructed constitute a proof that *primitive Christianity felt a need of gathering together the words of Jesus.* The question how far " stories " come from Q can be left on one side for the time being.

But this point of view brings us up directly against a problem. If sayings of Jesus had been collected at an earlier date, how would it come about that Mark was unacquainted with them ? Or if he knew the collection, why did he not include these words of Jesus in his Gospel ? On the other hand if the collection itself is of a later date than the Gospel of Mark, it must be dependent upon either an oral or written tradition. Then comes the question why Mark had not

[1] Wellhausen, *Einleitung*, p. 66 f. ; cf. also Wernle, *Die Synopt Frage*, p. 266 f.; Harnack, *Sprüche*, p. 121 ff.

used this tradition.   Such queries as Wellhausen has set down with great energy [1] threaten the assurance of the usual confidence in the source Q, and show of what great consequence a decision on this subject can be.   We must ask at once whether the Gospel of Mark really does intend to pass on the total tradition of the words as well as of the works of Jesus.

Amongst the sections in which Mark hands down sayings and speeches from the mouth of Jesus, the chapter of parables found in Mark iv, 1 ff., may rightly be regarded as specially characteristic.   Our analysis (cf. pp. 227 f. *supra*) has already shown that only the three parables of the sower, the self-growing seed, and the mustard seed, can be regarded as part of the tradition which the evangelist had received.   The introductory remarks depicting the circumstances, and the interpretation inserted, are an addition of Mark's.   *Thus Mark evidently valued a tradition which contained words of Jesus but which did not offer a narrative giving the context.*   The important point for our problem is that he introduces this tradition (iv, 2) with the remark " He taught them much in parables and said to them in the course of His teaching ", i.e. he is aware that what he now gives is only a *selection* or an *example*.

A similar case is found in xii, 38, where two short sayings against the Scribes follow upon the disputes between Jesus and His opponents in Jerusalem.   These sayings are introduced quite unconnectedly with the words " and He said in His teaching ".   In view of the small compass of these sayings it is quite evident that these are only intended to be a quotation from what Mark calls the " teaching " of Jesus.   No one would seriously suggest that all this is only fiction, i.e. that Mark knew no more than he set down, although such an assumption would perhaps be conceivable in the case of the speaking in parables.   Mark is not afraid elsewhere to append isolated sayings without introduction, e.g. ix, 49 f.   Thus he would seem not to have required any context if he had not wished

---

[1] Wellhausen, *Einl. in d. drei ersten Evangelien*, pp. 73, 84 ff.

to characterize the words as what they were, viz. quotations out of a more comprehensive tradition. And indeed attention may be drawn to a third passage, where the parable of the wicked vinedressers is introduced with the words : " He began to speak to them in parables " (Mark xii, 1). Once more a richer tradition is assumed out of which Mark gives only one example. In the end the same holds good also of Mark iii, 23, where the metaphor of the kingdom and of the house divided against itself is introduced by " he spoke to them in parables ", and thus with a formula which really leads one to expect something more than two or, including the metaphor of the strong man, three sayings. These observations also throw a light upon the passages in Mark in which Jesus is described as teaching, but in which we learn nothing about His teaching, as, indeed, at the beginning of the incidents of the synagogue in Capernaum (i, 21 f.) or before the call of Levi (ii, 13), or in the synagogue at Nazareth (vi, 2). The evangelist's transition to the feeding of the five thousand (vi, 34) is very significant, " And when he came to the land he saw the great multitude and felt compassion for them, for they were as sheep without shepherds, and he began to teach them many things." In such passages it is simply assumed that Jesus taught, but nothing is said of what He actually preached to His hearers.

Obviously it is not part of Mark's plan to tell what the " teaching " of Jesus was. In the context of his narrative, of course, he gives many words of Jesus, but sometimes as we have seen, these words are characterized explicitly as pieces of a greater whole which remains outside Mark's book. Evidently *the handing down of the actual words of Jesus depends upon a law different from that which governed the gathering together of Mark's material.* We must trace out that law if we wish to know why Mark did not to any large extent include the words of Jesus.

This law can be enunciated. A number of observations makes it probable that the words of Jesus were handed down under other conditions than were the narratives of His acts. Early and regularly in the primitive missionary activity a tradition was spread in which, as can be proved, the words of Jesus also played a part. We are concerned here with the primitive Christian " Exhortations". What was suggested in Chapter II about the probability of such a primitive Christian Halakha must now be demonstrated in a wider connection.

Paul often concludes his letters to the Churches with a hortatory section (Rom. xii, xiii ; Gal. v, 13 ff. ; vi, 1 ff. ; Colossians, iii, iv ; 1 Thess. iv, 1 ff. ; v. 1 ff.). As a rule this section is in a style widely differing from that of the rest of the letter. It contains no far-reaching discussions based on religion or theology, but special caveats often in the form of proverbs either loosely strung together or simply following one another without connection. One is reminded of other texts which contain hortatory proverbs, e.g. the first chapter of James, the first section Didache, Pseudo-Phocylistes, Tobit iv and xii, also the relevant chapters of the Archikar novel, or Isocrates (*ad Nicoclem*) and Pseudo-Isocrates (*ad Demonicum*). The hortatory sections of the Pauline letters are clearly differentiated in material from what Paul otherwise wrote. In particular they lack an immediate relation with the circumstances of the letter. The rules and directions are not formulated for special churches and concrete cases, but for the general requirements of earliest Christendom. Their significance is not factual but actual—not the momentary need but the universal principle. This difference, by means of which we first learn more closely to understand the literary category of the Pauline epistles, has a special significance in our connection. It shows the inner relation between the hortatory sections of the letters and the preaching of Paul. What is to be found in those chapters of the epistles arises from a didactic habit. In his missionary work itself the apostle was accustomed to impress upon fresh converts the fundamentals of a new Christian life in the form of such directions. When later the apostle, or his pupils, paid a visit these directions were revised and extended in the churches. The hortatory sections in the Pauline letters to his churches are nothing else than such divisions and extensions.[1] Our view is altogether credible in itself and is moreover supported by Paul himself when he warns the Thessalonians (1 Thess. iv, 1): "Since you have received it from us how to walk and to please God, and since you already walk in such a fashion, so may you now in these things continually approach perfection, for you know what exhortations we gave you through the Lord Jesus Christ." With these words Paul opens the hortatory section whose aim is thus only to bring back to memory what is already known and practised. Even in those places where Paul could not refer to his own mission or to the work of his pupils, e.g. in Romans, he assumes that his readers have received similar teaching (vi, 17; cf. the footnote below on this page) and, trusting to that, he brings forward his own exhortation (Romans xii, xiii). Exhortation, therefore, had a broader basis than the Pauline mission. It was the common property of Christendom, i.e. it was the general duty of the primitive missionaries to give such directions to their churches, or at least to the churches composed of Christians of heathen origin to whom it was most necessary.

Thus we see that the hortatory sections of the Pauline epistles have nothing to do with the theoretic foundation of the ethics of the Apostle, and very little with other ideas peculiar to him. Rather they belong to tradition. In this respect Paul is like the other Christian missionaries, for it is further to be noticed that these Pauline chapters are

[1] These are the "ways" of Paul of which Timothy is to remind the Corinthians and which Paul was accustomed to teach in each Church (1 Cor. iv, 17). We are also dealing with the exhortations where Paul speaks in Romans of a teaching which has been transmitted to the Romans (Rom. vi, 17; xvi, 17). This is seen from the fact that in the first passage the connection requires a reference to ethical cautions (cf. further, A. Seeberg, *Der Katechismus der Ur-Christenheit*, and my commentary to 1 Thes. iv, 1, in *Handbuch Zum N.T.*).

remarkably related to certain sections in James, 1 Peter, 1 Clement, the Didache, and Hermas. In these cases also we have to do with the writing down of the general primitive exhortation. Its mediators are patently those *teachers* who are often mentioned in primitive Christian literature. The composer of James, a writing which contains much exhortation, shows (iii, 1) that he is himself to be recognized as a teacher. The activity of the teachers appears to have been of great significance for the spreading of the ethical tradition. But at the same time, consciously or unconsciously, they helped to preserve and to gather the tradition of Jesus.

The primitive Christian Churches were prepared for the disappearance of this world and not for life in it. They were therefore in no way prepared for the necessity of bringing forward hortatory sentences for every-day life. However, Judaism had been at work. Often dependent upon Hellenistic models, its teachings as given to proselytes required only slight change or filling-out of a Christian character in order to become usable among Christians. And with their special treasure in the *words of Jesus*, Christians had a storehouse of warnings and teachings directed, or at least capable of being directed, towards the most varied everyday relationships, even when their teachings were by no means sufficient for all requirements of exhortation.

We meet these words again, sometimes in isolation, sometimes in numbers, in the Christian exhortations. To name only very illuminating examples, we may mention one in the undoubted hortatory section of Romans, where alongside many echoes of words of Jesus is the saying "Bless those who persecute you" (Rom. xii, 14) which is obviously a variant of the well-known saying of Jesus. In James v, 12, we read "Swear neither by heaven nor by the earth, etc.", which is nothing else than a second or perhaps more original form of the prohibition of Jesus in Matthew v, 34 ff. The collection of sayings in Didache 1, 3 ff, which is a Christian interpolation into the Jewish "ways", consists largely of words of Jesus,

without its appearing that anything from our Gospels lies
beneath.   Yet we should not think of dependence on one
of the synoptics, because the sayings here share a remarkable
characteristic with the isolated words already mentioned,
viz. lack of any formula showing it is a quotation.   We may
not conclude, however, that the teachers had not already
known those words as words of Jesus, for in that case the
frequency of such sayings in the Didache would be altogether
too significant a coincidence.   Rather we should remember
that all the sayings of Christian exhortation were regarded
as inspired by the Spirit or by the Lord.   Thus all of them
appeared as exhortations " in the Lord ", if not as exhortations
of the Lord.   In such hortatory connections it could therefore
appear unimportant whether or not isolated cases of such
sayings were handed down as authentic words of Jesus, and,
therefore, it was possible to do without emphasizing such
words by express quotation.   Of course this stringing together
of genuine sayings of Jesus with other Christian words of
exhortation could become a source of error.   In certain circumstances at a later date, other words standing in the neighbourhood of the authentic sayings could be held equally authentic
and so increase the number of genuine words of Jesus by
a few spurious ones.   But that could only happen on the
assumption that authentic words of Jesus were as a matter
of fact to be found among the pieces of advice in the
exhortations.

But the words of Jesus were not only included without
differentiation in the series of exhortations, they were also
collected explicitly as words of Jesus.   Indeed, this took place
not from a historical or theological, but from a hortatory
interest.   Once more it is Paul who gives the proof.   When
he quotes words of Jesus his point is not to support a Christological demonstration, nor to give an authentic reference
for the plan of redemption.   With the exception of the
eschatological passage, 1 Th. iv, 15 ff., which possibly comes
from an Apocalypse and the citation of which moreover serves

a practical purpose, he twice introduces words of Jesus
1 Cor. vii, 10, and ix, 14 (the passage dealing with the Last
Supper, 1 Cor. xi, 23 ff., does not belong as narrative in this
connection). These two sayings of Jesus' are intended to
strengthen the exhortation. The first occasion concerns
a marriage question, and the second deals with the support
of missionaries. And when in 1 Cor. vii, 25, Paul remarks
" concerning virgins I have no directions of the Lord ",
we may probably deduce that he had received a number of
such " directions of the Lord ", and that the two sayings of
Jesus which he cites in this letter belong to them. Amongst
these directions he finds no word about virgins, and we may
hear almost a tone of regret as he confirms this lack. Hence
he revises either the sayings which he has in his memory—
this possibility has already been proved (cf. p. 39 *supra*)—
or else he looks through the leaves of papyrus which he
carries. Thus there were not only words of Jesus alongside
of other sayings contained in the framework of exhortation,
but also collections which contained exclusively sayings of
Jesus, and which were given to the missionaries orally or
fixed in writing. Naturally such collections serve the purpose
of exhortation, but of course the sense of their authority
operated in the fact of their composition. It was desired to
hand down certain directions not only in the spirit or the name
of the Lord—as would hold good in the end of every Christian
exhortation—but also as His authoritative sayings. The
presence of these tendencies alongside that which holds all
hortatory advice of equal value should not appear strange.
From the beginning, regulatory conceptions have existed
in Christianity alongside inspirational ones, and in the same
way, alongside of the spiritual interest, for which all Christian
exhortation had one divine origin, there stands the appreciation of tradition, of authenticity, and of authority.

There is probably a trace of these collections of Jesus'
words in 1 Clem., xiii, 2 (cf. also Polycarp ii, 3). The firm
outline of the Form of these sayings of the Lord almost

excludes the possibility of there being only incidental combinations of citations from our Gospels. With a certain amount of probability we may also include here the citation of a saying of Jesus in 1 Clem. xlvi, 8. All these sayings are introduced with similar formulas of citation: " Remember the words of our Lord Jesus, when He said " (1 Clem. xlvi); " Being mindful of what the Lord taught when He said " (Polycarp); " above all mindful of the words of our Lord Jesus, when He spoke teaching kindness and patience for He said (1 Clem. xiii)." The same formula is found to-day in Acts xx, 35, in Paul's farewell at Miletus, " Remember the words of the Lord Jesus how he himself said . . ." The citation which then follows, " it is better to give than to receive," is so much the more important, since the saying is neither in the Gospel of Luke, who composed Acts, nor in the other Gospels. In this speech the saying stands in connection with an exhortation to help the weak, and this connection, which is obviously quite fixed, meant that the author cited the saying in this hortatory speech although he had not included it in his presentation of Jesus' work.[1] Thus in all these passages we recognize hints of collections of Jesus' words which were expressly described as such, and were employed in exhortation with a typical formula of citation.

Hence we can say that at an early date, viz. already in the time of Paul, words of Jesus had been collected for hortatory purposes. And here again, as in the case of the Paradigms, the results of analytic work offer a proof to those reached by the constructive method. For what literary criticism has revealed as the source containing the sayings (Q) in Matthew and Luke gives a rough idea of such a collection. These texts show clearly that the collection was made with the object of passing on to the church directions

---

[1] If we attribute this speech at Miletus to Paul we harmonize the passage with the evidence, already discussed, from the Pauline letters. Moreover, we must also reckon with the fact that the method of citation is due to the author. Paul quotes in another way, and the formula used in Acts xx, 35, is typical of a later style, as the parallels show.

and teaching from the lips of Jesus. Two observations should be made here.

(1) In the whole of the Q material recognizable by us there is no reference to the story of the Passion. If the tendency of one source were toward narrative, we ought surely to expect a Passion story. According to all witnesses the Kerygma, the only sketch upon which a narrative description could be based, laid special emphasis upon the data of the Passion story, and a narrative of Jesus which ignored His death is scarcely conceivable in the interpretation which was added to the Passion story. Thus the Q material which we have received shows in its essential content no narrative interest. We must infer as this source little else than speeches, mostly indeed isolated, i.e. sayings without context. And where it appears different, careful examination shows that in what Matthew and Luke have in common, in what is therefore really from Q, the narrative impulse was scarcely present. For in the record of the message of the Baptist to Jesus (Matthew xi, 2; Luke vii, 18) there is just an introduction to a collection of sayings which puts together various pronouncements of Jesus concerning the Baptist. The collection is made more particularly in a practical interest. It serves to regulate the relation between the Christian community and that of the Baptist.[1] And in the case of the temptation, the synoptic narrative shows that the common text only begins with Mark iv, 3; Luke iv, 3, and contains only the dialogue between Jesus and the devil. Thus the source is intended to give the answers of Jesus rather than anything else. It is the Evangelists who invented the beginning and the conclusion of the narrative, each in his own manner. A similar observation can be made in regard to the Tale of the Centurion of Capernaum. The complete agreement

---

[1] That this tendency already dominates the source is seen from the conclusion in Matthew xi, 11. For the words "The least in the Kingdom of Heaven is greater than he" ought to be understood not from the historical stratum of Jesus but from the circumstances of the Church. Cf. my *Die Urchristl. Ueberlieferung v. Joh. d. Taufer*, pp. 13 ff.

extends only to Matthew viii, 10 = Luke vii, 9, and thus does not include the cure. The text of the source which probably assumes the cure without question (just as Matthew viii, 22 = Luke ix, 60, assumes that the questioner became a disciple of Jesus) concluded with the word of Jesus which praises what the centurion had said because it is the evidence of a faith which is not to be found in Israel.

Thus the total content of the groups of material which we deal with in Q still shows clearly the original tendency of such collections. Their purpose is not to deal with the life of Jesus, but to give His words in order that they may be followed and in order that they may instruct. Nevertheless it may be granted that the collection used by Matthew and Luke already shows traces of a more advanced development.

Thus passages appear to have been included which, though of totally different origin, have still the same office in this connection, viz. the handing down of the sayings of Jesus, to show and to prove who He was whose words had been gathered in the churches. The inclusion of the temptation narrative serves this purpose and so also does that word of revelation in Matthew xi, 25–30, which comes from an entirely different sphere. It represents Jesus as similar to a Hellenistic redeemer god, calling men to himself (cf. Chapter X). Finally, also, we ought to mention the sayings of Matthew xxiii, 34–9, which, as the Lucan parallels show, come from the source Q, and perhaps even there were connected together. These sayings are ascribed to Jesus or, if Luke xi, 49, is authentic, to " the wisdom of God ", and hurl a violent accusation against the Jews, for it is they who have always and everywhere persecuted those whom God has sent. In this connection the accusation is naturally calculated to explain why the Jews denied Jesus. Of retrospective significance also are other words of Jesus which have been collected and edited in the sayings of Q.

Thus the pronouncement of Jesus about the Baptist, Matthew xi, 7 ff.; Luke vii, 24 ff., came to its place when the words of Jesus about John furnished references to present events (cf. p. 244, note 1 *supra*) and the parable of the complaining children is made to refer to Jesus and John by means of an allegorical interpretation.

All this is naturally conceived not in a historical, or biographical, but in a practical interest. But this particular practical interest outweighs the one which brought about the gathering of the sayings of Jesus as already discussed. The immediate object was to obtain from the words of Jesus not only solutions of problems or rules for one's own life, but also to derive from them some indications about the nature of the Person who had uttered them. Speaking in the Jewish idiom, one may say that what had first been regarded as containing Halakha were now seen also to contain Haggada. We have already observed the operation of similar tendencies in the collection of stories by Mark. It is even not altogether out of the question that these special features of the source Q came into being under the influence of the Gospel of Mark. Granted, we cannot say anything certain about the matter, because the date of Q, and especially the chronology for its development, is altogether unknown to us.

But the tendencies just depicted have not been able to obscure the original character of this collection of the words of Jesus. It is perfectly certain that the sayings were not brought together at first for the sake of their Christological interest. Indeed, the passages which are to be claimed for Q show themselves on the whole to have a completely different interest. It is the same interest as we have already observed in Paul, viz. *the sayings of Jesus were originally gathered together for a hortatory end*, to give the Churches advice, help, and commandment by means of the Master's words. This typical interest was dominant both in the origin of this special source and also in the gathering together of the words of Jesus everywhere. The nature of the formulation and of the collection prove this interest.

We must first of all point out that tradition preserved numerous words of an hortatory content. This corresponds doubtless to a large extent to the nature of Jesus' preaching. The forms which Jesus most often employed are maxims (proverb, gnome), metaphor, parabolic narrative, prophetic call (beatitude, woe, eschatological preaching) short commandment, extended commandment given with a basis like Matthew v, 44 ff.; Luke vi, 27 ff.; Matthew vi, 25 ff.; Luke xii, 22 ff.; with a promise like Matthew vi, 2 ff.; with a threat, like Matthew v, 29 f.; Mark ix, 43 ff.; Matthew xviii, 1 f.[1] Of these six categories which are determined on purely formal grounds only the last few are unconditionally imperative. But we must also emphasize that so very many maxims and metaphors and, indeed, even parables are spoken in the sense of warning. This hortatory character of many words of Jesus was emphasized and strengthened by tradition. The words about salt and light are preserved in Mark (iv, 21 and ix, 50) and Luke (xiv, 34 f.; xi, 33; viii, 16) as pure metaphors. Mark iv, 23, urges understanding and application of the formula of alertness, "He who has ears to hear let him hear." In Matthew the personal appeal has been added: "You are the salt of the earth," "You are the light of the world," and over and above all this is the exhortation, "So let your light shine before men" (Matthew v, 13, 14, 16). We must also mention here the probable transforming of the Beatitudes. The Lucan form with its direct address may be regarded as the original. The form in Matthew is of richer content, and does not address those who are called blessed but describes them in the third person. But an exhortation

---

[1] Bultmann, *Gesch. d. synopt. Tradition* divides the words of the Lord into "Logia" (Jesus as a teacher of wisdom), "Prophetic and apocalyptic sayings" and "Commandments and rules for the church"; also "Sayings in the first person" and "Parables and the like". These categories are, in fact, characteristic of the content of the gospel, but formal criteria, as well as those of content, crisscross when we attempt to demonstrate these categories. Thus, according to Bultmann, Matthew v, 44, and vii, 1, belong to the Logia—although they have an imperative form. He also regards the parable of the ten virgins as a prophetic warning, and among the Logia he ranges general sayings (Matthew xxii, 14) as well as metaphors like the kingdom and the house divided against themselves.

lies in that very fact, viz. be ye spiritually poor, be ye com-
passionate, for this is your reward. At the same time modifi-
cations could not be omitted. Instead of the poor, we have
the poor in spirit ; instead of the starving we have those
who hunger after righteousness ; and a like modification
was preferred in the beatitude on the persecuted.

A similar hortatory tendency is seen also in the tradition of
certain parabolic narratives. The story of the deceitful
steward (Luke xvi, 1 ff.), who, by means of a last deceit before
his discharge, makes his future sure, contains an example
of decision. Translated into eschatological terms it offers
doctrine and warning to the Church of the disciples faced
by the great change. It contains no exhortation for common
life. And yet, just such an exhortation in Luke xvi, 9, formed
the conclusion, " Make for yourselves friends of the mammon
of unrighteousness." The parable of the meal proclaiming
salvation to the disinherited but condemnation to the apparent
subjects of the king, has been filled out with the parable of
the Wedding Garment (Matthew xxii, 11–14), whose hortatory
significance is clear : whoever is invited to the kingdom
must provide a " wedding garment " (i.e. something which
shows that he is a subject of the kingdom). The effort to
provide the Churches with as many exhortations as possible
sometimes occasioned complete misunderstandings of parables.
The exhortation freely to take the lowest place at the wedding
was doubtless originally meant as a parable intended to ward off
false-righteous claims before God. As found in Luke xiv,
7–11, it must be understood as an exhortation to ready
humility at a feast to which one is invited. And thus a rule
for conduct at table has grown out of an eschatological
warning. In the same way, the advice to come to terms with
an opponent while on the way to the court was originally
meant eschatologically and, therefore, introduced by Luke
xii, 57, with the words " Why even of yourselves judge ye
not what is right (i.e. probably from your own circumstances) ? " The point of the saying is that one must not

delay until the divine judgment but rather take early pre-cautions. This counsel of commonplace caution which Jesus applies parabolically, has become in Matthew v, 25 f., a rule valuable in itself, and so in the Sermon on the Mount, between the antitheses about the law, there stands advice to accept the cautious custom of the man in the street as Christian praxis.

The paranetic value set upon the words of Jesus has occasionally altered their content. The prohibition of divorce in the Gospel, as the sayings of Mark x, 9; Luke xvi, 18, show, is radical and unconditional, but is to be understood as a fundamental requirement from the eschatological standpoint. In Matthew it stands as a rule for the Church, and therefore an exception is foreseen. Adultery of one partner makes divorce possible even for Christians (Matt. v, 32; xix, 9). A modification which makes it practically possible to fulfil the commandment to love one's enemies lies also in the rationalization which is found in the variation of the com-mandment in Didache 1, 3,[1] " Love those who hate you, and you will have no enemy." The vigorous imperative of the Sermon on the Mount, never altogether capable of fulfilment since it requires that love should compel even natural human instinct, is now bent round into the practical and moral exhortation to set enmity aside by love.

A particular extra proof of their paranetic character is offered by the parables of Jesus. First of all in this connection we must be clear about the possibilities given to preaching by the use of metaphor ; the division into analogy, parable, allegory, example, with which Julicher's work on the parables surmounted an antiquated interpretation, gives no picture of the multitude of applications. We must first observe the *differences of Form*.

1. The comparison in the present (the mustard seed in Mark iv, 30 ff.). This is very close to the metaphor. But a genuine comparison says something about the reference

---

[1] From the Christian collection of sayings mentioned on pp. 240 f. *supra*.

of the picture,[1] whereas the short metaphor can stand unexplained, and hence remain as a problem for interpretation.[2] But naturally we must reckon with the possibility that in the Church a certain paranetic character was given to puzzling metaphors by an explanatory sentence, or by introduction into special context.[3]

2. The comparison in the past (the yeast in dough, Matthew xiii, 33 ; Luke xiii, 20 f.). Such a comparison makes the event happen once ; thus a quite small narrative arises. The parable of the mustard seed in Luke's form (xiii, 18 f.) shows that there is no necessary material difference from the first group. What stands in the present in Mark is here given in the past. Since Matthew offers a mixed text, we may trace the narrative form of the comparison to Q, the source of sayings.

3. Short didactic narrative (the house on rock and on sand, Matthew iv, 27 ff.).

4. The detailed, comparative narrative of a Tale-like character. The difference between this group and the three already mentioned consists, above all, in the poetic fullness of the present type. The great parables in Luke come now into consideration. The Good Samaritan, the Prodigal Son, the Unjust Steward, the Pharisee and the Publican,

---

[1] e.g. the saying about serving two masters, Matthew vi, 24 ; Luke xvi, 13, is a real comparison. In spite of the fact that it begins like a metaphor, " No one can serve two masters," it clearly expresses the application, " You cannot serve God and Mammon." We have pure metaphors in the sayings about the harvest (Matthew ix, 37 f. ; Luke x, 2) and the hand on the plough (Luke ix, 62). The latter case was connected only by the evangelist with the saying about followers (cf. p. 160, note 1).

[2] The relatively few sayings whose original reference is quite enigmatic are almost all unexplained metaphors : " Give not what is holy unto the dogs, nor cast your pearls before swine " (Matthew vii, 6; late application to the Lord's Supper, Didache ix, 5) ; " Wherever the carcase is, there the eagles gather " (Matthew xxiv, 28 ; Luke xvii, 37) ; " Everyone must be salted with fire " (Mark ix, 49; altered in the variants and related to sacrifice).

[3] In Luke xiii, 24, the saying about the narrow door still stands as a metaphor, and is only more closely defined by an introductory question. Matthew vii, 13 f., has begun to speak of life and destruction so that the whole feels like a comparison. The city on a hill (Matthew v, 14) is only explained by the context, for the saying itself an independent metaphor. In Luke xi, 34 ff., the saying about the eye is only joined by λύχνος to another saying by means of a proverb used as a connective. In vi, 22 ff., Matthew helped to give it meaning by placing it between the sayings against Mammon-worship, but the question still remains whether the original sense of the saying has thereby been brought out.

the Great Feast; also some in Matthew: the Labourers in
the Vineyard, the Talents.[1] We are dealing with the most
comprehensive matters in the words of Jesus. It is not
astonishing that these narratives have been retained in the
tradition. They are in fact particularly suitable for retaining
in memory in consequence of their clear and orderly construction. Their narrative style has ever and again drawn painters
and poets to depict the story by the means appropriate to
their art. But the poetic fullness of this style does not consist
in equal and uniform detail, but in expanding what is essential
and abbreviating what is secondary. In the parable of the Good
Samaritan the misfortune of the traveller is told quite shortly,
but each of the three who pass by is given in an independent
sentence. In telling of the kindness of the Samaritan the
narrator cannot quite do enough in enumerating all his kindly
measures. In the same way, in the fate of the Prodigal Son
the presupposition of his return, viz. his riotous life in the far
country, is only briefly suggested. The stress of the poor
fellow in the far country requires more space, but his reception
at home is given in full detail.

As contrasted with the short didactic narratives these
parables appear as popular compositions with a well-defined
style, and the epic laws of folk poetry can be observed in
them in large measure.[2] Sometimes we may suppose that Jesus
took up a narrative already known and filled it with a new
meaning. In the story of the steward and of the rich man,
exegetical considerations make conclusions of that character

---

[1] The parable of the Feast is in Matthew; that of the Talents in Luke, by the
interpolation of allegorical traits points to its meaning, so that the actual wording in
the parallel which is certainly older, always comes into consideration first for our
special purpose.

[2] I mention the law of (i) *repetition*—the speech of the Prodigal to his father
is given both when the return is planned and when it is carried out. (ii) *antithesis*—
Pharisee and Publican, Dives and Lazarus, two debtors, two servants in debt, two
sons, three delegations to the wicked vinedressers (?), three men who pass by the
man who has been robbed (Good Samaritan), three servants to whom money has
been entrusted. The two last-mentioned cases show the law of " Three " in comparison with that of " *worthy of honour* " (" Worthy of Honour " when combined
with the number *three* is the foremost mark of folk composition. Olrik, 1909, p. 7).

probable. Recent researches into some of the parables have
led to tangible results.[1]

The full significance of the differentiation of the parables
as just now put forward only appears if we take account of
the content. Here we must first observe the *differences of
material.* The story of the parable may contain :

1. What is commonplace, as in the parable of the dough.

2. What is typical, as in the parable of the Complaining
Children (Matthew xi, 16 f. ; Luke vii, 31 f.) and of the Sower
(Mark iv, 3 ff.).

In the first case, in the narrative of the commonplace
events, what is said is unimportant in itself, for it is always
happening. In the second case, it is brought out because
it is frequent, and it is noteworthy, but not remarkable, in the
common sense of the word.

3. What is extraordinary.

4. Imaginary cases.

Both of these deal with remarkable matters ; the third
group with isolated events in real life ; the fourth with
improbable, or indeed with impossible, happenings which
have been imagined in order to serve a didactic purpose.
The great parables in Luke belong in general to the third
group. It is not easy to classify some other parables, because we
cannot answer the question of the possibility of the events
concerned. Thus the interpretation of the parables of the
virgins (Matthew xxv, 1 ff.) and of the labourers in the vineyard
(Matthew xx, 1 ff.) depends, in the first parable, upon whether
a real wedding custom is to be presupposed, or in the second
whether it is a possible mode of payment, or whether in both
cases usage and custom have simply been imagined.

But in each case it must be emphasized to what degree
the material of the parables portray the world of Jesus. From
the agrarian interests of the person and their social limitation,[2]

---

[1] Cf. Bousset, *Gött. Nachr., phil.-hist. Kl.,* 1916, p. 484. Gressmann, *Abhandl. d.
Berl. Akad.,* 1918, phil. hist. Kl., No. 7.

[2] That the farmer has only one servant both for his farm and for service at a meal
(Luke, xvii, 7) ; that the other employer (Matthew xx, 1) himself goes out to hire

we see readily that these narratives are racy of the soil, and this holds good of the whole group just mentioned. Our general impression can be strengthened by a multitude of parallels which show mostly not that Biblical parables are dependent upon old Jewish ones, but only that they had a common life and viewpoint.

Only on the basis of the observations here suggested in regard to the material of the parables can anything be said about the *differences in the application* of the material, as they become especially clear in the narrative parables. And now also the criteria are justified which have become the common possession of research by Julicher's exegesis of the parables. The following applications may be observed :

1. The story of the parable contains the didactic thought in its very application, as in the narrative of the Good Samaritan (Luke xxx, 29 ff.) and the Pharisee and Publican (Luke xviii, 9 ff.). The former had doubtless a paranetic sense : " Go and do thou likewise." The latter wants to show the true attitude of man to God by the picture of the Publican and by the antithesis of the Pharisee. The explanation lies in establishing that the Publican was " justified ". But, on the other hand, it corresponds with the paranetic tendency of tradition that a moral is added even when this is established : " He who exalts himself will be abased, and he who abases himself will be exalted." Thereby the parable receives a commonplace ethical meaning which is far removed from its wording.

2. The " story " really clothes the leading thought. Hence the action takes place not by its own right, but as dictated by the didactic conception. In this way the parable of the tares can be explained (Matthew xiii, 24 ff.), which introduces the "enemy" as if he were a known personality. He is not a hostile neighbour of the farmer by any means, or the narrator would have to

---

labourers; that the woman (Luke xv, 9) so greatly rejoices over the recovered drachma, and that the father of the prodigal (Luke xv, 23) causes *the* fatted calf to be killed—all this shows that the pictures were taken from the lives of peasant farmers.

explain the cause and beginning of the enmity, but he is the arch-" enemy," the devil. Thus we have here an allegory in spite of the fact that, for example, the servants are not " explained ". The clearest mark of allegorical purpose is the fictitious character of the narrative, which cannot be altogether understood from itself alone. For this purpose, the differentiation we have already made (cf. pp. 249 ff. *supra*) is of much value.

3. The story exists by its own poetic right. But an element of the action is concerned with the idea of teaching, although this belongs to quite another sphere than the action of the comparison. This is the nature of parable in the special sense of the word.

The question arises here whether the concern must always be confined to one point. The groups mentioned under 2 and 3 do not appear to be separated unconditionally from each other. An allegorical comparison like that of the Tares contains elements which are not " explained " (cf. under 2), and a parable like that of the Prodigal Son is intended to apply its teaching not only to the reception of the prodigal, but also to the rejection of the angry brother.[1] Of course we may always ask whether the second point was only intro- duced into the text by an extension of the original comparison. And indeed we must often reckon with the fact that those who made use of the parables often extended and edited them. But certainty of decision is not possible because as a rule we do not know to what situation these parables were originally fitted. Even if we succeeded in eliminating later applications, the application then offered cannot always be regarded as original, because it seems sometimes too moralized, too little eschatological, too static, or too little dynamic. The moralizing tendency has already been remarked in the case of the parable of the Pharisee and the Publican. Similar things can be

---

[1] For what follows, and for a constructive exegesis of parables as such, cf. C. H. Dodd, " The Gospel Parables," in *The Bulletin of the John Rylands Library*, vol. xvi, No. 2, 1932.

seen in the Parable of the Talents. In Luke xix, 12–27, the
parable is concerned with the absence of the Lord gone abroad
to receive his kingdom—an allegorical reference to the
time until the parousia during which Christ lives in heaven.
The text presented in Matthew xxv, 14–20, contains no such
references, nor any other application. Hence at first glance
a moral exhortation constitutes the essential content of this
narrative : we must use the gift which God has given to
men. But does it require a whole story in order to bring out
an almost axiomatic moral ? And is it the nature of Jesus'
gospel to preach commonplace " human " messages of that
sort ? Should we not rather construe the sense of the parable
dynamically and find in it an accusation against the Jewish
people who do not know how to use the precious heritage
entrusted to them by God ? With such purely constructive
considerations we may perhaps approach the original sense
of many a parable. But in any case, we must reckon with the
fact that we do not know the original references of numerous
parables.

In this connection we should bring out another difficulty.
It is rooted in the fact that certain metaphors were already
customary in Jewish exhortation, and the hearer was therefore
prone to understand the words concerned in the usual sense,
even when the parabolic narrative gives no occasion to do so.
It would appear that the mention of a King—in Rabbinic
writings often described as a " King of Flesh and Blood "—
referred to God ; the mention of a vineyard to the people ;
a field to the world ; and certainly also—at least in apocalyptic
circles—a harvest to the Last Judgment ; a marriage to the
commencement of the Messianic era. Half-allegorical forms
might have arisen in this way, for in re-telling the parables
those metaphors might have been unwittingly employed ;
and also the recognized metaphorical words, perhaps occurring
in the text of the parable without special significance, were
allegorically transmuted.

An example is offered by the parable of the Talents in the

Lucan form which transforms the absence of the Lord into a royal journey (cf. p. 251, n. 1 *supra*). The parable of the Ten Virgins (Matthew xxv, 1–12) offers another example of such a hybrid form : here the wise bridesmaids approximate to the bride, who celebrates her marriage with the bridegroom, for Matthew xxv, 10, says " The bridegroom came, and those who were ready entered with him into the marriage, and the door was snut ". These are believers who wait for the Messiah, and these same believers now celebrate the " marriage " with him. Really these maidens are only the train ; really in this place only a mention of the bride was to be expected. All these points of a " pure " parabolic narrative retire into the background ; the hearer-reader has long ago passed from the parable to the thing, i.e. from the bridesmaids at a human wedding, to the bride, i.e. to the host of believers who marry the Messiah. The introduction of such metaphors into a parabolic narrative therefore must have led occasionally to a kind of allegory of which the narrator was probably scarcely conscious. But the style of the pure parable is considerably disturbed by this allegorization, and a type arises which can no longer be called pure parable-Form, nor yet allegory.[1] Perhaps this narrative class, hovering between parable and allegory, specially suits the oriental mind. For to him the metaphor is obviously closely related to the riddle, and, therefore, a premature indication of the meaning is welcome. We recognize that clearly in the song of the vineyard (Isaiah v, 6), for the owner of the vineyard betrays his identity prematurely, when he not only threatens the vineyard with what lies within human power, but also declares that he will forbid the clouds to rain upon it. It is Jahwe Himself who speaks here. From the standpoint of purity of style, such things might appear as objections to the laws of metaphorical speech ; but hearers and readers certainly found this previous hint of the solution of the secret as a special advantage.

---

[1] It seems to me that Jülicher's classic work, *The Parables of Jesus*, requires at least limitation in this direction.

To what extent such half-allegorical forms go back to Jesus is hard to say. But in any case we must reckon that the tendency of the Churches to derive *as much exhortation as possible from the words* of Jesus must have affected the handing down of the parables. We have already spoken of some transformations and misunderstandings (cf. pp. 248 f. *supra*). The development towards exhortation can be easily illustrated in the parable of the Sower (Mark iv, 2 ff.). The parable may be held as a short didactic narrative with a typical, but not ordinary " story "—for a single sower would not as a rule experience on one occasion all the misfortunes described here. But, on the other hand, the " story " contains nothing which is invented for the benefit of the explanation, for no one thinks of Satan in the case of the birds who devour the seed on the wayside, and no one thinks of " tribulation or persecution " (iv, 17) when the sun burns up the rootless stalks. Rather the narrative gives the impression that different results of sowing are described, and, thereby, that the kinds of misfortune are described with special vividness. If the parable existed originally without application, its meaning is certain : it was intended to give comfort and calm in the face of misfortune and failures—just as the parables of the mustard seed and the yeast in dough give comfort and calm in regard to the small beginnings of things (i.e. probably of the movement which Jesus initiated). But now the paranetic influence operates ; more was desired from the narrative than comfort and calm ; one wished to get out of it teaching or warning against misfortune, and so the different kinds of bad ground which gave no lastingly good fruit were explained. The change of the note in the explanation shows that the paranetic tendency has been interpolated. In the text of the parable the comforting words are : misfortunes are unavoidable, even the Sower does not escape them ; in the explanation the warning is sounded ; but not like those among whom the word does not find good soil. But this paranetic transformation is so axiomatic for the Christian

Churches and, as we have seen, lies so close to the growth
of tradition, that we can scarcely conceive the parable in
tradition without its explanation.   When the text became
current, it was made capable of paranetic use.   We owe the
preservation of the words of Jesus in this case also to the
desire for exhortation.

We have already shown by the parables of the Steward
and of the Pharisee and of the Publican that parables received
a hortatory conclusion.   The narrative example of the Rich
Fool (Luke xii, 13-21) is also significant.   It describes nothing
else than the sudden end of all the schemes of the rich farmer.
It is " moral " in the paranetic sense, if the warning be added :
" Thus it happens to one who lays up treasure for himself,
and is not rich towards God."   For nothing was said in the
parable about lack towards God.

It has become clear what an important rôle is given to
exhortation in the preserving of Jesus' words.   The paranetic
interest can also be seen in the *assembling and grouping* of
these sayings . . . In Matthew v, 21 ff., Jesus' antitheses
to the law are reproduced in the form of a definite group of
sayings with the lay-out : " You have heard . . . but I say
unto you."   Into this layout other sayings are interpolated
which belong to the theme (Matt. v, 23 f., 25 f., 29 f.).   On the
other hand, the layout sweeps round and fastens on sayings
which have been handed down by Luke without the framework
of such a layout (Matthew v, 38, 43).   Everything serves
the production of a long, hortatory, connected passage.   The
same holds good of the sayings about John the Baptist,
which were obviously present in the source bound together
with Jesus' answer to the Baptist (Matt. xi, 7–19 ; Luke vii,
24–35).   The practical purpose here is to teach readers the
inferiority of the Baptist's sect.   Thus to the extent that a
warning is contained therein—the warning to reject the claims
of the Baptist—this section may also be traced back to
indirect paranetic tendencies.   This is only properly the case
in the sayings which Matthew xviii interpolates into the

dispute of the disciples about rank ; here the point is about
saving what is lost, as well as the discipline which is to be
exercised upon a sinful brother ; from sayings of Jesus a
whole Church " ordinance " arose, into which the parable of
the unmerciful servant was interwoven.

Naturally not all the words of Jesus were put into immediate
relationship with exhortation. The prophetic exclamations,
like certain of the words in the first person (cf. Chapter X),
mostly escape paranetic transformation. But we should note
that both the prophetic exclamation against Chorazin and
Bethsaida, and the so-called apocalyptic passage occurs in
Luke, in a historizing connection it is true, and is applied
to the sending out of the disciples (Luke x, 13–15, 21 f.).
But in Matthew they stand together with the " speech "
about the Baptist in a context conditioned by the subject-
matter (xi, 20–30). This speech supplies material for warding
off opponents—in this case the Baptist's sect. The sayings
against Chorazin also ward off opponents, and the commencement of the apocalyptic passage says that " this "
(salvation) is hidden from " the wise and prudent ". And,
since in Matthew xii, 1 ff., two Sabbath disputes follow, we
have a pledge that we have rightly understood the relationship of the sayings in Matthew xi, 20–30, viz. the whole
passage, Matthew xi, 2–xii, 14, deals with opponents (even
the Baptist as the patron of his disciples is an opponent),
and hence is conditioned by practical and paranetic interests.

Only when the standpoint is clear in accordance with
which the formulation and assembly of Jesus' words took
place can we understand the historical process of handing
down which interpolated these words into the narrative
of Jesus' works. Only when we perceive that narrative
material and speech-material were complexes of tradition
originally orientated quite differently, can we comprehend
that these complexes were only quite gradually interwoven.

In this connection, we must touch once more upon the
problem at first sight so severe, of the *relation between Mark*

and the tradition of the sayings. If we begin by noting that Mark obviously did not intend to write down the words of Jesus in their totality, we must see that this was not on account of personal prejudice, but because this tradition of the actual words had been preserved, in a way quite its own, separated from the handing down of general events, and kept for quite special purposes. The combination of the two webs of tradition was therefore not so inevitable as it appears to us to-day. The fact that Mark does not give the material which we find in the Q sections of Matthew and Luke is not at all strange. Rather the question could be asked why Mark gives any saying of Jesus in a form already in various passages arranged in little speeches.

This question is to be differently judged according to the nature of the particular word of Jesus with which we are dealing. I hope I have already shown in the previous chapter that Mark endeavoured to explain the Passion of Jesus beforehand by means of practical remarks and also by carrying through his theory of a Messianic secret. The inclusion of such words as Jesus speaks in dispute with his enemies obviously serves this interest of the evangelist, e.g. Mark iii, 22 ff., against the reproach of being in league with the devil; vii, ff., concerning ritual cleanness, and x, 2 ff., concerning divorce. We have also seen to what extent Mark's Gospel is a book of secret epiphanies. As such an esoteric revelation to the circle of the trustworthy, Mark included a whole apocalyptic speech (Mark xiii, 5 ff.). As a revelation which is comprehensible only to the initiated, he similarly introduced the parables in iv, 10 ff. In this way these words always appear in a historical context transformed to some extent into narratives. The conception is not far off that Mark included also sections of the heritage of the actual words either because they were already transformed into narratives or because he could so transform them. Quite obviously is this the case in the sections dealing with the dispute about rank (Mark ix, 33 ff.) and about the greatest commandment (xii, 28 ff.). These narratives are really only words of Jesus in a narrative setting.

The scene in Mark xii, 35–7, which speaks of the Messiah as the son of David, and which constitutes the conclusion of the disputes in Jerusalem, appears only in Matthew, however, as a conversation. But in Mark it is only a saying introduced into the text which was handed down as an example of Jesus' critique of scribal learning. It is improbable that in passing it on Mark had more in mind, e.g. to put forward a Christological theory, for the evangelist gives no hint of any such thing. He simply supplies the additional saying with his biographical framework. Perhaps the narrative of " the widow's mite " (Mark xii, 41 ff.) can be traced back to a saying of Jesus, and especially to a parable.

Even the story of the Canaanitish woman (vii, 24 ff.) may belong here.[1] In this way Mark included in his book a part of the tradition of the actual words, but under recognized points of view. If we have rightly understood the matter (cf. pp. 236 f. *supra*) he made no secret that he was only giving a selection, and that the greater part of the tradition of the words of Jesus was left out of account.

But in so far as Mark included in his book any words at all of Jesus from tradition, he began a development of the greatest consequence. What he offers elsewhere in his work is not the actual Christian preaching, but material for its support, indeed material already rounded off, fixed, and

---

[1] A comparison of Mark with Matthew shows that only words of Jesus and the reply of the woman correspond approximately word for word. The beginning and the end differ entirely. The assumption is therefore near that there was a source common to both, a source which contained only these speeches and which assumed the healing as obvious and natural—i.e. a primitive form such as we can also pre-suppose for the story of the Centurion of Capernaum (cf. pp. 244 f. *supra*), and which was probably handed down not among the paradigms, but among the sayings of Jesus. To what degree such passages were normatively, i.e. parenetically, understood or to what extent the attempt was made to see their value as fundamental data of differentiation from the Gentile problem is shown by the interpolation into the story of the Centurion (Matthew viii, 11 f.), of the promise that many Gentiles should eat at table with Abraham in the Kingdom of Heaven. We get the same impression of a fundamental application of the traditional material if we read the remark interpolated into the story of the Canaanitish woman : " I am sent only to the lost sheep of the house of Israel " (Matthew xv, 24).

interpreted. In part these texts, e.g. the Paradigms, were already formed for the purposes of preaching ; in part e.g. the Tales were of a different origin, but, as Mark's application of them shows they were used as proof-passages of Christian teaching and as witnesses to epiphanies of Jesus. The preaching itself, the " gospel of Jesus Christ ", can be only indirectly taken from the stories collected by Mark. At best in the interpretations do the ideas used in preaching appear openly. On the other hand the words of Jesus were collected in order to give candidates and those who were already Christians directions for practical life, and these words constitute a part of the Christian exhortation and therefore of the teaching itself. If Mark includes such words in his book, though still in small quantity and from a special standpoint, he thereby carries his book over the limits of a mere collection of materials, for it now contains a Christian message, though only in the most modest degree, and not only proof texts for this message.

Luke and Matthew advanced considerably along this road when they included the material gathered in Q, material reproducing the words or the conversations of Jesus either entire or in part. This they did, however, under completely different conditions. Luke is writing history, as elsewhere, in this connection. He places the sayings of Jesus in narrative contexts and puts them into the corresponding places, i.e. into those which seem to him historically probable. That he thereby approximated to the surrounding literature of the surrounding world, and assimilated the tradition of the sayings of Jesus to that of a " Chriae " kind, has already been shown in Chapter VI. But in this way he transformed the original style of the tradition of sayings in so far as by his framework he gave a narrative character to this tradition. The passages from Q are to some extent approximated to the Marcan type. Luke himself is perfectly conscious of this historical mode of writing in his work. In the prologue indeed he declares the purpose of his book is to give certainty to Christian preaching as far as this can be reached by means of narrating historical facts. This is an object which ultimately would be in place for Mark's Gospel.

Matthew did his work in quite another way. He brought together the tradition of actual words into long speeches, where he offers the words of Jesus arranged on distinct themes. And he ordered even the Marcan tradition, at least in the first half of his book, in cycles according to the viewpoint of the material. With him the main thing is not the narrative, but the systematic arrangement. For this reason, in contrast with Luke, he made the narratives of Mark to some extent approximate the style and type of Q. Naturally in doing so he did not act from literary considerations like Luke, but he followed a practical need of the churches for quite short narrative matters, in which however he transmitted the words of Jesus further and, in certain circumstances, commented on them. This is my explanation of the well-known tendency of Matthew's Gospel to abbreviate the narrative.

In this way were Tales separated from their secular connections, i.e. set free from the detailed descriptions which were to a large extent of a secular character and, as opportunity arose, transposed into an edifying key. We have already described this change of style in our examination of the Tales (cf. pp. 77 f. *supra*). The Paradigms appear to have been similarly shortened, at any rate in the narrative parts, whereas the words of Jesus seem to have been extended here and there. In this way the stylistic differences between the two narrative-categories have been obliterated, and the working out of the words of Jesus, as well as the systematic arrangement of the materials, change even the narrative vehicles of the traditional teaching in the sense of Q.

It is not at present my task to describe the special qualities of the evangelists. I will only attempt to bring out the important consequences which have followed upon introducing into the narrative description of Jesus' work a tradition of the actual words which had been gathered really for hortatory purposes. The word " Evangel " is the name given to the preaching of salvation, and the earliest Christians made no difference between the preaching of Jesus and the preaching about Jesus. Indeed at an early date they put Christological expressions like Matthew xi, 25 ff., on the lips of Jesus Himself. But this " Evangel " is something which on the whole still lies outside of the Marcan Gospel and to which the evangelist refers only as opportunity arises. Even the first expressions of his document signifying, if I understand the matter rightly, not his book but the Christian estimate of the story of the Baptist as " The beginning of the preaching of salvation ". St. Matthew's Gospel really offers some of the preaching, of course in a historical frame, but with a systematic pedagogic arrangement and cast. This is the earliest Gospel of which it can rightly be said that it contains " The gospel ".[1]

In the full sense of the term this is really true only with the appearance of John's Gospel. We may suppose that the books of Mark and Luke first received their own title as the Gospel according to Mark or Luke,[2] when they were brought together with Matthew or with Matthew and John.

With the penetration of the words of Jesus from the " exhortation " into the descriptions of the work of Jesus, a development begins which the composer of the fourth Gospel at length completed in his own way. The book which at first was only a supplement to the preaching thus became

---

[1] In this connection an old observation appears to gain significance. In xxiv, 14, and xxvi, 13, Matthew writes " this gospel " where Mark xiii, 10, and xiv, 9, has " the gospel ". " This gospel " naturally does not mean simply " this my book ", rather it expresses of course the very near relation of the book to the gospel, i.e. to the preaching of salvation. For Mark the gospel is something existing outside the book, but Matthew can rightly say : " This gospel which I proffer in my book." Should, therefore, the introduction of the word " this " be regarded as really only accidental ?

[2] We must, of course, suppose that Luke's work before being accepted into the canon had a special literary title with the author's name in the possessive case, for it is hardly conceivable that the author would mention the name of the person to whom the book was dedicated without mentioning his own. Only when it was counted among the Gospels did Luke's book receive a title corresponding to that of the other Gospels. Cf. Ed. Meyer, *Ursprung*, i, 3, and my *Geschichte d. urchr. Lit.*, p. 47.

its substitute : in the place of the oral entered the written evangel. Naturally even then the sermon was not exhausted, but it ceased to be the foremost vehicle of tradition. What unwritten tradition is still contained was in large part indeed taken up into the apocryphal Gospels.[1] In this way the river of tradition shrank more and more, and we gain insight into the first stage of this process when we observe the words of Jesus being written down.

[1] As far as the Gospel of Peter is concerned, cf. my *Geschichte*, chapter vii.

CHAPTER X

MYTHOLOGY

If I am right in my description of the foundation of the gospel tradition through preaching, the view is once more confirmed that the story of Jesus is not of mythological origin, for the oldest witnesses of the process of this formation, viz. the Paradigms, do not tell of a mythological hero.

It is interesting to pursue the question how mythological narratives about Jesus would appear. In this connection myths can only be understood to mean stories *which in some fashion tell of many-sided doings of the gods.* Not every narrative of mythical persons is a myth, but only such as is filled with a special sense or which depends upon a special relation, such as that between the original form and the rite rising from it ; or the narrative may depict the processes of the world's origin, of the starry heavens, of vegetation or of human fate after death. It may bring the nature of a god into typical form by means of a story. Any such a relationship gives meaning and value to the narrative about the gods as far as concerns the cult-community which narrates it. In such cases the story is a myth. Thus Christian myths would either represent the nature and the conduct of a strange god who had taken on the name of Jesus—this would be the Christianization of foreign myths—or else they would describe epiphanies of a Christian Son of God either in typical incidents, i.e. celebrated in the cultus, or taught by preaching. In such a case we should speak of myths of Christian origin. Neither of these possibilities is realized in the Paradigms, for most of them tell of commands and decisions of Jesus. *These, however, are not the words and the work of a god, but of a teacher.* And, even in the few stories of healing to be found among the Paradigms, the point is usually not the healing but the teaching about forgiveness of sins or breach of the Sabbath, which teaching Jesus confirms by the healing. Really the only exception is the healing in the synagogue (Mark i, 21–7), but here, as we have seen (cf. p. 57, n. 2 *supra*), the story cannot be logically carried through without obscurities. Rather we trace, at least at the conclusion, perhaps also in the motif of the demonic recognition of the Messiah, the pragmatism of the evangelist, which is indeed of mythological character.

The same view as that regarding the Paradigms applies also to another group of the most ancient tradition of Jesus, viz. the sayings gathered together for hortatory ends. What the Churches preserved of the words of their Master as rules and for teaching purposes shows *the sign of a teacher rather than a god*. It would be conceivable of course, when deeply affected by the blessings of such a teaching, that one would have carried back the sayings and the regulations to a god already honoured and recognized in his nature. This kind of linking of law and teaching into an already existing myth is not unusual. But it is impossible, at least in that time of religious romance, that a god would enjoy an epiphany in such sayings, or that in preaching a cult nothing else could be said of the god than the parables of Jesus or the words of the Sermon on the Mount. Paul brings a striking confirmation. He knows this tradition of the sayings and makes use of it when he desires to regulate the life of the Church. But where he preaches the cult of his God, i.e. of the " Lord " Jesus Christ, one looks in vain for a reference to any actual word of Jesus.

The letters of Paul are an unambiguous proof that there once was a *Christ mythology*. At the same time they are a proof that this mythology could not be supported directly from the tradition of the life of Jesus. For Paul knew this tradition to some extent (1 Cor. xi, 15), and if he had needed it he could have made its acquaintance much more closely but the Christ-myth through which for his churches he explains the great act of Divine redemption, had no need of the data handed down. This myth told the story of the Son of God who abandoned his cosmically intermediate place ; in obedience to the Will of God he suffered a human fate, even to death on the Cross ; he was finally raised by the power of God from the deepest humiliation to the status of " Lord " to whom all the world owed honour till He should come to conquer His enemies and to rule His Kingdom. The earthly life of this Son of God is only a stage. That He took this life upon Himself " in the form of a servant " is more important than *how* He lived it in detail. The happenings of His everyday life on earth are unessential as compared with the great cosmic turning-points of His path, viz. 1. In Divine form. 2. Arrival upon the earth. 3. Raised to a new heavenly glory. The earthly opponents disappear before the demonic, i.e. before sin, to conquer which He came to earth ; before the powers and authorities which bring Jesus to the Cross, but which, as arisen, He overcomes through His resurrection. It is of no particular importance to observe in this mythical connection that even the human life of the Son of God is full of blessed power. When we turn over in our minds the mythical journey of Christ from Heaven back to Heaven we shall not regard it as a miracle that the Son of God is superior to men but rather that He is like them.[1]

Paul is not the only creator of a Christ-mythology. He only makes a greater distinction than others between the revelation of the humiliation and exaltation of the Son of God on the one hand, and the human tradition of His earthly life on the other, thanks to that dualism which gives the special character to his Christianity. To others who had become followers of Jesus in a more human manner, and

[1] For further details I may refer to my *The Spiritual World in the faith of St. Paul*, 1919, and "The Worship of Isis in Apuleius", *Heidelb. Sitzungsberichte*, 1917. 4 S., 28 ff.

whose Christianity therefore was not of this character, the earthly life of the Master appeared to be the most valuable witness of His heavenly origin. It was the preaching of the eyewitnesses and of their disciples which must have had this estimate as its consequence. And perhaps even in their case, certainly in that of their hearers, this estimate might take on a mythical frame if it were not actually expressed in a mythical exposition of that very tradition.

A thoroughgoing mythological presentation of the life of Jesus, it is true, would have had to extend to the events in which the heavenly origin of the Master came to decisive expression. We should, therefore, have had to expect a mythological formulation of His descent upon the earth, and also of His death and of His liberation from death by resurrection and return to heaven. Of the events of His earthly life the most important for a mythological presentation would be the commencement of His work, and perhaps also a particularly significant moment in His activity. It is, however, significant for our tradition that this thorough-going mythical formulation has not been carried out. This shows how firmly at bottom this tradition kept its feet upon the ground. A mythology of Christ only gained place very incompletely within the description of the life of Jesus.

First of all there is lacking a mythological presentation of the *descent of Christ* upon the earth. The Legends of the shepherds and of Simeon bear witness to the greatness, and announce the future, of the child already born, but nothing is said about the way in which God became man. The Legend of Mary (Luke 1, 26–38) depends upon the secret of the divine origin of Jesus. But it tells nothing of true mythological happenings, and nothing of the theogamy or of the miraculous incarnation. It confines itself to announcing the soteriological event in the form of an intermediate report: the divine paternity of the Child in the body of the Virgin. Thus this Legend, resting upon a theologumenon of Hellenistic Judaism, avoids every kind

of presentation shaped mythologically : it is not a " mythological" but a " legendary" event which takes place.   Moreover
it is not written for the pleasure of writing, but paraphrases
and consciously veils the message. We know what a mythology
of the Incarnation would look like from the descriptions
in the Ascension of Isaiah (x, 18–xi, 11), and in the Epistula
Apostolorum xiii[1] : Jesus descends through the heavens
and takes on the forms of the angels through whose midst
He passes in the different spheres of the heavens. It is the
view which obviously Paul presupposes, when he says
in 1 Cor. ii, 8, that none of the rulers of this world knew
wisdom, "for had they known her they would not have
crucified the Lord of glory." But it is indicative of the conservatism of the Gospel tradition that such a presentation
of the Incarnation is lacking in the Gospels, although the
conception was to be found at least in certain Christian
churches.

In the same way, as is well known, a description of the
Resurrection of Jesus is lacking in the Gospel texts until the
time of the Gospel of Peter. In the place where it ought
to stand in the Passion story, there is to-day the Legend of
the empty grave. In this position formerly there was certainly
the record of the appearance of the Risen Lord to Peter.
The middle point of the Legend of the grave is the Easter
message of the angel. This Legend does not sound in any way
like a myth, and it leaves the question unanswered as to
when and where Jesus left the grave. Certainly Matthew
interpolated into the Legend of the grave a description of an
angel descending from heaven, and perhaps thereby intended
to indicate the resurrection (Matthew xxviii, 2, 3).   The
Gospel of Peter, however, gives a real description of the
resurrection (xxxv–xliv). This is mythologically conceived
throughout : two angels descend from heaven ; the stone
moves from the grave by itself; the Risen Lord is led by
the angels out of the grave, His head reaches higher than

---

[1] In the Kleine Texte, No. 152, pp. 11 f.

the sky—the cosmic dimensions of the mythological hero—
and the Cross follows Him. It is diagnostic of the faith of
the Church that, as Matthew xxviii, 2, 3, shows, need was
felt for such a presentation, but it is just as diagnostic of
the Evangelical tradition that it did not satisfy this need. Again
a further interest : the mythology of Christ does not come
to expression in the tradition, viz. the interest in the descent
of Christ into hell,[1] which undoubtedly was already in existence
but which was not satisfied immediately, because the descent
into hell, being an event outside the earthly sphere, found
no place in the Gospels amongst the records which confined
themselves to earth.

The only narratives in the Gospels which really describe
a mythological event, i.e. a many-sided interaction between
mythological but not human persons, are the records
of the Baptismal miracle, the Temptation of Jesus, and the
Transfiguration.

The Baptismal miracle would not be a mythological
narrative if the revelation from heaven originally and essentially
was meant for John the Baptist as is the conception of the
Fourth Gospel (John 1, 32, 34). But the earliest record
(Mark i, 9–11) makes Jesus Himself experience the heavenly
voice and the event interpreted by it.[2] The original sense
of this event is doubtless that Jesus at this moment was
instituted Son of God, and that this was made plain by the
descent of the Spirit upon Him. But if we are only dealing
with a solemn description of what Jesus already is, and
therefore with an epiphany, the Spirit would have to appear
as His possession. Here, however, the Spirit descends, and
Jesus receives Him as a lasting property, and thus the greatness

---

[1] There is also significantly lacking in the Gospel traditions every description of
Christ's stay in Hades, whether for conquering death or for preaching to the dead.
A hint of this preaching is found in the Gospel of Peter, 41 f., a hint of the liberation
of the dead perhaps (Matthew xxvii, 32 f.).

[2] That is the meaning of εἶδεν in Mark i, 10. The sky opens for Him, He sees
the Spirit. No question is raised about what the others perceived. But the idea in
εἶδεν is not that we have to do with a vision, i.e. with a subjective event in our
sense ; what is meant is the real, objective, perceptible presentation of the Spirit.

now proclaimed was not formerly proper to Him, rather He receives it only at this moment.   The story tells, therefore, of Christ's adoption as the Son of God.   That is also the meaning of the heavenly voice, for this employs a formula of adoption : " Thou art my beloved Son "—which means in Oriental legal language : Thou shalt be so, " I have chosen thee "— and therefore the institution follows.   In the pre-canonical form of this story the heavenly voice is given also in the form of Psalm ii, 7 : " Thou art my son, this day have I begotten thee." This wording which, by the emphasis on " this day " brings out the idea of adoption still further, did not get into the Gospels, but was preserved in the outside tradition and came from it, like many another, into the " Western " text of Luke (iii, 22, D. Itala). But at bottom it expresses materially nothing else than what the common text originally intended, adoption as the Son of God.

This idea of adoption, of course, could not remain in the two Gospels which had already described the child Jesus with full divine glory (as in Matthew and Luke).   Luke " nailed " the narrative down in literary interests (cf. p. 161 *supra*).   He excluded any doubt about the corporeal form of the dove (Luke iii, 22), and he reported finally that Jesus prayed when He left the water.   Here, as in ix, 28, before the Transfiguration, he brings the heavenly revelation into connection with the human and saintly activity of Jesus upon earth.   It is a characteristic diagnostic for the Lucan conception of Jesus, for he likes to supply Jesus with the virtues of human religiousness (cf. Chapter VII).   But by that means he transposes the whole narrative into the region of personal Legends.   Matthew, on the other hand, trans- formed the revelation to Jesus into a public announcement : " And behold the heavens opened," " This is my beloved Son " (Matthew iii, 16 f.). Thus out of the adoption he made an epiphany similar to the Transfiguration in all three evangelists.   Its content now is to make visible in a solemn moment the glory, otherwise hidden, of the Son of God.

It is and will probably always remain a question whether Mark united a special Christological idea with his reproduction of this adoption narrative. In no way had he brought to expression whether Jesus for him came to be baptised as already the Son of God, or whether He only received this glory by the Baptismal miracle (p. 231, note 1). Perhaps in this case he felt himself only a vehicle who had to hand on the traditional narrative. Out of this there arise the right and the duty for the exegete to understand the mythological traits of the narrative without regard to any theological ideas of Mark's Gospel which may be found elsewhere. The character of these traits is quite clear on the whole: the heavens open; the Spirit appears as a dove and descends upon Jesus; the heavenly voice says that God has chosen this Jesus for His Son. Details are questionable: especially do we not know whether and in what connection the dove stood as the symbol of the Spirit.[1] In the same way we cannot say anything provisorily about the sphere of ideas in which the reception of the "Spirit" makes one a Son of God.[2]

Beyond the canon the mythological elements of the narrative grew still stronger. According to "outside" tradition, as preserved in Justin (*Tryphon*, xxviii, 3) fire flashes from the Jordan. Ignatius unites mythology and mystery: "He was baptised in order that He might cleanse the water through His sufferings" (Eph. xviii, 2). The 24th Ode of Solomon provides the mythological event with the necessary cosmic background: the dove sings over the Anointed, then fear and the dread of death make the world tremble.

But long before such developments of a mythological

---

[1] Cf. Strack-Billerbeck, i, 123. "There is only very slight probability that it (the dove) was also regarded as a symbol of the Holy Spirit." In fact, none of the parallels brings forward anything decisive.

[2] The Jewish Messiah was apparently to be a vehicle of the Spirit. Cf. Michaelis, *Reich Gottes*, etc., 4 f.; but the term "Spirit" for the Spirit of God is un-Jewish; cf. Dalman, *Worte Jesu*, i, 166. The absolute τὸ πνεῦμα appears to be a term belonging to Greek Christianity. In any case, the beginning of the Messiahship of Jesus was meant.

character had entered in, mythology as such had become
historically localized in the earthly life of Jesus in connection
with the baptism of Jesus by John. We may even guess that the
miracle was never related by itself, but always in this connection.
A question how this had been reached can be answered
without the help of literary hypothesis, and also without
the help of psychological combinations. It is not credible
that the origin of the whole narrative goes back to what
Jesus Himself told of His inner experience at the
Baptism, otherwise the section would have been preserved
as a word of Jesus. The question why the Adoption
was brought into connection with the Baptism can be answered
automatically from tradition. For the Baptism of John
stands as the beginning both of the preaching of salvation
and of the work of Jesus (Mark i, 1 ; Acts i, 22 ; x, 37).
Thus it constitutes the terminus *ad quem* for the reception
of the Spirit ; but it is also the terminus *a quo*, because the
old tradition used nothing at all of a still earlier stage of
Jesus' life. But by its combination with the historical events
of the Baptism the miracle is certainly removed from the
purely mythological sphere and arranged in an earthly
environment, and thus the whole record has the effect almost
more of Legend than of mythology.

The forty days in the wilderness (Mark i, 12 ff.) is for Mark
a consequence of Jesus' possession of the Spirit ; the tempta-
tions occur continually during those forty days. Nothing
is said about a particular scene of temptation. But a conversation between the devil and Jesus was handed down in the
source Q, and that Marcan note which mentions the Temptation gave the occasion to Matthew iv, 1–11, and to Luke iv,
1–13, to narrate the dialogue here. Thus the framework of
the conversation became mythological ; the very homage
of the angels (Matthew iv, 11) makes this impression. The
conversation itself, however, is concerned with the question
of Messiahship. Its first point is to confirm the fact and the
reason why Jesus had not done certain miracles ; no miracle

of self-help, no miracle of display like casting Himself down from the Temple. It is intended in the same way to demonstrate that He had done nothing to obtain power by human means.[1] The conversation teaches that all this is of the devil and thereby it gives Christians an exhortation.

Analogies from comparative religion, particularly the temptation of Buddha do not come into question as sources. They only show that there is a law of biographical analogy (cf. p. 108 *supra*) according to which, before entering upon their office, holy men must come into some dispute with an opponent from the realm of the demons.

In the midst of the description of Jesus' works, there stands in all the Synoptics a narrative which expresses most clearly of all synoptic passages a Christ-mythology: the *Transfiguration of Jesus* (Mark ix, 2 f.). The analysis of this story in the latest research seems to me to suffer quite essentially when it is believed that the problems bound up with it can be solved altogether by separating out the various motives,[2] creating another context,[3] or another course of the action, or, finally, by teasing out a historical kernel.

Even if there were nothing to say as to whether and in what way Mark invented connections backwards and forwards at the beginning and the end of the narrative, the principal action would be described clearly and as a unity. Peter's word (Mark ix, 5) says something which is not to the point. The meaning is not that holy circumstances have arisen in which it would be useful to make tents for the holy man, for Peter's word is clearly enough characterized by Mark ix, 6, as a misunderstanding. The right understanding lies in the

---

[1] Thus there is a difference between the two first acts of temptation and the third. This can be explained by saying that in the third temptation the devil dropped the pretence of concern for Jesus' success and frankly suggests a compact. In this case the third temptation is certainly the last (the change in Luke is topographically conditioned) and can be well understood as the last.

[2] Cf. Lohmeyer, *ZNW.*, 1922, 185 ff.

[3] So Wellhausen, ad loc. K. G. Goetz, *Petrus*, 1927, pp. 76 ff. ; Goguel, *Jean-Baptiste*, 1928, 210 ff.; Bultmann, ii, 278. All regard the Transfiguration as an old narrative of the Resurrection which has been transposed into the life-time of Jesus.

opposite direction : only for a moment is Jesus seen for what
He is when in conversation with those prophets who have
not died a natural death but now already live in glory. In
order to be able to speak with them Jesus must appear for
a moment as a heavenly figure. Hence He is revealed as the
Son of God, and this " epiphany " is described (ix, 3). Then
God Himself approaches, present in the clouds as formerly
during the wandering in the wilderness, and proclaims the
Divine Sonship of Jesus : " Him shall ye hear." The words
spoken by the heavenly voice imply in no way adoption as
in the old form of the Baptist story, for Jesus is already a
Son of God when He becomes " epiphanes " (ix, 3).[1]

The verse which concludes the appearance (ix, 8) gives,
if properly understood, the end of the event. The disciples
can now look round again, i.e. the cloud which dimmed their
sight has disappeared [2]; only Jesus is " with them " ; this
implies that He has come back from the heavenly to the
earthly sphere ; thus He must have put on His earthly form
again.

From the passages which we have just examined we can
see at least the need which the narrator felt of making room
within the earthly life of Jesus for a mythology of Christ.
It is possible that this tendency influenced the formulation
or at least the understanding of the tradition of the Tales.
We showed in Chapter IV that Tales could arise either by
extending Paradigms, by introducing foreign motives, or
by borrowing foreign material. In every Tale we must
examine the elements upon which the breadth of its style
depends. We must ask whether these elements were originally
Christian, or if they are Christian but secularized, or if they
arise altogether from foreign and borrowed material. The
last supposition can only be accepted if the story as a whole
has no relation to the Gospel as is the case, for example,

---

[1] It is significant that here God does not say that He has chosen Jesus as at the
Baptism, but that men shall hear this His Son.

[2] From this it follows that the variant $αὐτῷ$ (Syr[s] for $αὐτοῖς$) in ix, 7, is
incorrect, for all three disciples were " overshadowed " by the cloud.

with the miracle of changing the water into wine at Cana.
The god whose epiphany is found in this miracle must be
a god of wine. One of those kinds of story might have been
told about him which, as mythology, perhaps contained a
fairy-tale motive.[1] When this wine miracle was transferred
to Jesus, a Tale about Cana, with its secular narrative manner,
grew from the myth. The evangelist supplied it with a footnote which explained the Tale in the sense of a " myth "
about Christ : " He revealed His glory and His disciples
believed on him." (John ii, 11).

We have already mentioned the story of walking on the
sea (Mark vi, 45–51) as an example of the secularization of
the Christian narrative by non-Christian motives (cf. p. 100
supra). In the motif of the epiphany " he made as if to pass
them by " (vi, 48), the narrative receives its special character
which does not accord with the Gospel. But this story could
have been understood as referring to the mythical waters of
death, and for this reason, then, the disciple Peter was made
to walk upon the water (Matthew xiv, 24–33) ; Jesus being
the mythological hero, and Peter the mystic who imitates
Him.[2] Naturally we are only dealing now with possibilities,
but that such possibilities lay near to the Christians is shown
by the Odes of Solomon, 39, where, in speaking of the
" powerful streams ", it says : " the Lord has bridged them
by His word, He walked and crossed them on foot. And His
footsteps stand (firm) on the waters, and were not erased ;

---

[1] Cf. p. 273, note 2, *supra*, for the possibility of a connection between mythology
and fairy tale.

[2] As already mentioned there is a Buddhist parallel to Peter's walking on the sea,
in the narrative of the lay brother who walks across the river Aciravati (cf. p. 116,
supra). But Peter is called by the Lord and walks on the water by His command
and thus it is his faith that holds him up. The Buddhist narrative is one of
miraculous self-help ; the river blocks the lay-brother's way and the ferryman is
absent. What holds up the brother is his joyful thought of Buddha. A Christian
parallel to this self-help is found in the narrative of Bisarion (*Apophth. Patrum.
Bisarion*, 2) mentioned on p. 175, note 5, *supra*—re the narrative of Peter,
we must prove that the walking on the water appears to belong to the typical
miracles in the contemporary miracle-literature. Cf. Lucian, *Philopseudes*, 13 :
τί γὰρ ἔδει ποιεῖν αὐτὸν (the Hypoboræan) ὁρῶντα διὰ τοῦ ἀέρος φερόμενον
ἡμέρας οὔσης καὶ ἐφ' ὕδατος βαδίζοντα καὶ διὰ πορὸς διεξιόντα σχολῇ καὶ βάδην.

they are as a beam that is firmly fixed . . . And a way has been appointed for those who cross after Him." [1]

How powerful is the mythological background of many a Tale narrative, can be recognized even in a trait apparently so harmless as the word of Jesus in the story of the Epileptic (Mark ix, 10). " You unfaithful generation, how long shall I be with you, how long shall I bear with you." Thus speaks the God who appeared only temporarily in human form quickly to return to Heaven. If more of the texts of the apocryphal Gospels had been preserved to us we should presumably be acquainted with far more myths and mythological motifs which had been connected with Jesus. In the synoptic Gospels, Tales open to such an influence found a place only alongside parables and sayings.

As we saw, Mark included them because they served as supports for his conceptions of Epiphany. And now we may even characterize this representation as mythological, for Mark narrates the story of Jesus under the conviction that the glorious heavenly mode of existence was proper to the hero of his narrative. Indeed, His disciples saw Him in this mode of existence at the transfiguration. In the time of His earthly life this glory is, indeed, hidden, and must be hidden —whence the theory of a secret. But the narrator rejoices in every moment in which at least to the eyes of his readers he can free Jesus from the earthly sphere and represent Him in His true worth. This is the significance of the recognition by the demons, i.e. the lower creatures of the spiritual world sense the Son of God. Without any doubt that is a mythological conception, as the Son of God is represented with a peculiarity characteristic of Him as a demon conqueror. But the extent of this conception in Mark's Gospel is only very small for it covers only the framing which the Evangelist has given to tradition. *Thus in the last analysis the Gospel of Mark is certainly a mythological book*, although what is true

---

[1] *The Odes of Solomon*, xxxix, 9, 10, 13. Engl. translation. Ed. Rendel Harris and A. Mingana, 1920, ii, p. 396.

of the Form into which it was thrown is not true of the material itself. *Only to the smallest extent is the tradition assembled in the Gospel of a mythological character* and this is confined to the epiphany narratives and a few Tales. In the majority of its sections Jesus does not appear as a mythological person.

It should not remain unmentioned that the mythological idea penetrated into the handing down of the very words of Jesus. It is to be seen everywhere where Jesus speaks as the risen Lord or as the " Lord " in full possession of His divine status. Even in the passages which must be ascribed to Q one such text is to be found, i.e. the revelationary passage, Matthew xi, 25–30.[1] Three closely connected strophes[2] depict the nature of revelation, (1) to whom it comes—not to the wise but to the foolish ; (2) who transmits it—only the Son ; (iii) and who invites to share in it—" Come unto me." That these three strophes belong together is sometimes disputed. The Semitic character of the first strophe is then insisted upon,[3] or else the Old Testament and Jewish character of the third[4] is brought out, and attention is drawn to the fact that the second strophe with its " Hellenistic " use of " knowledge " stands out between the other two like a foreign body. But the different coloration of the conceptions alone cannot furnish a decisive proof against the connection of these three strophes, for it is in accordance with the nature of Hellenism that Semitic conceptions should be reproduced in Greek language and united with material of another kind. In addition the conception of revelation,

---

[1] Norden, *Agnostos Theos*, p. 277 ff. appears to me rightly to have described the place of the logion religiously and historically, but his literary deductions on the other hand do not convince me.

[2] All three strophes are to be claimed for Q in spite of the lack of the third in Luke. They belong together in their material and the omission in Luke x, 21 f., can be explained, viz. the situation in which he has set the logion of the return of the 70 entirely excludes the giving of the third strophe. I leave on one side here the question whether in one of the strophes is a word of Jesus much transformed as supposed by Bousset and (with reservation) by Bultmann for the first and J. Weiss for the third strophe.

[3] Cf. Strack-Billerbeck, *Kommentar*, i, 606 f., ad loc. Bultmann, 2, 172.

[4] Cf. Strack-Billerbeck, ib., 608 ff.

and of the bearers of revelation, which stands behind the
second strophe arises like the other conceptions from the
Orient and not from Greece. Admittedly the three strophes
stand alongside one another to a large extent disunited. The
cause of this may be the different kinds of origin. To solve
this question we need to be able to prove what was intended
as the subject of the revelation in xi, 25, i.e. the content of
what was hidden from the wise, but revealed unto babes,[1]
and we can never know that. In Q, however, the three
stories obviously stood together, and would express a single
thought. Thus we have a right to equate the first strophe's
object of revelation with the knowledge (of God and the Son)
with which the second strophe deals, and to explain at one
time the whole three-strophed complex. This principle is
decisive, especially for understanding the third strophe.

The saying is recognized to be widely different from the
synoptic type of the words of Jesus. The Christological
content, the concentration on the ego of the speaker in the
third strophe, the mystic responsion in the second, [2] the totally
unevangelical idea of " rest " [3]—all this indicates the religious
and historical place of the text to be outside of the sayings of
Jesus. But what is still more important is that the whole
text serves for the self-recommendation of the speaker and
of the revelation brought by Him. We must not be led astray

---

[1] In the tradition of the words of Jesus it does not appear to be impossible that
a passage would begin with such an apparently unconnected ταῦτα. In the question
of authority, a passage which apparently belonged at first also to the tradition of the
words of Jesus, a similar ταῦτα was already firmly planted (Mark xi, 28), which
also had no immediate connection (cf. p. 45, note 1). Hence it does not necessarily
imply a context in Matthew xi, 25.

[2] In the non-canonical form of the text testified by Justin, Marcion, Irenæus,
" No one knows the Father except the Son and no one the Son except the Father ",
the second phrase is merely the customary responsion to the first. The theme is thus
the knowledge of the Father, and that may be the original because Jesus the revealer
from whom men should learn is not really the unknown, but rather God whom He
reveals. Not without purpose does the strophe begin "All is given me of my Father";
Jesus is thus the mediator of God for the world, and hence what is to be revealed
must be the knowledge of God. The reversing of the phrases in the MSS. puts
a Christocentric in the place of a theocentric context and in consequence speaks of
the secret of the person of Jesus in the first place.

[3] In this " rest " we are dealing with something which can be gained only by
revelation.

by the form of the first strophe: "I thank Thee O Father that Thou hast hidden this from the wise and prudent and hast revealed it to babes." Only in form is this a prayer of thanks but in fact it is a sermon on the true receivers of revelation, a sermon out of which we can see the nature of this revelation, —and at the same time now in actual fact the nature of the gospel of Jesus is most truly seen. The prayer-form has only the value of a demonstration somewhat as in the well-known prayer of Jesus at the grave of Lazarus, John xi, 41 f., which is only offered for the sake of the surrounding people in order that the close connection of Jesus with the Father may be evident to them. In the same way, the second strophe of our text brings a self-recommendation, for it serves to proclaim the " Son " as the exclusive herald of the revelation : " All things are given to me by my Father." The third strophe also stands in the same category, which, in the address to the " weary and heavy laden " and in the requirement of meekness and humility, is once more so similar to the gospel. But its essential content consists in a concentration upon Him who speaks and who imposes the " easy yoke ". But this is not the teacher who had spoken of the narrow door and who by his severe requirements had frightened many rather than drawn them. But *this combination of self-recommendation and of the preaching of conversion is the typical mark of the divine or semi-divine herald of a revelation in Hellenistic religiousness, i.e. of a mythological person.* In these ways speak sons of God and supermen who promise the world the only true salvation. Celsus, piling up examples and thus exaggerating, described their nature " I am God—or the Son of God— or the Spirit of God. I am come because already the world is failing, and you men must be destroyed on account of your sins, but I will bring salvation " (Origen, *Contra Celsum*, vii, 9). Similarly also the heathen Gnostic prophet in the *Corpus Hermeticum*, vii, 1, 2. " Why are you being kept away ? You are drunken . . . Stand firm, turn sober, look upward with the eye of the heart . . . seek a guide to

lead you to the door of the house of knowledge ; there
you will find the bright light which is pure from darkness ;
there none is drunken, but all are sober, and they look up
and see with the heart. Alone He should be seen.[1]

Little sermons of this character are also to be found in
Corpus Hermeticum, i, 27, and also in Philo " *De sacrificus
Abelis et Caini*, 70 ".   One is quite justified also in adducing
as a parallel the speech of the half-divine virgin in the thirty-
third Ode of Solomon : " O ye sons of men, return ye ; and
ye their daughters come ye ; and leave the ways of that
Corruptor and draw near unto me ; and I will enter into you
and bring you forth from destruction, and I will make you
wise in the ways of truth." [2]   He who can have such words
laid on his lips has no place on earth as the teacher of a people
or of a school, but he comes, himself of another origin and
nature, to the children of men in order to deliver them from
the destruction inherent in their nature. Here is proclaimed
the typical saving gospel of Gnosis. The form of the
Redeemer in this gospel, however, is of divine nature and
cosmic form—a mythological being.

In the Churches in which the passage Matthew xi, 25 ff.,
arose, the person of Jesus was looked upon in the light of
this redemption faith. That is why these words were put into
His mouth, and the collector of Q found that text in front of
him already as a word of Jesus and therefore included it.
That a need was felt for Jesus to proclaim Himself in such a
manner is proved above all by the extra-canonical tradition
which in this case also—as we have already similarly observed
in the narrative materials—more readily granted entry to

---

[1] English translation in Walter Scott, *Hermetica*, i (1924), pp. 171, 173. The
beginning of the translation is in its form an imitation of the passage Pseudo Platon-
Cleitophon, 407*a*. But it is precisely the comparison of this text (and of that in
Epictet, iii, 22, 26, which also quotes Cleitophon) with the Hermetic, which shows
how much more religious is the latter and how much more pessimistic its gnosticism.
The passage from Philo quoted above maintains about the mean between the tone
of philosophical apostrophe of the former and the latter from gnostic literature.
" Flee ye fools, to the only physician who heals the ills of the soul ; let all that go
which this suffering generation falsely calls ' help ' " (*de Sacrif. Abel. et Caini*, 70).
[2] Engl. trans. Harris and Mingana, op. cit., ii, p. 374.

mythological tendencies than did the canonical literature. Specially to be mentioned in this connection is the third of the sayings of Jesus in the Oxyrhynchus papyrus i, 1. " I entered into the middle of the world and appeared to them in the flesh and I found them all drunken and none found I among them who thirsted. And my soul is troubled for the children of men because they are blind in heart . . ." Here the characteristics of the passage of Matthew xi are to be observed in yet higher degree. Still more striking is the relationship with the phraseology of Hermetic preaching, and still more emphatic the status of the speaker in cosmic mythology. The significant association of self-recommendation and hortatory preaching has formed, however, a noteworthy expression in the ninth Ode of Solomon. If I am right, the Anointed Himself speaks there.[1] " Open your ears and I will speak to you. Give me your souls that I may also give my soul to you. The Word of the Lord and His good pleasures, the holy thought that He has thought concerning His Messiah . . . Be enriched in God the Father, and receive the intention of the Most High . . . for I announce peace, to you His saints ; that none of those who hear may fall in war. And that those who have known Him may not perish and that those who receive (Him) may not be ashamed.[2]

By a comparison with such texts we may perhaps trace a mythical attitude in other words of Jesus in the canonical Gospels. In particular is this true of the *missionary command* of the risen Lord, Matthew xxviii, 18 ff. The words stand in no historical situation since every question which the narrative text of Matthew xxviii, 16, 17, raises, remains unanswered : How does Jesus appear ? how does He disappear ? how does He deal with doubters ? which hill is meant ? On the other hand the union of self-recommendation and exhortation to preach is most striking here. The exhortation, however, is

---

[1] That the anointed one is mentioned in the third person is nothing to the contrary since it belongs to the style of these apocalyptic speeches to leap from the first to the third person. Cf. Matthew xi, 27a and b, 28 ; John v, 19, 30.

[2] Op. cit., pp. 259, 260.

an exhortation to preach, and is directed to the disciples, whereas the self-recommendation expresses unambiguously the dignity of the Risen and Ascended Lord, and therefore has a mythological character more unmistakable than Matthew xi : all power in heaven and on earth is given to the Risen Lord and His presence is assured to His own to the world's end.

Detailed research into the verbal tradition teaches us also to recognize one or another word of Jesus as a word of the risen Lord, as the language of a mythological person. This may be the case in the saying : " Where two or three are gathered together . . ." Matthew xviii, 20.[1] In a much more mythological form, perhaps influenced by legend, the motif of omnipresence is to be found once more among the words of Jesus contained in the Oxyrhynchus Papyri (i, 1, No. 4). There, following a saying imperfectly preserved, but which obviously had the same sense as Matthew xviii, 20, we read : " Lift the stone and there you will find me, split the wood and I am there." Among the Oxyrhynchus sayings we meet with the one which has a parallel in the Gospel to the Hebrews, and which I mention here because its language is remarkably related to the Hermetic. The saying is : " Let not the seeker rest until he find and when he finds he will be astonished, and when he is astonished he will rule, and when he rules he will find rest " (Oxyrhynchus Papyri iv, 654, No. 2).[2] It is true that the ego of the speaker retreats in this connection and one may suppose that the saying had first existed as a word of Gnostic wisdom, and then been placed on the lips of Jesus. It is well known that certain synoptic sayings such as Matthew xxiii, 34 ff. = Luke xi, 49 ff., xiii, 34 f., lead one to

---

[1] In this case we should compare the saying which the Mishna, Aboth, iii, 2, ascribes to R. Chananja b. Teradjon (second century, first half), " but if two sit together and occupy themselves with the words of the Torah, the Shekina is in their midst.

[2] Compare a " chain " with " seek—find—(present) " in the Kore Kosmu. (*Stobæus*, i, p. 386, 15, Wachsmuth), similarly with " Look—wonder—recognize ", *Corp. Herm.*, iv, 2. " Rest " as the object of " search " at the end of the prayer, *Corp. Herm.*, xiii, 20, and " think—believe—rest ". *Corp. Herm.*, ix, 10.

think of such a process of transference (cf. p. 246 *supra*) but I shall not enter here upon an examination of it, for even if these and other words be placed upon the lips of the risen Lord, nevertheless the mythological element in them properly so-called is not clear enough for us to speak of the influence of mythology upon evangelical tradition.

But it is possible to speak of such an influence in the case of the book in which the development here described first really reaches its conclusion, viz. the Gospel of St. John. The need constantly meeting us in the texts we last examined, viz. of letting the mythological Christ speak, is here satisfied and satisfied completely and this in Tales and revealing words which stand like strangers among the other sections of the tradition in the synoptic Gospels. Rather in the Gospel of John it is everywhere the post-existent who speaks. There is scarcely a word or a deed which does not express what Jesus the risen Lord is and brings to His own. The work of Jesus is here related really as the story of the Son of God, a story which is full of holy and esoteric relations to faith and worship. Here everything is mythological.

But this mythological formulation does not destroy the inherited content of the story. The Gospel of John relates the work of Jesus from the Baptism of John onwards to the Easter appearances. Thus his sketch is contained formally within the framework of tradition. And a little attention will discover many other traits of tradition in John, as is indeed generally granted in regard to the story of the Passion. Only it is surely not simply the synoptic tradition which comes to light here, but often another and more Tale-like heritage. But now it is no longer, as is the case in the Synoptics, that the combination of myth and tradition is brought about by the construction and the framework. Rather the evangelist has loosened the stereotyped from the tradition, and to some extent broken it up. He expanded it, added to it, interpreted it ; he linked it up with the self-revealing speeches of the Son of God and thus lifted it up into the mythological. In this way a new unity arose, not always and without exception a happy combination, although indeed fundamentally well carried out. This combination is most markedly different from the editing of tradition at the hands of the Synoptics.

The future belonged to this book. It conserved what was most valuable in the tradition, but *the tradition has entered into the realm of mythology*. The Gospel of John told of the same divine Saviour, who was worshipped and confessed in public worship. The development of the two entities, tradition and mythology, with their mutual influence, had reached its conclusion here. The two entities had bound themselves together, and as the development just mentioned shows, this combination was necessary and viable. And it is exactly in connection with research in John's Gospel that an understanding of the history of Gospel-Form leads to knowledge of historical origins.

CHAPTER XI

FORM, HISTORY, THEOLOGY

The fortune of primitive Christianity is reflected in the history of the Gospel-Form. The first beginnings of its shaping hardly deserve to be called literary. What Form was present was determined by ecclesiastical requirements arising in the course of missionary labour and of preaching. The Passion story, the most significant piece of tradition for Christian faith, was told relatively early as a connected story. Moreover isolated events from the life of Jesus, suitable for sermons, were told in short stories, and sayings and parables were used especially for a practical purpose. But pleasure in the narrative for its own sake arose and seized upon literary devices. The technique of the Tale developed, and lent meanwhile a fully secular character to the miracle stories. In addition, legendary narratives full of personal interest in the persons of the sacred story joined themselves to the periphery of the tradition. One told of these persons in the same way as similar narratives from the surrounding world spoke of other holy men. Already between the lines of the Gospel-Form one can see that the faith of Christendom moved from its fundamental strangeness in the world and its self-limitation to the religious interests of the Church, to an accommodation to the world and to harmony with its relationships.

And further, right at the beginning of the history of primitive Christian literature, there stood a tradition of an unliterary nature, consisting of short narratives and striking sayings, which were repeated for practical purposes. Those who gather them gradually try not only to give their context, but also to interpret them and, indeed, to make their point of view explicit. Thus it comes about at length that the mythological element takes charge of the entire material of evangelical history. But this also corresponds to the general development of primitive Christianity which passes from a historical person to his formal worship and finally to the cosmic mythological Christ of Gnosis, and to ecclesiastical Christology.

The Gospel Forms bear clear witness not only to these developments, but also to the *subject matter*. The earliest formal constructions, the Paradigms, give us insight into a class of man to whom all literary effort, every artistic aim, each emphasis upon personal impression in the course of the narrative, is completely strange. The writers of our present-day literature, who pay attention to individuality and psychological refinement, lack in general the inclination and the ability to reproduce an event simply and pointedly, and without admixture of their own. The narrative method of the " people ", however, avoids explaining the outer or giving the motive of the inner. And it is precisely this lack which we, unaccustomed to such an attitude in a narrator, find, in certain circumstances, specially attractive and artistic. As proof that this kind of oral tradition even to-day flourishes in the East, are the stories collected by Hans Schmidt and Dschirius Jusif in the winter of 1910–11 among the peasants of Bir-Zet in the mountains of Ephraim.[1] Besides the legends, sagas, and fables, there are " histories " and " experiences ", formulated for the purposes of handing down tradition. This collection constitutes the best examples of popular tradition-making in modern times.

But we must not be misled by the epithet " popular ", and without more ado classify (say) the Paradigms in the same category as those *folk-tales*. For what differentiates the primitive Christian type from that type of narrative must not be overlooked. I mean its explicit aim at propaganda. The

[1] Hans Schmidt u. Paul Kahle, " Volkserzählungen aus Palästina " (*Forschungen z. Rel. u. Lit. des. A. u. N. Test*, Hft. 17 and 18, 1915 and 1930.

Paradigms aim at proselytising, but the folk-tales aim at amusing and even perhaps impressing with a certain popular sagacity. For this reason the Paradigms are lacking in the playful freedom which characterizes the Palestinian and also other folk-tales, often in a complex way; a more earnest discipline has made itself felt in them. Witness is borne to that fact by all in the style which we perceive is due to devotional aims. Preachers and teachers were interested in preserving these stories. They would serve both for converting unbelievers and for teaching believers.

That the words of Jesus were preserved, that they were put together to form " speeches " with a single theme, and, not least, that the sayings and parables were edited in the interest of exhortation, shows the Church's concern for shaping life according to the commands of the Master. What was said at first only in face of the impending eschatological Judgment now gains significance for a lasting period and for the necessary consolidation of the Church in the midst of the world.

This consolidation had certain consequences; the Church came into contact with the world, and this contact was partly assimilative and partly defensive in character. Missionaries must guard themselves against compliance, teachers must arm themselves for explanation. One learned now to tell of Jesus in another way, a way already current in the world : Jesus was presented in His epiphany as Lord over illnesses and natural powers. Or else He was made to express the meaning of His mission in powerful language. And while the expansion of the Church was presenting itself in this way in the forms of its tradition, within the Church other narratives were growing up as evidences of devout intimacy with the persons of the sacred story, viz. Legends which were fitted to answer all questions of pious curiosity but which the earlier tradition had foregone.

But the significance of the history of the Form of the Gospels for the historical criticism of evangelical tradition is by no means exhausted with such an illumination of the circumstances. Indeed, the formal criteria seem to me perfectly fitted to exclude the subjective judgment which easily makes itself felt as a matter of experience in the examination of the historicity of the evangelical narratives. The undoubted impression that more trustworthiness belongs to certain stories than to others can be more exactly settled with the differentiation between Paradigms and Tales. It can be rooted in the nature of tradition and finally become a certainty. In their connection with preaching the Paradigms possess a means of protection against unhistorical extensions and other corruptions. Just because the simplest preaching of Jesus itself made use of it, it may be traced back as a category to the generation of eyewitnesses. Indeed, unprejudiced reading of these stories shows that their trustworthiness is not subject to such great questions as that of the Tales. The impression given to many unprejudiced readers of the life of Jesus in the Gospels, that it is narrated in a true, human, simple, and artless manner—this impression ascribed by many theologians to the Gospel of Mark—rests fundamentally neither upon all the Gospels nor upon this one, but to a large extent upon the paradigmatic narratives alone. To mention the most striking : miraculous elements are to be found only in complete isolation in these stories. Among the eighteen Paradigms mentioned (p. 43 *supra*) are only five miracles, and these five miracles, viz. the Healing of the Demoniac in the Synagogue, of the Lame Man, of the Withered Hand and of the Dropsical Man, and the Blind Man of Jericho, are all so recounted that it is not the miracle but the fundamental idea in Jesus' preaching which stands in the foreground. And simple cures are recorded whose historicity cannot at once altogether disappear even in an era of criticism and of scientific therapy. If one leaves entirely out of account the stories of healings religiously conditioned, like those at Lourdes and Bad Boll, nevertheless the healing process in cases of severe damage and mental disturbances occasioned by shellshock must be regarded as significant witnesses for the possibility of such rapid cures. The so-called therapy by domination,[1] with its influencing of the will, with the rapidity of the process and with the greatness of its result, has reminded not only theologians of the miracles in the life of Jesus. Of course, in such cases the difference between exact record and a narrative cast in devotional form must not be overlooked and the historicity of each cure narrated in a Paradigm should not be asserted out and out at once. At best only their possibility can be granted in view of those astounding psycho-therapeutic cures, and even this judgment tallies with the results of stylistic examination.

In the same way the historical understanding of the longer narratives, of the Tales, is put upon an assured foundation by knowledge of their Form. As a result of a bringing together of their stylistic characteristics, the impression of a certain inter-relationship is confirmed and illumined, an impression which the great miracles of the life of Jesus make upon the unprejudiced reader. This similarity is connected with the rise of a new style of narrative in primitive Christendom, and this development is just as much conditioned by certain requirements of the worship of Christ which needs epiphanies as by the increasing pleasure in graphic narratives, a pleasure whose pre-supposition is to find oneself in line with the world. The historical place of this new method of speaking about Jesus can be more exactly fixed. It represents Jesus as the miracle-worker, as has already been shown, and puts the powers and the means of the miracle in the foreground of observation. Thereby, its historical place is altogether in line with the Greek and the Oriental conception of Prophets, Magi, and wonder workers, all of a nature similar to the divine. These figures were, however, quite strange to pre-Christian

---

[1] Vgl. Willy Hellpach, "Die Psychotherapie der Kriegsneurosen," in *Der Tag*, 1918, No. 155; Micklem, *Miracles and the New Psychology*, 1922, etc.

Rome.[1] But this disguise was the appropriate means for making comprehensible to the world who Jesus was. Moreover, the extra-Christian conceptions did not operate to such an extent that the Synoptic Tales became collections of most capricious miracles. Most of them keep to a line not foreign to the essence of the gospel. Of all the great miracle stories in the Synoptics it is only the banishment of the demons into the swine which clearly puts the reader into a world outside Christian views and life. Our analysis of these Tales (cf. pp. 87 ff. *supra*) has shown that this general impression can be assured and sometimes explained by the method of Formgeschichte.

The historical reliability of the Tales·is in no way guaranteed by these demonstrations, rather analysis has already shown that the Tales are only to be used with great caution as historical sources. They lack the protection which preaching furnished to the Paradigms, and they were open to the invasion of foreign motives, since the shaping of their form was not influenced by missionary requirements, but by the pleasure of narrating the Tale. We have already discussed the various possibilities for the rise of the Tales in Chapter IV. A historical judgment, accordingly, must be reached afresh for each Tale ; a general critique appears impossible. At best we may here once more insist that the early rise of these stories would have been unthinkable if Jesus had not enjoyed the reputation of performing astonishing deeds of this character. According to John x, 41, it was known of the Baptist that he " had done no signs " ; but of Jesus obviously the very opposite was said. Thus the Tales had their point of origin in history.

How far that can be said of the Legends proper, i.e. the narratives examined in Chapter V, remains untouched, for

---

[1] Lembert, *Das Wunder bei den römischen Historikern*, S. 40 f., contends that " according to Roman belief God did not give men power to work miracles ". In the case of the miracles of Vespasian in Alexandria we are dealing with Oriental conceptions ; " Only when it is essential that the miracle-worker is the Roman Emperor is this movement set going in Roman dress."

here we are dealing with material of very different origin, all of which was shaped from the same standpoint. The Legends of the Childhood do not belong to the material of tradition about Jesus' work. Many of the other Legends were only shaped out in special honour of holy persons, but, of course, have their final basis in historical reality. I am thinking, for example, of the stories of Martha and Mary, or of Zacchaeus; and this origin is altogether clear in the Nazareth Legend, which contains the legendary form of material preserved also elsewhere. The estimation of the two Legends of finding the ass and the Passover Room depends upon historical judgment about the context, i.e. upon the criticism of the history of the Triumphal Entry and the dating of the Last Supper. But we must again speak of the self-limitation of the Legends in the Gospels. We have already brought it out that the motive of miraculous self-deliverance, a favourite theme of the Legends of saints, is still completely in the background in the Gospels (cf. pp. 105 ff. *supra*). But also other motives, diagnostic for saints' lives are lacking in the Legends of the gospel tradition.

General observations of this character are better able to show how conservative the tradition of Jesus really is than considerations of detail applied to passages of the New Testament. Moreover, this conservatism hangs naturally together with the *chronology*. At the period when eye-witnesses of Jesus were still alive, it was not possible to mar the picture of Jesus in the tradition. Chronology furnished a criterion for judging the evangelical tradition. Hence we must again indicate its limits here.

According to Luke iii, 1, the Baptist came on the scene in the fifteenth year of Tiberius. This appears to reckon the royal years according to the Syrian mode, and thus to be the year A.D. 27 to 28. According to Mark i, 14, Jesus' activity seems to have begun only after the Baptist's arrest. Hence we must place his first appearance in at least A.D. 28. All calculations which attempt to fix the duration of Jesus'

activity are idle. For no starting-point of reckoning can be
gathered from the individual passages, and the surrounding
remarks of the evangelists do not belong to the old tradition.
Hence, at best, we might estimate that Jesus was crucified
circa A.D. 30. If we now date Mark's Gospel only after the
destruction of Jerusalem, because his report of the signs in
the Temple and of the empty grave shows nothing about the
possibility of a cross-examination on the spot (cf. p. 195,
note 3, *supra*), its composition would fall in the eighth
decade, though others believe that an earlier date can be
accepted.   Then the whole process of developing the
evangelical tradition as far as the Gospel of Mark took place
within 40–5 years. The analogies of the Apophthegmata
Patrum examined in Chapter VI show the possibility of such
a process of tradition within so short a time including,
indeed, transcending the bounds of a language.

    We can go somewhat further: according to Galatians i, 18;
ii, 1, Paul's conversion took place about 15–17 years before the
so-called Apostolic Council—if we follow the reckoning of
the first years by the figures given in Galatians. The Apostolic
Council, however, is to be placed in 49–50.[1] Then it follows
Paul was converted within the period 32–5. At that time
as a Christian, or somewhat later when he became a missionary,
he received the traditions spoken of in 1 Cor. xi and xv, a
kerygma, and a record of the Last Supper which had already
been shaped. Thus as early as the fourth decade there were
already in existence texts in Greek about events from the life
of Jesus. At that time or later, hence perhaps in the fifth
decade, Paul must have also received collections of the sayings
of Jesus of which he made use in 1 Cor. vii and ix. Hence,
we may assert that the weighty elements of the tradition had
become fixed in the first twenty years after Jesus' death. We
may assume that all the elements of tradition of which Mark's

---

[1] The chronology founded upon the Gallio inscription (cf. Deissmann, *Paulus*,
2nd ed., 1925, pp. 203 ff.) furnishes for the date of Paul's arrival in Corinth
the year A.D. 50 or 51. The Apostolic Council is to be set at a corresponding distance
of time.

Gospel consists received their formulation in Greek at latest between A.D. 50 and 70. Thus the weightiest part of the tradition had been developed at a time while eyewitnesses still lived, and when the events were only about a generation old. It is not to be wondered at that this part of the tradition remained relatively unaltered.

The meaning of the point of view proper to " Formgeschichte " is not exhausted even with these historical demonstrations. The Formgeschichte of the Gospel leads finally to a theological outcome. For from the Forms it can deduce the leading interests of the tradition. It replaces the texts into the spiritual world from which they came. It believes, therefore, that it can show what significance the tradition of Jesus' words and deeds enjoyed when first it began to be told, and thereby it believes it can penetrate to the first and normative connection between history and belief in Christ.

The first understanding afforded by the standpoint of Formgeschichte is that there never was a " purely " historical witness to Jesus. Whatever was told of Jesus' words and deeds was always a testimony of faith as formulated for preaching and exhortation in order to convert unbelievers and confirm the faithful. What founded Christianity was not knowledge about a historical process, but the confidence that the content of the story was salvation: the decisive beginning of the End.

In saying this we have already touched upon the second theological goal of the standpoint of Formgeschichte. It undertakes to portray that understanding of the story of Jesus, by which the various formulations of the material are dominated. We showed in Chapter VII that the earliest Passion story, as far as it can be recognized in Mark, does not mean to present events in the historical sense. Although in a few places it depends upon the information of eye-witnesses, it does not purpose to narrate and prove the

sequence of events, nor to stir and exhort people by the
description of the Passion.   But, as is also quite obviously
the purpose of the editing by Mark, it proposes to describe
salvation, i.e. the fulfilment of God's will as revealed in the
Old Testament.   But this presentation could only be made
by one who had faith, i.e. the Easter faith.   In the sense of
history the undertaking would have been a tremendous
paradox.   Only he who in faith saw the continuation of the
events of the Passion, viz. the Risen Lord enter into His
glory with the Father and His return to earth as the Lord of
the Kingdom of God, only he could have undertaken so to
describe the shameful events of His arrest and execution that
an eternal counsel of God were visible in them.   The most
essential medium of such a presentation was to put forward
the agreement with Scripture, to show that the events accorded
with the necessity found in the Old Testament.   Thus it
could be generally emphasized that all had to happen in this
way because Scripture required it (Mark xiv, 21, 49), or,
again, in formulating the record, the agreement of an event
with certain passages could be expressed in a way that would
be clear to both readers and hearers even without express
citation.

   The same standpoint at a later date determined Matthew's
presentation.   This holds good of course only where he
himself shapes the material over and above his sources.
In certain remarks introduced between passages from his
sources, he depicts general circumstances and supports these
descriptions from the Old Testament, e.g. that Jesus lived in
Capernaum (iv, 15) ;   commanding silence about a cure
(from Mark, but already with an interpolated remark, xii, 16) ;
the method of speaking in parables (xiii, 35).   He incidentally
bases individual events also in this manner, e.g. the Triumphal
Entry ;   the acclamation of the children ;   the purchase of
the field of blood with the traitor's money (xxi, 5, 16 ;
xxvii, 9).

   It was not necessary to. give such a basis for the actual

happenings in Jesus' life, for the words and deeds of the active life in Galilee, because there was nothing paradoxical to tell here, nothing whose earthly and historical cause would have contradicted faith's understanding. Thus the great miracles, as narrated in the Tales, said to unbelievers what they said to believers, viz. that One who was armed with superhuman authority was at work here. But faith could say more. It could say whence that authority came which was overwhelmingly revealed in the great miracles of the Tales. When Mark included these miracle stories in his book, he doubtless understood them in this manner, i.e. in the sense of Christian faith. But as a rule he did not impress this understanding upon his text; rather he preserved and handed it on in all its mundane character. For even in this Form also the Tales operated as they were intended—as epiphanies of Christ. And when Mark included them he at the same time stamped the Christological character of his book. For the " epiphane " nature of Jesus' deeds stood in contradiction to the conclusion of Jesus' life. The more the fullness of revelation was presented in deeds and words, the more puzzling and incomprehensible became the final rejection of this revelation by the people who were blessed by it. Mark solved this contradiction by his theory of the Messianic secret. He put not only the great miracles but the whole activity of Jesus under the standpoint of a secret epiphany.

This gave the decisive standpoint for the theological understanding of the material of Jesus' life. For the idea of an epiphany was understood by the world and was, therefore, available for the Christian *mission*. But the decisive concern of *faith* also came to expression in the idea of epiphany, and thus the standpoint of this idea was not lost again from the Church, but, especially as formulated by the Fourth Gospel, was carried even further.

It was useful for missionary work, for the thought that God would send salvation to a world thirsty for redemption by revealing Himself in an historical person was not foreign

to the age, but rather was brought continually closer to
it disguised in Emperor worship and distorted by miracle-
workers of all sorts.   Hence the Christian missionary could
introduce his message about the life of Jesus in the way Acts
makes Paul commence his speech upon the Areopagus,
" What you ignorantly worship, that I preach to you."

In this way the missionary expressed a thought or conception belonging to effective propaganda and at the same
time the real concern of faith.   For preaching dealt not only
with the salvation which was to come, but—and it was
emphasized increasingly the longer the parousia of the Lord
delayed—with the salvation already accomplished.   The
life of Jesus became increasingly the decisive phase of salvation,
whereas it had formerly been only the opening bar.   A heavenly
light radiated ever more fully round the existence of the Son
of Man upon earth, the traits of the Risen Lord became ever
more visible in the countenance of the Master of Capernaum.
This new emphasis made good also in the tradition of the
words of Jesus.   The more they were combined together
by their theme, the more they ceased to be sayings of Jesus
uttered on particular occasions, and the more they became
Jesus' law for His Church.   And thus the mythology about
Christ came to expression although it was only in some few
words and stories (cf. Chapter X), but it began to place itself
like a framework round the life of Jesus, and then the union
of the tradition of the life of Jesus with Christology was completed.   On the one hand, the Risen Lord could be regarded
as the subject of the tradition, and on the other, as much
as tradition offered could be said about the revelation of the
Lord on earth.

It scarcely needs to be said that John's Gospel took part
in this union in a decisive fashion.   For this Gospel referred
the glory of the resurrection back to the earthly life of Jesus
and presented Jesus as Lord and Revealer in the situations
offered by tradition.   But then the question appears to remain
unanswered why the Jews refused to follow a Master who

came forward with such claims to authority. John solves this problem not by concealing the epiphany like Mark, but by describing the understanding of the hearers as completely perverse. In their blindness they would not see the one whom God had sent with special authority. Thus both the majesty of God's emissary and the rejection of this emissary by His people became comprehensible. The gaps in the New Testament close up ; the Gospels reporting about Jesus came to be understood as documents of Christology as this was found in the Epistles.

There remained, it is true, a certain difficulty in the fact that for Paul the earthly life of Jesus was not the locus of revelation, but the sphere where the soteriologically necessary humiliation of God's Son took place. Hence Paul needed only to know about the life of Jesus, that it took place, and that Jesus in that life was obedient even unto the Cross. What lies between the Incarnation and the Crucifixion is overcast, but the Gospels tell how this very earthly life was lit up ever and again by heavenly glory which in speech and work broke through every concealment. The variance between the two standpoints was not overcome. Rather this variance provided the theme of the Church's doctrinal disputes on Christology. This variance is found to the present day in the fact that the traditions which the Gospels reproduce from the life of Jesus as signs of revelation are entirely unmentioned in the Creed, because they are not regarded as soteriological facts. Nevertheless we may say that the idea of epiphany guaranteed to the entire biographical material of Christ its meaning for the Church, and to this extent effected its preservation. That nevertheless this thought exercised little influence on the Form of the tradition shows to what degree tradition was already definitely shaped. It told of Jesus of Nazareth and called Him the Son of Man. On the other hand the title " Lord ", which is congruous with the idea of epiphany, found only occasional place in the Gospels of Luke and John. The title " Son of Man " really points to the future parousia, but in John it takes on the meaning of the perfect tense, and is quite obviously applied to the descent of God's Son, to live an earthly life. Here we may trace the change from an eschatological into a soteriological characterization. This understanding of the life of Jesus has been carried through here, viz. the life of Jesus is the epiphany, is the decisive revelation of God.

This must be emphasized all the more since still another possibility exists of estimating the tradition of Jesus' life. We recognize it most clearly in the Lucan presentation of Jesus' suffering, which gives the Passion the character of a martyrdom. Jesus is the hero who in patience maintains His faith (cf. p. 201 *supra*). This is not a theological but a literary standpoint, which elsewhere also has incidentally shaped Jesus' biographical material. It rises from the need of speaking about Jesus in the manner elsewhere employed in speaking of the heroes of Legend. The analysis proper to Formgeschichte has shown how this interest maintains itself in all sorts of little changes especially in the Passion, but without changing the essential substance of the tradition. Here the point is not soteriology, but the edifying description of a person. Of course, this change of emphasis in the tradition had a certain value for propaganda since a certain sympathy for the hero of these events could in this way be made to flow into non-Christian circles. But a primary interest of the Christian Church did not here come into its rights. For the Church was not interested in what Jesus proved but in what He brought. Nevertheless, when the " household list " (1 Peter ii, 21 ff.) puts forward the suffering Jesus (who " when he was reviled did not revile, and when he had to suffer did not threaten ") as an example for the slave who is bearing injustice, we see how even this view of Jesus' suffering came to its place in the preaching of the Church. But at the same time the rarity of such references shows that this standpoint reached no decisive significance.

We must remember that the Gospels did not intend and

ought not to describe the story of an exemplary saintly person. Hence we ought not to raise questions about the tradition preserved in them, i.e. questions which arise from these interests. Apart from the exceptions already mentioned our records refuse an answer if we inquire into them about the character, the " personality ", or the qualities of Jesus. This very refusal over against such secular interrogation reminds us once again that the tradition did not belong to literature. The standpoint of Formgeschichte is able to make clear the unworldly character of the original tradition. It shows also how the tradition gradually accommodated itself to the world by developing Forms more widely current— the Tale, the Legend—and by composing and providing a framework in Forms which stood closer to literature proper. Here we are dealing with a literary proceeding, but a further process becomes clear in it. The fact that it is recognizable precisely in the formulation and the changing of the Forms gives the point of view of Formgeschichte its theological justification. This further process is the propagation of the gospel in the world.

GENERAL INDEX

Abbot Poimenus, 173

Aboth of Nathan, 108 n., 136

Acts of the Apostles 3, 16, 19, 21;
  speeches in, 16, 25, 26, 111

Acts of John, 106

Acts of Paul, 23 n., 106

Actus Petri cum Simone, 89, 106

Aelian, 82 n. 2

Aelius Aristides, 96 n., 175

Analogies to Gospel Forms, Ch. VI
  passim; Rabbinic, 133–151; Hellenistic, 151–172; Patristic, 172–7

Antioch (on the Orontes), 20, 29, 30,
  34

Apothegms, 151, 152, 153, 156

Apophthegmata Patrum, 172–7, 190 n.,
  294

Apollonius of Tyana, 89, 91, 97

Aretalogy, xii, 96, 151

Asclepius, 82, 83 n., 96, 97, 165, 167,
  170, 171

Asita, 127

Aufhauser, 175 n.

Augustus, 128, 130, 131 n.

Baba Qamma, 138

Beleth, 104 n.

Berakhoth, 83 n. 2, 91 n., 134, 145, 150

Bickell, 160

Bisarion, 174–5

Blenkenberg, 94 n.

Bousset, 18 n. 2, 172, 173, 226 n.,
  253 n., 275 n. 2

Buddha, 107, 127, 275

Bultmann, 6, 46, 54, 68, 156, 247 n.,
  275 n. 2, 3

Burkitt, 214 n.

Büschel, 214 n.

Cadbury, 11 n., 16 n.

Campbell Bonner, 85 n. 2

Celsus, 281

Chria, xii, 40 n., 152–172 *passim*;
  definition of, 152; origin of, 156;
  relation to Paradigms, 156 ff.; and
  Sayings of Jesus, 160 ff.; style of,
  152 ff.

Christ - Mythology, Ch. X *passim*,
  298; definition of, 266; examples,
  271 ff.; extra-canonical, 273;

Fourth Gospel in, 285 f.; Paul and,
  267–8; words of Jesus and, 279 ff.

Christology, 123, 131, 197, 198, 199,
  211, 241, 246, 261, 273, 280, 288,
  298, 299

1 Clement, 24, 29 n., 240, 242

Corpus Hermeticum, 281–2

Dalman, 32 n., 273 n. 2

Deissmann, 6

Didache, 29 n., 238, 240, 241, 249,
  250 n.

Dieterich, 85

Diogenes Laertius, 152, 153 n. 2

Disciple, the Beloved, 216 n. 2

Dodd, 254 n.

Easter-Story, 113, 179, 199

Easton, B. S., 31 n.

Eleazer, 84, 89

Epidauros, 82, 90, 166, 167, 168, 170,
  172, 175

Epiphany, 43, 94, 95, 97, 100, 102, 117,
  131, 150, 151, 230, 231, 232, 260,
  262, 266, 267, 271, 272, 276, 277,
  278, 279, 289, 291, 297, 299

Epistula Apostolorum, 270

Erdmann, 131 n.

Erubin, 145

Fayoum Fragment, 160, 181 n.

Fiebig, 82 n., 140

Form, 2, 4, 6, 8, 13, 26, 38, 54, 58, 119,
  141, 142, 164, 165, 217, 222, 242,
  243, 249, 279, 286, 288, 290, 291,
  295, 297, 301

Formgeschichte, xii, 5, 6, 60, 148, 292,
  295, 300, 301

Gaster, 134 n., 137 n.

Gemara, 134, 135, 138

Gethsemane, historicity of, 211–13

Gnome, xii, 153, 247

God-Fearers, 14, 30

Goetz, 275 n. 3

Goguel, 163 n., 275 n. 3

Gospel of the Childhood (Thomas's),
  106

Gospel, Fourth, 3, 40, 193, 204, 264,
  298

INDEX OF SCRIPTURAL PASSAGES

(a) OLD TESTAMENT

(b) NEW TESTAMENT

(i) *Self-contained Paragraphs* (cited only by the first verse and where possible as found in Mark, and otherwise in Matthew, Luke, and John respectively).

Mark

(ii) *Single Verses*